W9-CLV-637

3 3311 00227 490 2

THE RISE OF THE HISPANIC MARKET IN THE UNITED STATES

THE RISE OF THE HISPANIC MARKET IN THE UNITED STATES

CHALLENGES, DILEMMAS, AND OPPORTUNITIES FOR CORPORATE MANAGEMENT

LOUIS E.V. NEVAER

M.E.Sharpe
Armonk, New York
London, England

99808146912

HF 5415.33 .U6 N47 2004

Nevaer, Louis E. V.

The rise of the Hispanic
market in the United States

Copyright © 2004 by M.E. Sharpe, Inc.

All rights reserved. No part of this book may be reproduced in any form
without written permission from the publisher, M.E. Sharpe, Inc.,
80 Business Park Drive, Armonk, New York 10504.

Material was reprinted from Anthony DePalma, *Here: A Biography of the New American
Continent* (New York: Public Affairs, 2001). Copyright © by Anthony DePalma. Reprinted
by Permission of Public Affairs, a member of Perseus Books, L.L.C.

Library of Congress Cataloging-in-Publication Data

Nevaer, Louis E. V.
   The rise of the Hispanic market in the United States : challenges, dilemmas, and
opportunities for corporate management / Louis E. V. Nevaer.
      p. cm.
   Includes bibliographical references.
   ISBN 0-7656-1290-9 (cloth: alk. paper) — ISBN 0-7656-1291-7 (pbk.: alk. paper)
      1. Hispanic American consumers. 2. Market segmentation—United States. 3. Target
marketing—United States. 4. North America—Economic integration. I. Title.

HF5415.33.U6N47 2004
658.8'34'08968073—dc21

200305053

Printed in the United States of America

The paper used in this publication meets the minimum requirements of
American National Standard for Information Sciences
Permanence of Paper for Printed Library Materials,
ANSI Z 39.48-1984.

BM (c)   10   9   8   7   6   5   4   3   2   1
BM (p)   10   9   8   7   6   5   4   3   2   1

AUG 3 0 2004

Table of Contents

its two rosters: victims and victimizers," Randall Robinson, a distinguished African-American political leader and thinker, writes in *The Debt: What America Owes to Blacks*.[4] Although it may not be as well recognized, ethnicity can produce similar challenges that differences in social class and national origins produce, as Robinson suggests.

But what, pray tell, is a "Hispanic"?

Why are people from Guatemala Hispanic, but those in neighboring Belize are not? On the island of Hispaniola, shared by the Dominican Republic and Haiti, the Dominicans are Hispanic, the Haitians are not. Mexicans and Chileans are Hispanic; Jamaicans and Bahamians are not. The people of the Iberian peninsula—the Spanish, Basque, Catalan, and Portuguese—are all Hispanic, as they have always been called for more than a thousand years.[5]

The term "Hispanic" first came into widespread use in Europe in the tenth century. Saxon writer Hroswitha of Gandersheim, a nun who was familiar with the court of Holy Roman Emperor Otto I, coined the phrase "the ornament of the world" to describe the cultural and political achievement that Cordoba represented: "The brilliant ornament of the world shown in the west, a noble city newly known for the military prowess that its Hispanic colonizers had brought, Cordoba was its name and it was wealthy and famous for its pleasures and resplendent in all things."[6] Six centuries later, throughout the colonial era in the New World, the name "Hispanics" distinguished those people who were becoming acculturated to Western norms from those who resisted Western civilization. Throughout Latin America, historically, "Hispanic" refers to the process of becoming Christian and learning Spanish; one can be a full-blooded Zapotec and, by virtue of being Christian and speaking Spanish, not be "indigenous" or "Native American" but simply "Hispanic."

To understand what makes a person Hispanic in the United States, it is instructive to understand what makes Americans so accepting of religious diversity. The simple answer is that this nation's beginnings as a British colony were, in no small part, to provide a refuge for religious minorities who were unwelcome in England. No one religious sect was dominant, and the result was the creation of a society in which religions could flourish. This ideal of inclusiveness is embodied in the separation of church and state in the American Constitution.

This process of tolerance has its counterpart in Hispanic thought. Why, for instance, are Hispanics so accepting of racial and ethnic diversity? Why would Celia Cruz (black) defend Desi Arnaz (white) so passionately? Why is Salma Hayek no less Hispanic than Tito Puente? Why are Oscar de la Renta and Oscar de la Hoya both Hispanic? The simple answer is that the history of Spanish America is the history of one chronic labor shortage after another, and Spain desperately sought to populate its colonies, welcoming anyone who had a pulse. Look at the map and see how large the geography is: When Mexico declared its independence from Spain, for instance, little more than 3,000 people lived in what is now California! As a result of this labor shortage, for centuries Spain encouraged immigration to its colonies from the whole of Europe.

As a result, the demographics of Spanish America consisted of:

1. Spanish administrators who made up the political hierarchy;
2. Catholic missionaries (who came from various European nations) who were charged with spreading Christianity;
3. immigrants from many lands who, seeking economic opportunities, petitioned to emigrate and settle in the various parts of New Spain, regardless of whether they came from Spain or the Ottoman lands, Germany, or Italy
4. millions of indigenous peoples who were, to varying degrees, integrated into society; and
5. thousands of Africans brought over as slaves, primarily to the Caribbean and, by the Portuguese, to Brazil.

When Christopher Columbus set sail for the New World, his crew consisted of Spaniards, Italians, and Frenchmen, among other nationalities, and included North African blacks and one Jew—who was fluent in Arabic.[7] More than a century later, such diversity would be absent aboard the *Mayflower.*

The net result was that it was impossible for any single racial or ethnic group to dominate the others, though, in theory, New Spain was "Spanish." This, of course, does not mean that to be "Spanish" means one is "Spanish." Spain's King Juan Carlos is Italian by birth, and Queen Sofiá speaks Spanish with a German accent, presumably because she was born in Greece. This is not uncommon in European history; at Buckingham Palace, Prince Philip was born in Greece, and Queen Elizabeth is of German ancestry. Princess Diana, curiously enough, had more "royal" blood in her veins than does Queen Elizabeth. The splendid nature of life informs the Hispanic worldview, where humanity is seen to fall within a wide range of possibilities. Mexico's census form, for instance, omits race but emphasizes ethnicity. In the United States, "Hispanic" was first used in the 1970 census, at the direction of the Nixon administration, as an attempt to understand the phenomenon of a permanent Spanish-speaking population that refused to assimilate and become "Americanized."

A general observation, which one alluded to in market research on the Hispanic market throughout corporate America, is that U.S. Hispanics can be roughly divided into "Mexican Hispanics" and "Caribbean Hispanics." A further general observation is that the majority of Mexican Hispanics are, to varying degrees, of Native American and European ancestry. The majority of "Caribbean Hispanics," on the other hand, have varying degrees of African and European blood. These are generalizations, of course, but few California and Texas Hispanics of Mexican ancestry have African blood, and even fewer Puerto Ricans, Cubans, and Dominicans have Native American blood.

The content of their worldview and their character are more important than the color of their skin. What makes Sammy Sosa and Cameron Díaz equally Hispanic is their mindset. The emergence of the Hispanic market in the United States thus offers Americans a different way of looking at society, the marketplace, and the corporate world. Is it possible for corporate America to think of the consumer marketplace "outside the racial box"?

The short answer is yes.

The polarity between blacks and whites in American society does not exist in the same way in Latin America, nor does it exist within the Hispanic market. Hispanic society is not immune to racism, of course, but has had a centuries-old process of integrating hundreds of Native American peoples, as well as Arabs, Jews, and Asians, throughout the whole of Latin America. Whereas American society has experienced the tensions inherent in segregation—free whites, enslaved blacks, and excluded Native Americans—Spanish America had a far less conflictive and dysfunctional model.

The qualities that we think of as "Hispanic" reflect the cultural, social, political, and economic integration of indigenous peoples, and the inclusion of former slaves in societies that have offered them more economic and social mobility. In this respect, Hispanic society has a different historical, cultural, and social experience, one that differentiates not primarily on the basis of race, but on other criteria altogether. The "land mines" that corporate America needs to understand about the Hispanic market, the Hispanic worldview, and the Hispanic cultural legacy have their own nuances and prejudices, but they are not based exclusively on race.

As we shall see, Hispanic society is free of racism (as it is understood in the United States's experience), but it is rife with discrimination (in a way that is fundamentally different from how it manifests itself in the United States). The discussion presented here offers an analysis of the Hispanic market—of the Hispanic consumer's worldview and how it informs Hispanic consumer behavior.

This approach is instructive, for corporate America has stumbled in trying to come to terms with what the "Hispanic" market means. Consider the results of a million-dollar market research study conducted by the R.J. Reynolds Tobacco Company. The R.J. Reynolds marketing department, in a market analysis designed to increase that company's market share among Hispanics, concluded:

> An interesting distinction surfaces when the United States Hispanic population is divided into its two broadest components: Mexican versus Caribbean Hispanics. Likely due to factors both environmental and hereditary, the Caribbean Hispanics possess a "passionate intensity" that seems largely absent from the Mexican personality. They are loud, assertive, impatient, emotional, and highly charged. The Mexicans, by contrast, tend to be accepting, passive, and less inclined to assert themselves or make demands. Even the Cubans in this study (the only market probed on this issue) agreed that the Mexicans were the humblest of the Hispanic sub-groups. Perhaps related to this "humility" on the part of the Mexicans is that in both Los Angeles and San Antonio jobs are difficult to find and the unemployment rate among these people is high. Consequently, even their dreams are meager. While the younger Puerto Rican adults might wish for all the money in the world and all the "good things" it could buy, and while their Cuban peers are fueled with grand career ambitions, the younger Mexican adults wish for little beyond basic job security.[8]

In other words, some Hispanics are timid, but others are assertive. Some Hispanics are high-school dropouts, and others have graduate degrees. Some Hispanics are underachievers, and others are overachievers. Some Hispanics are humble, but others are ambitious.

How, then, can a unified campaign be developed to reach "underachievers" who have graduate degrees? Or timid consumers who are also ambitious? Or humble consumers who assert themselves? The sheer diversity within the Hispanic market necessitates contradictory and mutually exclusive marketing and merchandising strategies, a realization that opens a Pandora's box of possibilities and pitfalls. Of equal concern, why does the R.J. Reynolds analysis seem so harsh and disparaging, relying on sweeping generalizations that label millions of consumers in unkind terms? Is this evidence of a lingering bias throughout corporate America against the one group of consumers in the United States who, by demanding to be spoken to in Spanish, challenge America's history of assimilation?

What is a marketing director to do?

The R.J. Reynolds market analysis—which is quoted here because it entered the public domain as a result of a civil lawsuit against the tobacco giant—reveals the muddled thinking going on throughout corporate America as managers come to terms with Hispanic ascendancy. It is clear that corporate America's traditional approaches to market research offer few insights other than the realization that Hispanics, as a market, are as diverse as society at large. The results of R.J. Reynolds's research, however, are the norm. In the course of working for more than a decade with Fortune 100 companies interested in "understanding" and "quantifying" the elusive "nature" of the Hispanic market, it has been my experience time and again that corporate America stumbles over the question of ethnicity, which it unerringly confuses with race.

The emergence of the Hispanic market means that corporate America—like American society at large—has to learn to think outside the racial box. To understand the Hispanic market, it is necessary to understand the cultural and historical forces that inform the Hispanic worldview. To be fair to R.J. Reynolds, if this market analysis offers little in the way of helping managers reach the Hispanic market, it is because of the underlying premise: The market research was based on previous studies to determine the differences between black and white American consumers!

The State of Race Relations, with a Hispanic Twist

Language is only one part of the challenge that Hispanic ascendancy represents, though it is the one sweeping social force that has transformed the United States into a bilingual nation. The other part of the challenge is how corporate America understands, in terms of both human resources and corporate social responsibility, how diversity is achieved. For more than a quarter century, along with the American military, corporate America has been at the forefront of championing diversity in society in general. Glass ceilings have shattered, race barriers have been overcome, and it is often in the workplace that Americans have the chance to interact with people of other races, ethnic groups, and nationalities.

Randall Kennedy, a Harvard professor who explored interracial marriages in *Interracial Intimacies* (2003), reported that marriages between blacks and white were a mere 0.6 percent of total marriages in the United States in 1998. Outside the workplace and school, Americans do not socialize with people of other races. In Robert Putnam's *Bowling Alone*,[9] Eileen McDonagh, a political scientist, is quoted as asking, "Is it better to have to have neighborhoods legally restricted on the basis of race, but with everyone having everyone over for dinner, or is it better to have neighborhoods unrestricted on the basis of race, but with very little social interaction going on between neighbors?" The same question, although not as challenging, can also be asked about ethnicity.

The state of race relations in the United States remains a work in progress. Hispanic ascendancy, however, represents a direct challenge to how the United

States thinks about the nature of race. Clearly, there are similarities between race and ethnicity, at least along some dimensions. Consider how Anthony DePalma, reporting on his experiences as bureau chief in Mexico City for the *New York Times*, describes the Hispanic race-neutral self-perception:

> Mexicans and their country are torn between the twin poles of their identities, trying to be modern but falling back on ancient ways of work, courtesy, and corruption. They are proud of their Indian roots, but no number of statues of the warrior king Cuauhtemoc or other Indian heroes can hide their shameful treatment of today's descendants of the Aztecs. I saw this firsthand when a friend, Henry McDonald, an American real estate executive in Mexico City, told me of his experience when he tried to take his family to dinner at an expensive restaurant in Mexico City not far from the monument to Mexico's Indian past. They were turned away because he had brought along his dark-skinned Indian housekeeper. It wasn't a sophisticated rejection, nor a veiled objection. The maître d' simply told Henry that no tables were available at the time. Henry kept an American schedule in Mexico and arrived at the restaurant at about 7 p.m., when it was practically empty. Mario Padilla, the restaurant manager, later told me quite openly that the restaurant policy was for the benefit of patrons, most of whom have servants but would never bring them along. However, some people "lack discretion," he said, obviously referring to Americans like Henry who wouldn't know not to bring a maid to dinner at a fine restaurant.[10]

If there isn't racism, as racism is understood in American society, in Hispanic society, then there certainly is *discrimination*, which is not the same thing. Not all discrimination is objectionable, one reason we admire people who have "discriminating" taste. The difference between racism and discrimination, for purposes of this discussion, is that from a Hispanic perspective, racism connotes hostility or prejudice against someone simply because of his or her race. Discrimination, on the other hand, suggests a negative reaction because of something specific, such as objecting to someone who is inappropriately dressed for a social event, or is too loud, and so on. How Hispanics differentiate between the two—and the role of what we now classify as "lookism," which is a bias against the old, overweight, homely, short, or dark-skinned—constitutes the single most important human relations land mine that corporate America confronts with Hispanic ascendancy in the United States. America's baggage of racism, however, weighs down Hispanics, who suffer the backlash of this unfortunate legacy. Hispanics who live in the United States resent being in a "twilight zone," where society is race-obsessed, as archaic as if one entered a theme park where people were walking around dressed as seventeenth-century Puritans or espousing the discredited nineteenth-century social Darwinism of Herbert Spencer. Make no mistake, however, for Mexican and U.S. Hispanic sensibilities about race are defining how "race" will be lived in the United States in the twenty-first century, eclipsing previous historical concerns in which black-white relations were center stage.

These unfolding fundamental changes are of such economic consequence that many companies throughout corporate America have taken proactive steps to position themselves for this brave new marketplace. Indeed, corporate America, recognizing the defining challenges in this development, are for the first time thinking of *one* unified Hispanic marketplace across all three NAFTA nations. In a bid to "dramatically increase our market share" of the remittance market between the United States and Mexico, for instance, Bank of America chairman and chief executive officer Kenneth Lewis announced the acquisition of 24.9 percent of Grupo Financiero Santander Serfin in December 2002 for $1.6 billion in cash.[11] Bank of America, of course, was playing "catch-up" to Citigroup, which, in May 2001, purchased Banamex, Mexico's second-largest bank, for $12.5 billion. "Today's announcement represents Citigroup's commitment to Mexico and to the belief in the potential of this country, to the belief in the further integration of Mexico and the U.S. economy, and to the grander vision of the North American economy," Robert E. Rubin, Citigroup vice chairman, said at the time. "Mexico will have a world-class banking system which, for all practical purposes, is invulnerable to shocks. . . . In my view, the vision of NAFTA—the vision of these two countries being inextricably linked together economically—is a vision that is now well advanced."[12]

In due course, Citigroup's rivals answered the challenge that the acquisition of Banamex represented. "Bank of America says it will compete with Citigroup for Mexican and Mexican-American customers in the United States," Tim Weiner reported in the *New York Times*, signaling the emergence of a single North American Hispanic market.[13] It is clear, then, that corporate America understands that the "Hispanization" of the United States—and the whole of North America—constitutes a sea change, for it represents fundamental changes in how consumer markets compete throughout the whole of North America.

Managers throughout corporate America are also struggling to make sense of the economic implications of Hispanic ascendancy in the United States—what this means for the business community and how companies will conduct themselves as they fulfill their missions to be good corporate citizens. This book offers an interdisciplinary analysis of the business consequences of the emergence of a single Hispanic market in the North America Culture

Area (NACA), which consists of Mexico, the United States, and Canada. Now the largest minority in the United States, through NAFTA's success, Hispanics are poised to become half of the entire North American consumer marketplace by 2025. The sweeping demographic and economic consequences will reverberate throughout the American—and continental—economy as this century unfolds.

For corporáte executives, who throughout the twentieth century were often overwhelmed by social events—the political ascendancy of women in 1919, the civil rights movements spearheaded by African-Americans in 1964, the breakdown of the American family with divorce and substance abuse exploding since the 1970s—the implications of the "Hispanization" of the United States, while far less dramatic, are no less significant. "It is a turning point in the nation's history, a symbolic benchmark of some significance," said Roberto Suro, director of the Pew Hispanic Center, a Washington-based research and policy analysis organization, of the emergence of Hispanics as the largest minority. "If you consider how much of this nation's history is wrapped up in the interplay between black and white, this serves as an official announcement that we as Americans cannot think of race in that way any more."[14]

It is impossible to distinguish much longer between "Mexico" and "U.S. Hispanic," particularly in light of the fact that two out of three U.S. Hispanics are of Mexican ancestry. The discussion presented in this book assumes a fundamental knowledge of consumer markets and a general understanding of the Mexican economy. These subjects provide a crucial background to developing appropriate strategic planning over the next decades, both on a policy-making level and for how robust growth in consumer markets in the three NAFTA nations can be sustained. Consider one sobering fact: Under present immigration law, one in three Mexicans in Mexico—almost 34 million people—can make a legal claim to establishing permanent residency in the United States. That few choose to exercise this right is another matter, but it underscores the demographics that will affect the fates of the United States, Canada, and Mexico.[15]

We often forget the power of the ideas that swept through the Western world during the Age of Reason. In the United States, for instance, Thomas Jefferson wanted the Declaration of Independence to begin with "we hold these truths to be sacred." It was Benjamin Franklin who objected to this wording, reminding the men who were about to become the founding fathers that their efforts were to assert the importance of Reason in our lives, and to remove the political process from religious belief. This is how "these truths" became "self-evident." In the Spanish-speaking world, likewise, suddenly the world was divided between those who held Reason above all else, and those who were still "enslaved" to religion, superstition, and mysticism—

to their Passion. This obsessive distinction between Reason and Passion lives on linguistically: In Spanish, the phrase, "you're right," is *tienes razón*, which literally means "you have reason." The distinction between who is "reasonable" and who is "unreasonable" will be explained further in the appropriate section, but suffice it to say that Hispanics are inclined to size up a person as being "reasonable" or "unreasonable," and then discriminate accordingly, accepting the former as equals, dismissing the latter. This differentiation defies America's notion of "racism" but still creates societies rife with "discrimination."

Whereas American society is divided along the basis of race (skin color), Hispanic societies are divided along the lines of varying degrees of "reasonableness"—mindset and education. The distinction has sweeping implications for the American economy. Merchandising and marketing in the twenty-first century therefore requires an interdisciplinary approach, one that combines retail anthropology with basic marketing. "With ethnography, a consumer is viewed using products in his or her natural environment," argues Marvin Matises of the Galileo Idea Group, a company specializing in the development of new-product concepts for consumer product companies. "Perhaps the greatest benefit of such an ethnographic approach is marketers' ability to view the consumer actually using the product, taking the concept of a 'taste test' to a whole new realm. . . . Rather than having a consumer test a product and provide feedback, consumers are using the product where and when they are most comfortable."[16]

Language barriers can be overcome through the incorporation of techniques employed by anthropologists and ethnographers. Market research that seeks to better understand consumer behavior in the twenty-first century is a more complex matter. In fact, consider how nuanced this market research becomes when linguistic and cultural differences have to be factored into the analysis: Whereas in the United States callers are advised to "Oprima dos para español," consumers in Mexico are not advised to "Press 2 for English"—yet. That our continental neighbors do affect us—Americans now eat more salsa than ketchup—is often discounted, if for no other reason than that it is easy to cross a bridge until one arrives at it. Citigroup and Bank of America are not alone in realizing that corporate America has now arrived at a Hispanic bridge. But it does not lead from Washington to Mexico City, or Los Angeles to Guadalajara, or Houston to Monterrey. It leads from Chicago to San Antonio, from Boston to Miami, and from New York to Los Angeles.

This book is a guide to crossing that bridge successfully. It offers insights into the anthropological and ethnographic retail marketing aspects of the Hispanic consumer market, affording managers and marketers the skills they need to perform their jobs successfully under NAFTA in the Hispanic market in the United States and the Mexican marketplace. For corporate managers in the United States and Canada, it is imperative to make sensible strategic decisions in this heightened competitive market, particularly given the consolidation and expansion of the European Union. To understand what Hispanics mean for the United States—particularly as the North American economies accelerate their integration during NAFTA's second decade—it is necessary to think in terms of the American economy *and* the North American economy.

Part I takes the insights presented in the survey of Hispanic thought and then applies these lessons in an analysis of what the "Hispanization" of the United States means for corporate America. Chapter 1 examines how marketing and merchandising are undergoing fundamental changes in response to Hispanic ascendancy. With an estimated purchasing power expected to approach approximately $1 *trillion* by 2010, these 38 million consumers represent a market that cannot be overlooked. Corporate America's strategy, to provide Spanish-language advertising in print and broadcast media, has had the unintended effect of exacerbating the debate over language as Spanish spreads throughout the United States, making the nation no longer a monolingual consumer market.

The question of language has several components. Foremost is the enormous market in educational services, primarily to teach Hispanics English and to allow them the opportunity to pursue higher education. Of equal concern, however, are the structural changes in how corporate America does business, for Hispanics resist surrendering their language, the means through which they "self-segregate." Furthermore, Hispanic thought is predisposed to favor the view that the proper role of government is to be an active agent in the economy. Hispanic consumer behavior revisits the twentieth-century debate between John Kenneth Galbraith and Milton Friedman. Galbraith advanced the idea that the proper role of government was to intervene in the economy to ensure that "public needs" were satisfied to serve the greater social good. Friedman, on the other hand, argued that allowing individuals to pursue "private wants" would itself ensure a superior societal outcome. Thus, the great debate among economists throughout the twentieth century centered on how best to balance the competing interests between "private wants" and "public needs." How these ideas affect Hispanic "aspirational" consumer behavior, which challenges traditional marketing research in its wholesale repudiation of the race-based premises, is a stark challenge to how goods and services are merchandised in the United States.

The next chapter builds on consequences of the linguistic and cultural fragmentation of the North American market. The processes of Hispanization entail the proliferation of *normas hispanas*, or "Hispanic norms," which were the processes by which the Spanish acculturated indigenous peoples throughout Latin America over the course of centuries. The staggering purchasing power of Hispanics in the United States ends Anglo America's ethnocentric conceit. Building on the social forces reinforced by the forces unleashed by NAFTA, the Hispanic presence in the United States, along with the French influence of Quebec in Canada, is further fragmenting the North American Culture Area into five distinct markets.

The cultural-linguistic fragmentation of the continental marketplace accentuates the specific externalities that shape Hispanic consumer behavior. It is in a mature, fragmented consumer marketplace that Galbraith's arguments enjoy a renaissance, for it suggests that, left to its own devices, the pursuit of private wants does not satisfy compelling social needs, particularly when consumer behavior is influenced by cultural externalities. Corporate America's understanding of how externalities influence consumer behavior, in essence, is undergoing a seismic shift, because the Hispanic response to externalities is fundamentally different from how African-Americans respond to the same externalities. Indeed, this chapter examines briefly the political-economy characteristics of pre-census 2000 that are being swept away now that African-Americans have lost their privileged position forevermore.

Chapter 3 addresses the impact on business imposed by restrictions on the movements of labor. The success of nation-states in rendering the movement of entire labor markets criminal constitutes interference in the market economy. This is not to say that nation-states do not have the obligation to protect their borders.[17] What is germane to NAFTA is that there are superior ways of addressing immigration. The way in which Canada and Mexico have managed to create a "guest" worker program is superior to the manner in which the United States and Mexico currently handle this issue. Policymakers in all three nations recognize the need for immigration reform. Business leaders are frustrated by chronic labor shortages and, in the United States, at least, have at times conspired to traffic in human beings in order to satisfy market demands. "The NAFTA nations should learn from the example of the European Union," Fernando Margain and Walter Russell Mead wrote in a *New York Times* op-ed piece. "Worried that migrants from Spain, Portugal and Ireland would flood into the richer E.U. nations, the union provided loans and grants for large-scale development and public works programs to create jobs for these workers in their own countries."[18] It is imperative that the NAFTA partners apply the lessons of the European Union to the model developed by Canada and Mexico. The labor of the businesses throughout the United States and the dignity of the individual are safeguarded through legislation that reforms and rationalizes how labor markets across North America operate, which is particularly germane given that the Hispanization of the United States is fast creating a single continental consumer *and* labor market.[19]

Part II describes the processes driving the Hispanization of the United States, underscored by the ascendance of Hispanics over African-Americans as the largest minority in the country. How this Hispanization is tied to sustained growth in Mexico after a decade of NAFTA, and how Canada-Mexico relations continue to strengthen, proves instructive in understanding the processes transforming the economic landscape of North America.

Chapter 4 reviews the growing presence and influence of Americans in Mexico and how these effects flow back and forth across the border as continental economic integration accelerates. The growing presence of American expatriate communities throughout Mexico, coupled with the globalization of the Mexican economy, is giving rise to a convergence in lifestyle among Mexico's middle classes that emulates more closely the consumer patterns of their American counterparts. Merchandising, then, is changing to reflect the standardization of consumption habits of the relatively affluent consumer.

Chapter 5 addresses the emerging intellectual life that NAFTA has fostered, and which is now flourishing among U.S. Hispanics. An understanding of this topic is necessary for American managers for two simple reasons. Foremost, unlike the United States where intellectuals are mostly relegated to academic pursuits, in Mexico (as in Canada) intellectuals often enter political and public life, where they wield considerable power and influence.[20] Over the course of the second half of the twentieth century, Canada and Mexico have forged a remarkable "alliance" between two nations that, though historically different, are remarkably like-minded, and it has only blossomed under NAFTA. This alliance stands to change the political dynamics within the United States, for Hispanic ascendancy reflects the higher profile of intellectuals, not unlike what is found in Canadian and Mexican societies. Furthermore, by having a general overview of the disparate roles intellectuals play in Mexico and the United States, American managers will be able to understand the patterns that emerge as political and regulatory debates emerge in Mexico.

To this end, chapter 6 analyzes the Hispanics of Mexican ancestry, who account for most U.S. Hispanics. This is the most difficult chapter, one that dissects the narrative and psychology of Americans of Mexican ancestry (AMAs). What is the "baggage" that Hispanics have brought with them from Mexico? What is the baggage that is thrust upon them by American society? Are Hispanics, by being transformed into a "minority" by virtue of being in the United States, a diaspora? Chapter 6 addresses the five themes that inform and suffuse Hispanic thought in the United States. These themes, which are not flattering, constitute more a dissection than a portrait; for they analyze the cultural and historical forces that shape the predominant Hispanic worldview in the United States.

For the Mexican diaspora, the five issues that permeate their lives reveal the forces that compelled them to emigrate to the United States and the challenges that they encounter navigating the subtle racism of American life. The question of "rootlessness" speaks to the frustration that U.S.-born Hispanics face in feeling alienated from their ancestral culture by virtue of their parents' lack of formal education. The Mexican-Americans, whose families arrived in the United States with less than a high school education, were raised in homes where cultural histories were absent. That many are not fluent in proper Spanish frustrates efforts to find their histories. Latinos often disparage their heritage, a practice that is common among Latin Americans who have "poca cultura," or little culture. One strategy ameliorating these feelings of inadequacy has been the proliferation of mythmaking evident in much Chicano writing, which is largely based on the cult of "victimology" that has gained favor in the United States since the 1980s.

To complicate matters further, Hispanics in the United States face the double sting of discrimination. The dispiriting consequences of racism and the adverse social consequences of "lookism" have worked to encourage the phenomenon of Hispanic "self-segregation." Hispanics use language to create a barrier to defend themselves from the greater Anglo society. Consider how this resistance to acculturate and become American influences something as simple as filling out a census form.

Another "influence on perceptions of who is 'white' originates among the so-called Hispanics," Orlando Patterson, a professor of sociology at Harvard, wrote in the *New York Times*. "For political and economic reasons, including the benefits of affirmative action programs, the leadership of many Hispanic groups pursues a liberal, coalition-based agenda with African-Americans and presses hard for a separate, unified Latino classification. This strategy is highly influential even though nearly half of Hispanics consider themselves white."[21]

It would be irresponsible to write a history of the United States and omit discussing the Civil War simply because it was an unpleasant event in the nineteenth century. It would be equally a disservice to discuss the Hispanic ascendancy without presenting the background that informs the Hispanic worldview and how cultural ideas influence consumer behavior across Hispanic market segments. Throughout this book, reflecting the overwhelming majority of U.S. Hispanics that are of Mexican ancestry and the rapid integration of the Mexican and American economies as a consequence of NAFTA, proportionate emphasis is placed on U.S. Hispanics of Mexican ancestry. Finally, corporate managers need a fundamental understanding of the cultural forces that make Hispanics Hispanic, lest corporate America be condemned to spend millions of dollars on market research studies that yield platitudes that have little market value. This task is the more urgent, given that U.S. Hispanics yielded $600 billion in purchasing power in 2002.

1

The Future of Marketing and Merchandising in the United States

Abstract

The "Hispanization" of the United States signals a seismic shift in how managers will develop marketing, merchandising, and customer service programs. More than recordings that say, "press '1' for English, press '2' for Spanish," the changes in American society are profound. Reaching consumers in their own language is a sound business practice, made more urgent by the decision of Hispanics to self-segregate themselves linguistically. The question of language is important, for it not only creates a barrier that divides Hispanics from the rest of "Anglophone" America, it also limits the ability of Hispanics to prosper, since they trail significantly in pursuing higher education. Corporate managers, thrust into the linguistic flux of the twenty-first century, also need to recognize two social phenomena that accompany the Hispanic acculturation. (How this acculturation takes place is shaping how quickly the United States will become a bilingual nation as this century unfolds.) Foremost is the ambivalent relationship Hispanics have toward paternalism, where Hispanic thinking favors an activist government, along the lines advocated by Galbraith, but there is a strong desire for the material goods that can best be provided by an unfettered market economy as envisioned by Friedman. The second is the blossoming of entrepreneurship, one that approximates our standard understanding of "aspirational" consumer behavior, minus the subtext of race. Hispanic ascendancy challenges how corporate America can do business as the United States quickly moves from

*being a monolingual nation, and one where the divisive "black versus white"
paradigm of the American worldview is no longer as relevant.*

Why does the Hispanic market exist at all? Why have Hispanics not assimilated into America's legendary melting pot and become part of the mainstream? Why is there a segment of Americans—among the fastest-growing
in the demographics—that makes the conscious decision to opt out linguistically from mainstream American life? Why has the United States become a
bilingual nation, one whose youth increasingly speaks Spanish?

On the Nature of the U.S. Hispanic Market

These questions have puzzled marketing executives and social critics since
the 1960s when the Cubans arrived in south Florida. The Cubans explicitly
said that, however grateful they were for the exile afforded them by the United
States, they were so proud of being Cuban that they kindly declined the invi-
tation to become Americanized by "melting" in any "pot."[1] Jorge Mas Canosa,
founder of the Cuban-American National Foundation and an adviser to presidents on policy toward Cuba, explained:

> For us, as a people, it was important to succeed in the United States, but
> not necessarily abandon our own identity. When my family arrived in
> Miami, blacks weren't allowed to sit at the cafeteria counter in the down-
> town Woolworth's; Jews were not allowed to play golf in the Coral Gables
> Country Club; and Americans placed a misguided importance of a "ca-
> reer" over the well-being of their family. We didn't want to "integrate"
> into any society that was openly racist, where anti-Semitism lingered and
> where the moral values were such that children and our older parents had
> to be neglected. We love and are grateful for the economic opportunities
> of this great country, but we are not interested in forsaking our social and
> cultural values.[2]

Cubans, in essence, decided to protect the integrity of their community by
self-segregating through the act of speaking in Spanish *in public*. Never before had a Hispanic group, whether Mexicans in Los Angeles or Puerto Ricans
in New York, decided to take a radical move. To be sure, there were millions
of Hispanics who spoke Spanish in the United States, but the reason they did
not speak in English was that they did not *understand* English or were unable to negotiate their way in society by speaking English in public. They,
along with policymakers and the public at large, saw this as an educational
deficiency, one that could be resolved through bilingual education and teaching

English as a second language to adults. In short order, Hispanics would learn English, just as every other immigrant to the United States had done.

The Cubans, however, for the first time explicitly said no, they would instead speak Spanish on the civic stage of public life. Writing about the differences between Cuban-Americans in Miami and Mexican-Americans in Los Angeles, Joan Didion argues:

> This question of language was curious. The sound of spoken Spanish was common in Miami, but it was also common in Los Angeles, and Houston, and even in the cities of the northeast. What was unusual about Spanish in Miami was not that it was so often spoken, but that it was so often heard: in, say Los Angeles, Spanish remained a language only barely registered by the Anglo population, part of the ambient noise, the language spoken by the people who worked in the car wash and came to trim the trees and cleared the tables in restaurants. In Miami Spanish was spoken by the people who ate in the restaurants, the people who owned the cars and the trees, which made, on the socioauditory scale, a considerable difference.[3]

This made a considerable difference to whom? To those who believe that Latinos—Mexicans and Mexican-Americans—are destined to be part of the blue-collar working class, clearing tables and pruning shrubs but never in a position to dine at upscale restaurants or own homes whose gardens must be tended? To those who presumed that Hispanic immigrants would follow in the steps of every other immigrant group and adopt English as their primary, if not exclusive, language?

In Miami it is the Cubans and Cuban-Americans who are doctors, engineers, architects, and attorneys and run City Hall; the socioeconomic success of these Hispanics is exceptional. How Hispanics of Cuban descent see themselves and their place in American life is far different from how Americans of Mexican ancestry see themselves. Didion explains what she means in an answer to her implied question of why Spanish was "so often heard" that is itself instructive in how Hispanics "fail" to meet the expectations of American society:

> An entrepreneur who spoke no English could still, in Miami, buy, sell, negotiate, leverage assets, float bonds, and, if he were so inclined, attend galas twice a week, in black tie. . . . [And among] Anglos who did not perceive themselves as economically or socially threatened by Cubans, there remained considerable uneasiness on the matter of language, perhaps because the inability or the disinclination to speak English tended to undermine their conviction that assimilation was an ideal universally shared by those who were to be assimilated.[4]

In other words, for Hispanics to speak Spanish is a repudiation of assimilation into mainstream society, a direct challenge to the historic social contract of American life: the "huddled masses" who wash up on these shores are welcome, provided they embrace an "American" identity in due course.

Furthermore, Cubans who have a more sublime command of English than many native English speakers, chose, time and again, to speak in Spanish in public and *demanded* that they be answered in Spanish. Whether it involved placing a phone call to City Hall or making an airline reservation, government and the private sector alike realized that to serve the taxpayers and to court paying customers, they needed to provide Spanish-language customer services. "When it comes to breakfast cereal," the Cubans seemed to say, "our decision will be decided by which one advertises to us in Spanish: Post Raisin Bran or Kellogg's Corn Flakes." Thus, the reason the Hispanic consumer market exists in the United States at all is a deliberate cultural act whose sweeping economic consequences rippled across the economic landscape of the United States.

Corporate America, taken aback by the realization that a prosperous community refused to speak English, decided to regroup and consider what this meant. The initial response was straightforward enough: begin providing some Spanish-speaking customer service personnel, and develop Spanish-language advertising. That, however, was not enough, for cultural nuances mandated that different strategies be devised if the loyalty of Hispanic consumers was to be secured. Regardless of their language skills, Hispanics feel more comfortable in Spanish, almost as if their emotional needs are better satisfied living life in Spanish than in English. Time and again, Hispanic consumers indicated that although they "thought in English," they "felt in Spanish."

As any brand manager knows, consumer behavior is predicated more by feelings than by thoughts. "I feel like having a Coke" is more conducive to inculcating brand loyalty than "I think I'll have a Coke." Consumer loyalty is greater to brands for which there is an *emotional* connection rather than an *intellectual* one. The Roslow Research Group (RRG) studied the effectiveness of television commercials among Hispanics to understand better what was going on. In a series of research studies, the first completed in 1994, when NAFTA was first initiated, and the second in 2000, when the U.S. Census confirmed Hispanic ascendancy, the results were startling. Despite their language skills, Hispanics who were completely bilingual still preferred advertisements in Spanish.

In RRG's analysis, the methodology of both the 1994 and 2000 studies was identical. The research examined three components of effectiveness of advertising: unaided ad recall, communication (defined as "main message recall"), and persuasion. The findings indicated that:

- *Unaided ad recall:* Spanish-language ads were 61 percent more effective than commercials in English
- *Communication:* Spanish-language ads were 57 percent more effective than commercials in English
- *Persuasion:* Spanish-language ads were four times more persuasive than commercials in English.

Furthermore, RRG found that:

- Language comprehension was not an issue; yet fully bilingual and acculturated Hispanics were more influenced by advertising in Spanish than in English
- The findings of the 2000 study were almost identical to those of 1994, signaling that these differences are of a *cultural* nature, not one of either language skills or level of acculturation or assimilation.

The 2000 RRG report concluded simply that "these results strongly suggest that Hispanic rating points delivered via an advertising schedule on English-language television should be adjusted down to compensate for substantially reduced effectiveness."

The unexpected nature of these findings, which indicated that the traditional ideal of the "melting pot" of American immigration had been broken, compelled corporate America to find new ways of understanding how the consumer markets were changing, and what Hispanic ascendancy meant. "The melting pot is out; the salad bowl is in," Gary Berman declared in *Sales & Marketing Management* in October 1991. "Here's how to make sure your Hispanic marketing program provides the right dressing." Then, declaring that "key words now are 'target,' 'micro,' 'segmented,' 'niche,' and 'Hispanic,'" he argues that with a "homogenous marketplace" long gone, "marketers are focusing their efforts on a process called 'demassification.'" He points out, however, that Hispanics cannot be treated as a "subgroup," like the African-Americans or Jewish-Americans have been in the past.

When this strategy of demassification was implemented, in fact, corporate America failed to produce desired results. "As corporations realized the profit potential of minority markets, they developed the position of 'target market specialist' within their bureaucratic structures," Berman wrote. "These individuals were responsible for both Hispanics and African-American segments, as well as other groups such as the mature market. Unfortunately, these same individuals generally didn't possess an in-depth understanding of the similarities and differences between Hispanics, African-Americans, and the general market."[5]

Other researchers offered rather complicated answers. One group favored an "Ecosystem Model" and sought to "explain" the Hispanic market in a way only academics could love. Hispanics differed from the rest of the population in their emphasis on family life ("microsystem"); their relationship with institutions, such as work, peer groups, extended family ("mesosystem"); their interactions with social institutions, such as the government and religious institutions ("exosystem"); and their ideas and cultural beliefs ("macrosystem") (Figure 1.1). Hispanics' microsystem, mesosystem, exosystem, and macrosystem, according to this model, were fundamentally different from the microsystem, mesosystem, exosystem, and macrosystem of mainstream society, or Anglophone Americans.

Another group of observers thought the Ecosystem Model was a bit confusing, and they offered a simpler model, the "Hispanic Cultural Concepts" interpretation. Hispanics are reluctant to acculturate, this theory explains, which is understandable, given that Hispanics never completely sever their relationships from their homeland. They have one foot in America and another foot in their country of origin, shifting their weight back and forth in an undulating process of slow assimilation and often incomplete acculturation.

Furthermore, Hispanic cultural concepts of *machismo* and *marianismo* impede their acculturation into America's mainstream, according to this theory. Machismo was a characterization of how Hispanic males saw their role as financial providers and protectors of their families, and their duty to be the point of contact between their family and outside authorities and strangers. Cultural values of machismo were said to include being courteous, responsible, strong (emotionally), and virile. Marianismo, on the other hand, defines a woman's role in Hispanic culture. Hispanic females are expected to sacrifice their own ambitions and desires for the good of their family. Their self-sacrifice is a badge of honor, the way the Virgin Mary placed her responsibilities to the Holy Family above her own interests, a phenomenon often called the "Maria Paradox."

Marianismo reverses the cultural directives of machismo, exacerbating gender roles and the inherent conflict between the values of their former lives in the "old" country and the modern demands of assimilating to life in the United States. "Adapting to life in a new country is in some ways more complex now than a century ago, when immigrants typically broke most ties with their native lands," Donatella Lorch wrote in the *New York Times*. "Home-country ideas are reinforced by Spanish-language cable television channels, newspapers and radio talk shows and several new Spanish-language women's magazines published in the United States. And because many of their native countries are relatively close, many immigrants can see friends and relatives regularly. Even the Internet helps some keep in touch."[6]

Figure 1.1   **The "Ecosystem Model"—Hispanics Versus Anglophone Americans: Is This a Tautology?**

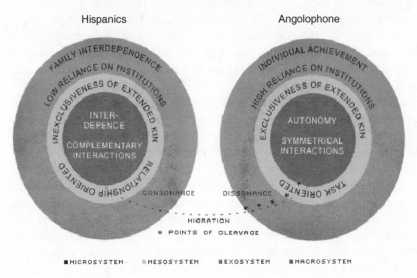

Into this conflict between machismo and marianismo, enter Generation Ñ (defined as Hispanic youth between ages fifteen and twenty-five), a term that gained currency in 1995 when Hispanics reached a critical mass. Generation Ñ is fully bilingual and bicultural and, furthermore, is the cultural bridge between their parents and mainstream American society. They are the ones who will make America's "salad bowl" into a "melting pot" once again, the theory's proponents argued. But as RRG's research indicates, this is not the case. All generations of Hispanics default emotionally to Spanish, regardless of where they were born or how complete their command of the English language.

The problem with these approaches, of course, is that they are wrong. The Ecosystem Model is tautological and the Hispanic Cultural Concepts theory continues to be disproven: The more Hispanics become bilingual and bicultural, the more they self-segregate away from mainstream American society and mainstream consumer behavior. Thus corporate America confronts a dilemma that centers on the resistance to assimilate. It is therefore not surprising that one of the more successful companies in the Hispanic consumer market is Goya Foods, a New Jersey–based Hispanic business. "Certain foods and ingredients cross over with each Hispanic group even though each group has certain preferences and cooking styles," Joe Pérez, vice president of purchasing is quoted as saying. "For example, fruit nectars containing guanabana, pineapple and mango are enjoyed by all Hispanics from Mexico, Caribbean, Central and South America."[7]

Is it that simple? Goya management's innate understanding of the Hispanic market is natural, since it is a Hispanic company. Its success in the United States, however, is evidence that corporate America can provide the goods and services of this community, in spite of its daunting diversity. Goya's success, rest assured, has nothing to do with long strategy sessions discussing the "exosytem" of this or the "mesosystem" of the other. "Marketers must understand that the three largest Hispanic groups are the Mexicans, Puerto Ricans and the Cubans, who comprise three-fourths of the total U.S. Hispanic population," Morton Winsberg, a professor of geography at Florida State University, told writer Susheela Uhl. "However, we also have to be aware of the 'other' Hispanic cultures who constitute one-fourth of the . . . Hispanic consumer market."[8]

The Hispanic Cultural Concept takes universal gender roles, presents them as a unique phenomenon of Hispanic culture, and runs into a brick wall. Males have dominated most human societies, and human history since the Age of Enlightenment has included the struggle to enfranchise women. There is also an undeniable aspect of prejudice to this theory, for it plays into stereotypes about poor, uneducated people. Despite what advocates of the Hispanic Cultural Concepts theory suggest, it is possible to be a Hispanic male in America without being an insensitive brute who is opposed to women's rights. It is possible to be a Hispanic female without being a long-suffering creature at risk for mental health problems. And it is possible to be a member of Generation Ñ without becoming a de facto ambassador between one's Hispanic heritage and America's melting pot. It is possible to understand the Hispanic market—as Goya Foods does—without resorting to simpleton reductions.

This brings us back to the beginning: Why do Hispanics self-segregate by language? Why do they refuse to embrace becoming Americanized? Why do working-class Mexican immigrants in California show little interest in becoming American citizens? Why do professional Cuban millionaires in Miami recoil at being labeled as "Americanized"? Why do Puerto Ricans in New York refer to themselves, first and foremost, as "Puerto Rican," regardless of how many generations in their families have been born in the United States?

Why is there a "Hispanic" market in the first place? And what does Hispanic ascendancy mean?

The Use of Spanish to Self-Segregate

The Hispanic market in the United States exists simply because the Spanish language is spreading throughout the nation, and an increasing number of Americans are bilingual. Hispanics constitute 38 million consumers in the United States (Figure 1.2). Of these, Hispanics of Mexican ancestry account for two-thirds (Figure 1.3). When one considers that Central American im-

Figure 1.2 **Consumer Market in the United States, 2003**

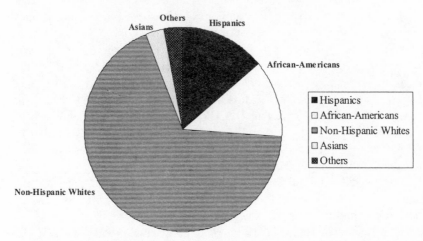

Source: Access Worldwide Cultural Group; U.S. Census Bureau, 2000; International Credit Monitor, 2002.

Note: "Non-Hispanic Whites" includes all Americans of European, Middle Eastern, and Jewish descent.

Figure 1.3 **Hispanic Market, 2003: 38 Million Consumers**

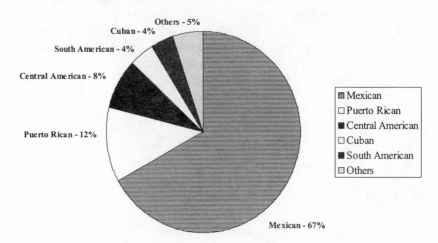

Source: Access Worldwide Cultural Group; U.S. Census Bureau, 2000; International Credit Monitor, 2002.

Note: "Others" includes Hispanics from regions not listed—the Caribbean, Spain, and Portugal.

migrants to the United States come primarily from Guatemala, El Salvador, and Honduras—part of the Maya Culture Area—then the bulk of Mexican and Central American immigrants share a common indigenous background. U.S. Hispanics of Mexican and Central American origin are 75 percent of all Hispanics. The next significant groups are Puerto Ricans, who account for 12 percent, and Cubans, with 4 percent. The remaining 9 percent of Hispanics come from South America, Caribbean nations, and Spain.

In the United States, as in Mexico and Canada, debates rage on bilingualism and bilingual education, particularly since significant numbers of these countries' respective citizens speak minority languages. The question of how best to teach minority students the dominant language is an emotional one. It is also a political one. It determines how acculturation and assimilation are able to take place. Throughout American history, immigrants have become fluent in English, one of the milestones in becoming American. Hispanics have broken that pattern, however. In 2003, fully 27 percent of Hispanics were not proficient in English, meaning they did not know enough English to order a Big Mac at McDonald's in English. Another 63 percent were only "partially acculturated," meaning they knew enough English to perform their jobs and get by, but their primarily language remained Spanish (Figure 1.4). These statistics are expected to *increase* by 2025 (Figure 1.5).

More and More Hispanics Will Speak Less and Less English in Public as this Century Unfolds!

One thing is certain: The NAFTA nations are undergoing a linguistic revolution in the twenty-first century not seen since the Norman invasion of England in the eleventh century. As Robert McCrum says in *The Story of English*, the democratization of the language—the free incorporation (one could say the "migration") of foreign words—strengthened and invigorated English. "Between 1600 and the present," McCrum writes, "in armies, navies, companies, and expeditions, the speakers of English—including Scots, Irish, Welsh, Americans and many more—traveled to every corner of the globe, carrying their language and culture with them."[9] It is a process best exemplified by the Norman invasion of 1066 that, centuries later, made English the preferred international language of commerce. As a consequence, the Oxford English Dictionary lists more than 500,000 words—with an equal number of technical and scientific words. By comparison German has fewer than 200,000 words, and French half that figure.

Consider how English itself is already a bilingual language. After William the Conqueror established his rule in 1066, the established language of the conquered—"Old English"—was flooded by the arrival of the Norman French.

Figure 1.4 **Acculturation Among U.S. Hispanics, 2003**

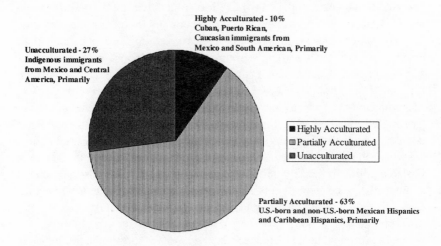

Highly Acculturated - 10%
Cuban, Puerto Rican,
Caucasian immigrants from
Mexico and South American, Primarily

Unacculturated - 27%
Indigenous immigrants
from Mexico and Central
America, Primarily

■ Highly Acculturated
▥ Partially Acculturated
▨ Unacculturated

Partially Acculturated - 63%
U.S.-born and non-U.S.-born Mexican Hispanics
and Caribbean Hispanics, Primarily

Source: Strategy Resource Corporation; International Credit Monitor, 2002.
Note: "Unacculturated" refers to Hispanics who are not proficient in English.

Figure 1.5 **Acculturation Among U.S. Hispanics, 2025**

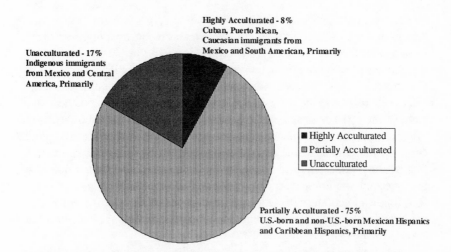

Highly Acculturated - 8%
Cuban, Puerto Rican,
Caucasian immigrants from
Mexico and South American, Primarily

Unacculturated - 17%
Indigenous immigrants
from Mexico and Central
America, Primarily

■ Highly Acculturated
▥ Partially Acculturated
▨ Unacculturated

Partially Acculturated - 75%
U.S.-born and non-U.S.-born Mexican Hispanics
and Caribbean Hispanics, Primarily

Source: Strategy Resource Corporation; International Credit Monitor, 2002.
Note: As the United States becomes "bilingual," acculturation declines.

As these tongues mixed and mingled in speech and writing, an ingenious solution evolved as a matter of commerce and law: to ensure that everyone understood everyone else, two words were used for everything. Attorneys advise us, for instance, to have our "last will and testament" in order. If a "will" is a "testament," why the redundancy? The answer is that "will" is Old English, and "testament" is from the Latin and French. If a resident of London in the eleventh century was not familiar with one word, he would be familiar with the other. In matters of commerce, the same convention emerged. A property owner, for instance, could make it known that he had property available to rent, or to lease. "Rent" is Old English, and "lease" is an Anglo-French invention. As a general rule, shorter words with many consonants are Old English, and longer words with many vowels are Norman French or Latin in origin.

The bilingualism of English has, since the eleventh century, given way to the multilingualism that emerged over the centuries, to be sure. Although conservative activist Phyllis Schlafly reiterated her demand that Spanish be banned from government and that "foreign" words be "forcibly" removed from English spoken in the United States when I spoke to her, I have yet to hear an American child protest the "contamination" of the English language by the Aztec origin for the word "chocolate."[10]

The linguistic phenomenon that the United States is living within this century is different from the Canadian model. Whereas in Canada, bilingualism is the result of a *political* compromise between the Quebecois and their English-speaking compatriots, in the United States the spread of Spanish is the result not of legislation, but of *economics*. Whereas French is mandated by federal authorities in Canada, in the United States the use of Spanish in public is the result of corporate America (and local governments) trying to meet the needs of consumers (and constituents), driven by the marketplace. This makes a considerable difference, for in a capitalist market economy, supply and demand finds its own equilibrium, including in markets where the sale depends on speaking a different language.

In 2003, one out of three consumers in North America is Hispanic (see Figure 1.6). By 2025, one out of two consumers living in North America will speak Spanish (see Figure 1.7). Concerns over "bilingualism" center on how to educate children, and how corporate America should manage the use of languages other than English in marketing, advertising, and the corporate workplace. Let us consider how each in turn affects corporate America.

Bilingual Education

"What is the best way to teach bilingual students, in English or their native language?" Kenneth Cooper asked in a *Washington Post* article in 1991.

Figure 1.6 **Hispanic Market Across North America, 2003**
(1 of 3 Speak Spanish)

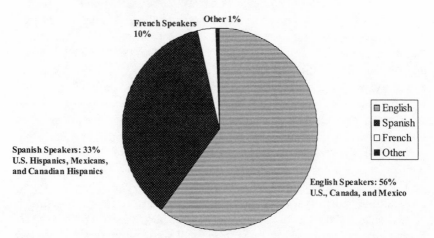

Source: Access Worldwide Cultural Group; U.S. Census Bureau, 2000; Statistics Canada.

Notes: Language designations denote fluency in language. "Other" denotes individuals who speak indigenous languages and are not fluent in one of the other three.

Figure 1.7 **Hispanic Market Across North America, 2025**
(1 of 2 Speak Spanish)

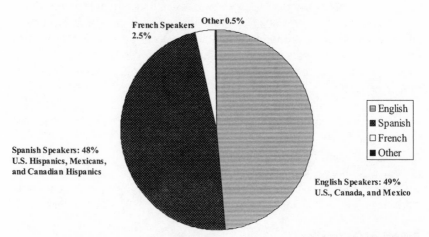

Source: Access Worldwide Cultural Group; U.S. Census Bureau, 2000; Statistics Canada.

Notes: Language designations denote fluency in language. "Other" denotes individuals who speak indigenous languages and are not fluent in one of the other three.

A diplomatic answer to that controversial question comes from an Education Department study that concludes Spanish-speaking pupils learn at about the same rate, regardless of how much English their teacher uses. The four year study . . . compared three bilingual methods involving 2,000 elementary students in five states. Under those methods, a teacher's use of English varied from almost all of the time to almost none of the time.[11]

The answer, then, resides in the *quality* of the teachers' instruction, not the language used. Almost a decade later, these findings were confirmed in an exciting real-world experiment. "Two years after Californians voted to end bilingual education and force a million Spanish-speaking students to immerse themselves in English as if it were a cold bath, those students are improving reading and other subjects at often striking rates, according to standardized test scores released this week," Jacques Steinberg reported in the *New York Times.* "I thought it would hurt kids," Ken Noonan, founder of the California Association of Bilingual Educators, who opposed the drive to end bilingual education and is currently the superintendent in Oceanside, California, told reporters. "The exact reverse occurred, totally unexpected by me. The kids began to learn—not pick up, but learn—formal English, oral and written, far more quickly than I ever thought they would. . . . Here are kids, within nine months in the first year, and they literally learned to read."[12]

A generation ago, in contrast, this kind of acculturation required individual drive. This is how Pete Hamill describes how Henry B. González, who served in the House of Representatives for thirty-seven years, sought to educate himself:

At the same time, young Henry B. [González] was coming up against the prevailing American bigotries of the era. He learned the hard way that some Americans thought of him and his father and his family as "greasers," or "messicans." His skin was brown, the color of the earth, and people with pink skins too often treated him as if he were dirt. . . . Schools were rigidly segregated. The use of Spanish was punished. Mexican customs were subjected to sneers. And on blazing summer afternoons, Henry B. and his friends were barred from public swimming pools. . . .

In spite of the derision, Henry B. began to forge an alloy of his Mexican heritage and his American identity, and followed the traditional path out of the ghetto. It was the same path followed by the American children of the Irish and the Jews and the Italians and all the other enriching streams of American immigration: education. From the age of eight, he haunted the public library.[13]

It is clear that two generations of Hispanic youngsters have been deprived of the opportunity to succeed by misguided social scientists and unscrupulous educators who sought to increase their power by using minority children as pawns in a political game. In fact, the test scores reported by California are also a measure of the competence, or lack thereof, of "bilingual" teachers. Of the dozens of such instructors with whom I have spoken over the years, it is clear to me that far too many are illiterate in *both* English and Spanish, making it impossible for them to teach properly in *either* language.

Furthermore, bilingual education, of course, presumes that these children's native language is Spanish. "Rufino Dominguez is well known in California for a special expertise. A native of a Oaxacan village, San Miguel Cuevas, he speaks Mixtec, an indigenous Mexican dialect still spoken in the small villages of southern Mexico," Joel Millman writes in *The Other Americans*. "Mixtecs have been coming to California in ever-increasing numbers of the past decade [1990s], establishing their own critical mass. In articles in the *Los Angeles Times* and *New York Times*, Mixtec Indians have been portrayed as the new Okies of the state's harvest, part of an historic chain of exploitation that links California's biggest industry to Mexico's oldest pockets of poverty."[14]

One explanation for the failure of children *taught* in Spanish is that they don't *speak* Spanish that well, if at all. If English is as foreign to them as Spanish is, then it is logical to teach them English and then *in* English. But the power of the teachers union—where bilingual education has often been used as an instrument to create employment and dispense political patronage to Latinos—resides in keeping certain political ideologies alive. "It's premature to comment on which ultimately works better," Dave Crowles, superintendent of schools in Vista, California, told reporters. "If these results are indicative of how students learn best, then we have to take them into account when we talk to parents."[15] Crowles, of course, declined to identify how many instructors in his school district were bilingual—in English and *Mixtec*.

This should be kept in mind when we talk of politicians as well. If (a) children learn as quickly when taught in either language, and (b) children taught in Spanish in California consistently fail to learn, then it naturally follows that it has nothing to do with bilingual education, but rather that it is a question of incompetent teachers. Now the question becomes, who benefits from the proliferation of incompetent teachers? It is not the students, obviously. It must therefore be the teacher unions and boards of education throughout the United States that derive their authority from the proliferation of programs that conform to their political ideology, regardless of whether minority children learn or not.

Language in Consumer Marketing

As for corporate America, it will continue to increase its use of Spanish as required to improve customer service and to reach new customers. "Some ethnic marketing initiatives use foreign-language advertisements, especially as a strategy for reaching the Hispanic population, since Spanish remains by far the most popular non-English language in the United States," Marilyn Halter writes. Furthermore, she notes that fully 70 percent of "Hispanic residents were born abroad; an equal percentage speak Spanish at home."[16] Despite the growing number of bilingual Americans, corporate America is uneasy about how best to proceed. "Many mainstream national advertisers remain reluctant to speak directly to a market that they perceive as linguistically and culturally complicated," Stuart Elliott reported.[17] Business life is often complicated, however reluctant one may be to accept this fact.

Reluctant or not, reaching consumers in their own language is a sound business practice. "The growing interest in Spanish, school administrators said, is a function of how widespread the language has become in New York," Mirta Ojito reported in the *New York Times* in 1999. "Spanish is everywhere these days—from labels identifying food and produce in the city's busiest supermarkets to the signs on city buses advertising shows on WNJU, Channel 47, the local affiliate of Telemundo, one of the country's two Spanish-language networks. . . . The New York Police Department is now exploring options to offer Spanish classes to all those on the 40,000-officer force who wish to take them. . . . Doctors at Metropolitan Hospital Center in East Harlem started taking Spanish lessons at work almost two years ago. A teacher from the Spanish Institute goes to the hospital three times a week."[18]

Although Latino activists decry the fact that there are no "amigos" on NBC's hit television series *Friends*, they overlook one simple fact: Hispanics do not need to be on ABC, CBS, or NBC to be "visible," by virtue of their having two national Spanish-language television networks broadcasting continuously. Indeed, this complaint makes as much sense as complaining that there are no men in the women's restroom—forgetting to mention that men have their own restroom.[19] That Hispanics freely choose to resist assimilation by self-segregating linguistically is more a political repudiation of what Hispanics find reprehensible about American society than it reflects an inability to learn English.

"The phenomenon of assimilation alongside cultural affirmation is not unlike that experienced by other ethnic groups as they set roots in this country," Mireya Navarro reported in the *New York Times* in 1999. The question of assimilation signals how rapidly Spanish is spreading into mainstream culture, whether it is the Terminator saying, "Hasta la vista, baby," or a chihuahua declaring "Yo quiero Taco Bell." "But the Hispanic population is likely to make its presence more deeply felt, these experts say, because Latinos make up the largest ethnic and linguistic group to arrive; they retain ties to their geographically close countries of origin, and the migration is continuing. All those factors reinforce Hispanic culture and the Spanish language while at the same time, assimilation dilutes them."[20]

When novelist Peter Schneider wrote in praise of "the specter of English," he confessed: "I myself have come to welcome the English specter as a friendly ghost that is forcing—no, luring—the Europeans back to a common language for the first time in about 500 years. Establishing a new lingua franca is the most significant milestone on the road to a unified Europe—more important even than the euro." He wrote those words in a foreign language; Philip Boehm had to translate it into English, suitable for publication in the United States.[21] That Boehm himself is not fluent in English but ponders that English is overtaking the European imagination, has its parallel in the United States, where Anglophone Americans decry how loud Spanish is becoming on the "socioauditory" level of American life. As "English Only" initiatives provide amusing entertainment, so do all Sisyphean efforts. In the debate over the surreptitious spread of Spanish in the United States at a time when English is spreading in other countries, there are unintended, but delicious, ironies.

Bilingualism in the Workplace

In the workplace, there are sufficient market forces—and business success—that will shape how English and Spanish coexist. "As socially acceptable as Spanglish is in Miami, it can cause problems for U.S. companies operating in Latin America and Spain, appearing sloppy or even snooty to Spanish-speaking customers," Jennifer Hull writes: 'When you send an e-mail with 20,000 [grammatical] mistakes in it, the thought is, I'm dealing with an illiterate guy,' says Dario Gamboa, senior vice-president in charge of human resources at Visa International for Latin America and the Caribbean."[22]

There is, however, the overriding concern of being able to communicate with one's customers. "I feel, in order to really communicate, to explain products and new approaches, I need to know Spanish," Jack Lass, who owned a paint store in Wheaton, Maryland, explained more than a decade ago. "My attitude is, these folks are going to be here, we should respect them. I absolutely agree they should learn English. But in the meantime, I'm in business, and it doesn't hurt you to know another language. I think we should all learn something, just to expand our tiny constricted little minds—Spanish, Japanese, something."[23]

Corporate America's ability to "smooth" linguistic transitions is historic. Robert Putnam writes:

> In the thirty years between 1870 and 1900, nearly 12 million persons immigrated to the United States, more than had come to our shores in the previous two and a half centuries. In the following fourteen years nearly another 13 million would arrive. In 1870 one-third of all industrial workers in America were foreign born. By 1900 more than half were. In 1890 immigrant adults actually outnumbered native adults in eighteen of the twenty cities with a population over 100,000. . . . By 1890 the cacophony of strange tongues and strange customs of newcomers had triggered a national debate about "Americanization" and ethnic identity, similar in many respects to the debate about "multiculturalism" and "English only" today.[24]

There are business pros and social cons to "Spanglish," however. On the pro side, writes the *New York Times*, "Spanglish can reflect impressive bilingual verbal skills as speakers choose from two languages. Switching back and forth between Spanish and English, or 'code switching' as linguists call it, people will often use Spanish to express emotions and English for analytical thoughts."[25] On the con side, it can create tension with English-speakers in an office, and it can alienate other Hispanics who are offended by the "cliquish" nature of Spanglish as a form of snobbery.[26] For those conversant in Spanglish, there is an overriding concern: remaining *literate* in both English and Spanish.

Racism and Why Hispanics Self-Segregate

Hispanics use Spanish as a defense against "America's baggage of racism," to use Anthony DePalma's apt phrase. America's legacy of slavery and racism places corporate America at a competitive disadvantage when it comes to understanding the Hispanic consumer market. Consider how R.J. Reynolds ended its "research," concluding that "Mexican[s] feel fortunate—even awed—at the prospect of life in America, and are less inclined to make waves . . . [the group] is distinguished by its relative lack of hostility toward the White race."[27] Cubans, on the other hand, are "relatively well established . . . [and are] clearly the most educated and upscaled of the four major [Hispanic] markets. And young adults here are remarkably aspirational and career-oriented, when compared to [other Hispanics, though] it does not follow that the Miami Cubans have become 'Americanized.'"[28]

Most of these Cubans are white, which is why it is not necessary to remark upon their "hostility," or lack thereof, toward the "white race."[29] More instructive still, why were the Cubans ("white") queried about their opinions about Mexicans ("people of color"), but not the other way around? And is the answer offered by R.J. Reynolds—Cubans "agreed that the Mexicans were the humblest of the Hispanic sub-groups"—not consistent with what American Caucasians have always said of African-Americans, but in harsher, more incendiary, terms?

It is evident that this analysis has a *racial* subtext, one based on a "black and white" paradigm at work throughout corporate America. The phrasing in this research report reveals more about the state of mainstream thinking in corporate America than it does about the consumer behavior of the polyglot Hispanic market. What is transparently clear, furthermore, is that corporate America insists on imposing a black-white paradigm on the formulation of its marketing strategies, something that is no longer appropriate given America's post–Census 2000 demographics. Indeed, this primitive analysis is as misguided as it is ignorant of understanding the distinct cultural heritages of Hispanics, and it underscores why corporate America has to move beyond thinking in terms of race.

Such "out of the racial box" thinking has been done before, in other fields. William Lambert, an authority on cross-cultural psychology at Cornell University, contends:

> Throughout the 1950s and 1960s when cross-cultural psychology was in its infancy, evaluation results were very strange. The tests showed a tremendous gap in the scores of Westerners and people from other cultures, suggesting that non-Westerners were stupid or mentally impaired. How could such disparities among people possibly exist? One knew *instinctively* that there was something very amiss—not with people, but with our method of testing them. But when we approached cross-cultural psychology from a different perspective—assume the human mind is the same across cultures—then psychologists began to make progress in understanding how culture affects human development and why societies are structured the way they are. This approach has added tremendous rigor to the discipline and it helped completely change the way we understand the world.[30]

Consider two incidents, half a century apart, that illustrate why Hispanics recoil at the thought of being forced to see the world through the lens of race, and thus opt out of discussions of race, expressing hostility for the American penchant of thinking inside the racial box. When in the 1950s Desi Arnaz portrayed Ricky Ricardo on *I Love Lucy*, his fictional character was a bandleader whose signature song was "Babalu." "Babalu" is a deity in the Afro-Cuban religion of Santeria, which has its origins in the beliefs of the Yoruba people of western Africa. That Arnaz, a white European-descendant male, chose to sing the music that was born of the Cuban experience of slavery was not an issue, then or now. No one in Cuba (or Little Havana) would challenge his right as a human being to embrace and perform a music genre of his choice.

Now consider what happened in the United States almost fifty years later, when another white European-descendant male decided to embrace a musical genre associated with blacks. Eminem's decision to perform rap created a firestorm, with detractors charging that he had no "right" to "appropriate" an African-American musical form. The "issue" was debated in the pages of the *New York Times*, on MTV, in cable talk show after talk show, and the controversy continues, with the element of race clearly in the middle. Who is white and who is black, and what can a white person do and what can a black person do, are all a matter of contention in this country.

Hispanics point to differences between how Desi Arnaz and Eminem are perceived by others in their respective societies and argue that this is evidence that there is no racism in Hispanic society. "This kind of controversy does not exist in Cuban culture," Celia Cruz,[†] the famous Cuban singer who was black, said of the uproar over Eminem, "Music belongs to everyone equally, and everyone has the right to sing any song he wants to sing."[31] When asked how she would answer someone who challenged Arnaz's right to "appropriate" a black musical genre, she replied, "I would answer that that is a question only an ignorant person would ask, and that the question itself was racist! Why is everything about race in this country? When will the United States transcend this maddening insistence of labeling everything and everyone by skin color?"[32]

Hispanics thus choose not to think inside the racial box that otherwise dominates American life. This is infuriating, and problematic, for corporate managers, for it challenges the assumption upon which the consumer marketplace in the United States is understood.

Of Puerto Rican "Grandmothers" and Mexican "Gringadas"

Recall how Cuban exile leader Jorge Mas Canosa berated Miami when his family arrived—"blacks weren't allowed to sit at the cafeteria counter in the downtown Woolworth's"—and thus his family's conscious decision *not* to become "Americanized" if becoming American required adopting such values. Other Hispanic groups have chosen to set themselves apart from mainstream American society as a way of defending themselves. To counteract the pressure to live inside the racial box of American society, various His-

---

†Celia Cruz died on July 16, 2003.

panic groups have developed mechanisms to cope with daily humiliations of living in a country where racial tension is part of everyday life. Roberto Suro writes in *Strangers Among Us: Latinos' Lives in a Changing America*:

> For me, Spanish and everything that went with it belonged at home and with family friends and relatives; and the language came to life most powerfully on our trips back to Puerto Rico and Ecuador. English belonged in all other places. . . . For me, Spanish could belong to one world and English to another, and the door between them was open. We were light skinned and middle class, and I could switch from one language to another, from one world to another. By becoming culturally ambidextrous, I fulfilled my parents' aspirations. When I passed through the door into America from my Spanish-speaking home, I did it quietly and no one much noticed.[33]

Suro, whose father was Puerto Rican and mother Ecuadoran, grew up in the suburbs of Washington, D.C., in the 1950s and, by virtue of being "white" to other Americans' eyes, had an easy time of living in the United States. Most Hispanics, however, are "people of color," meaning, neither entirely Caucasian nor Native American nor black. What Suro describes, however, is not an unfamiliar process to Hispanics who are white or can pass as white. When Raquel Tejada, a Bolivian-born immigrant, wanted to increase her odds of succeeding as an actress, she changed her name to "Welch" and projected a "white" public persona. When Ramon Estevez, another Hispanic with acting ambitious, pursued his dreams, he changed his name to "Martin Sheen," although his driver's license still identifies him by his "real" name.[34]

But what of the vast multitudes of Hispanics who are "people of color"? To understand how completely America's race-obsessed worldview offends— and impacts—Hispanics, consider the following story about another society marked by racism. When apartheid was the law of the land in South Africa, a British friend of mine was sent to Capetown, part of a nonprofit, humanitarian program to teach black youngsters. Upon arriving in South Africa, because he was scheduled to remain in the country for an extended period of time, he had to register at the local police station, where certain paperwork was requested of him. One question asked him to indicate his race. He left it blank, a deliberate omission on his part.

A few days later, a police officer showed up at his residence. The police officer explained that he had to indicate his race. He resisted, saying he found the question immaterial and offensive. The police officer then explained to him that he was *required* to indicate his race, and that if he chose not to comply, the police officer would simply mark the box "Caucasian" on his behalf. My friend objected, saying he would complete the form and return it the following day. The police officer left, and the next day, he turned in his completed paperwork at the police station. Several days later, two police officers showed up at his residence again. The paperwork was not acceptable, they explained to him. My friend, who had indicated that his "race" was "human," was ordered to write in "Caucasian." An argument ensued, and a few days later, the police officers were back. They informed my friend he had fifteen minutes to pack his belongings. The police officers would drive him to the airport, where he would be deported, or they would drive him to the police station, where he would be arrested and jailed. He was deported, simply because, on principle, he did not want to comply with the requirements of institutionalized racism.

At times one's self-perception differs greatly from how others see one. It is therefore instructive to try to understand how others see one, and it may not always be complimentary. That said, the following may come as a surprise to non-Hispanic America, and if Hispanics do not state it so bluntly, perhaps out of a certain embarrassment, it is nonetheless what they think and how they feel. With Hispanic ascendancy a fait accompli, however, it is necessary to articulate publicly what generations of Latin Americans say privately.

It is this: *The United States is the only nation in the hemisphere that fought a civil war over the question of abolishing slavery; the United States is the only country in this hemisphere that legally sanctioned segregation; the United States remains traumatized over the question of race.*

Every other nation in the hemisphere, to varying degrees of success, moved in a more honorable and humane way to abolish the institution of slavery and then proceeded to incorporate the blacks into their respective societies. When people from Latin America emigrate to the United States, family and friends gently remind them not to adopt *valores anglosajones*, "Anglo-Saxon values," a euphemism for adopting American anti-black attitudes. This compels Latin Americans to demonstrate their lack of this kind of prejudice by refusing to surrender their language, regardless of how fluent in English they become, regardless of how acculturated they become: *How Americans saw South Africa under apartheid is how most Hispanics see the United States.*

This is the most important lesson anyone in corporate America can take from this book: *This is the moral imperative that drives the Hispanic worldview in the United States. It is a fear that, if one becomes "Americanized," one runs the risk of losing one's innocence, one's language, one's soul.*

This is the cultural backlash against the infuriating insistence of Americans imposing a "black and white" racial paradigm on the world. "When we came to the United States, we filled out a form and it was as if labels had been stapled to our foreheads. I was 'white' and my daughter was 'black,'" a Venezuelan woman, who is a successful advertising executive in New York, explained. "What kind of way is that to devalue a family?"[35] Hispanics resent this aspect of American life, though Americans take it as a matter of course. The singer Lenny Kravitz, whose father is white, tells how his mother taught him that he would be considered "black" in America, and treated as such, and he had to know how to "survive" being a black man. The actress Halle Berry, whose mother is white, tells of the "life lessons" imparted by her mother, who taught her she would be treated differently by society because of the color of her skin. These facts of life are what fuel the single most widespread Hispanic presumption—or prejudice—about Americans: that an element of racism runs through the American character, a lingering remnant of the "white man's burden."

Hispanics use Spanish both to resist "Americanization" and as a defense mechanism against racism. This does not mean they are fully insulated from the racial discrimination of American society, however. Hispanics understand this well. They are therefore loath to acknowledge how they are victimized by America's "creeping racism." Only recently, however, have Hispanics begun to speak openly about their feelings. "I'm seek (sick) oaf (of) the way jew (you) relate everything to skeen (skin) color, Lauren. It's so . . . American," Elizabeth, who is South American and black, complains to Lauren in Alisa Valdes-Rodriguez's *The Dirty Girls Social Club.* "In Colombia, nobody cares." Then, with a roll of her eyes, Lauren sets the record straight about the truth of America's insistence on forcing everyone to live inside a racial box. "I find that very hard to believe. Plus, she's here now, and America cares."[36]

America cares about the color of your skin more than the content of your character: Hispanic literature thus mirrors the racial nature of the lives Spanish speakers in the United States are forced to live in the real world. "Havana, sometime before 1994: As dusk descends on the quaint seaside village of Guanabo, two young men kick a soccer ball back and forth and back and forth across the sand. The tall one, Joel Ruiz, is black. The short, wiry one, Achmed Valdés, is white. They are the best of friends," Mirta Ojito reported for the *New York Times*'s series of articles "How Race is Lived in America," which was awarded a Pulitzer Prize for national reporting in 2001. "Miami, January 2000: Valdés is playing soccer, as he does every Saturday, with a group of light-skinned Latinos in a park near his apartment. Ruiz surprises him with a visit, and Valdés, flushed and sweating, runs to greet him. They shake hands warmly. . . . [But i]n ways that are obvious to the black man but far less to the white one, they have grown apart in the United States because of race. For the first time, they inhabit a place where the color of their skin defines the outlines of their lives—where they live, the friends they make, how they speak, what they wear, even what they eat."[37]

The Hispanic men, once best friends, now have to define their lives within the racial box of American life.

Being forced to play racist games that one finds reprehensible is an unpleasant fact of life at times. "While the de facto segregation has been a pernicious part of this society since the end of slavery, in our case, it became an unbearable assault on our family bonds," Juan Gonzalez, a columnist for the New York *Daily News*, writes in his book, *Harvest of Empire: A History of Latinos in America*, describing how Puerto Ricans in New York were forced to step inside the racial box of American life. "'*Y tu abuela, donde esta'* ('And your grandmother, where is she?') is a familiar Puerto Rican refrain and the title of a popular poem by Fortunato Vizcarrondo. The phrase reminds us that black blood runs through all Puerto Rican families. Puerto Ricans resisted the sharp racial demarcations so prevalent in this country, and their implicit diminishment of our human worth."[38]

González then describes how generations of Puerto Ricans and other Hispanics have been forced to make a Faustian bargain: become accepted by American society by becoming racist. He describes the haunting realization of what America demands this way:

> But gradually, almost imperceptibly, I watched my aunts and uncles begin to adopt antiblack attitudes, as if this were some rite of passage to becoming authentic Americans. "A hostile posture toward resident blacks must be struck at the Americanizing door before it will open," is how writer Toni Morrison so aptly describes it.
>
> The social imperative to choose a racial identity, and then only in purely black-and-white terms, impelled those of us in the second generation at first to jettison our native language and culture, to assimilate into either the white or black world.[39]

Puerto Rican "grandmothers" are a defense mechanism, one way Puerto Ricans remind themselves and each other that they need to defend themselves from being boxed in and becoming caught up in the unresolved trauma of slavery that continues to haunt Americans.

Hispanics of Mexican descent—who constitute the vast majority of U.S. Hispanics—for the most part do not have a choice, for few are able to "pass" as white and are therefore unable to assume a white public identity. Hispanics of Mexican descent are simply "people of color," and treated as such. Rodolfo Acuña writes of California in 1994 in *Anything But Mexican:*

> At the heart of the tension between Latinos and the white community was numbers. By the year 2020, the Latino population in California would in-

crease from 27.3 percent to 36.5 percent, while the Euroamerican population would fall from 52 percent in 1993 to 34 percent. Prop[osition] 187
was based on the color of Latino and Asian skins. No one mentioned the
Irish, Polish or Canadian undocumented workers [in California]. . . . In
other words, Prop. 187 went far beyond scapegoating immigrants for the
state's economic woes. It signified a profound resurgence of legalized racism in response to a historic national upheaval [occasioned by Hispanic
ascendance].[40]

California Hispanics, who are overwhelmingly working class, have little
political clout, one reason they remain an easy target. When Dianne Feinstein
was mayor of San Francisco in the 1980s, she used the race card to exploit
white fear of the Latinos in the Mission District. Her administration lashed
out against Hispanics, banning "low riders" parades that Mexican Hispanics
favored and opposing Hispanic cultural events in Dolores Park. Her anti-
Hispanic policies were calculated to curry favor with San Franciscans alarmed
by the influx of Central American refugees, part of the "Sanctuary Movement" that sponsored people fleeing civil wars in Guatemala and El Salvador. When she ran for a seat in the U.S. Senate, she exploited white xenophobia
and prejudices, falsely claiming that "3,000 illegal aliens" entered California
every night, and that Proposition 187 was the "solution" to "stop our state"
from being "overrun" by this "invasion."

"Gringadas," a word derived from the word "gringo," is a term Mexican
Hispanics and Mexicans use to describe biased or prejudiced speech or actions. When Dianne Feinstein uses anti-Hispanic rhetoric to advance her political ambitions, her speech is described as a "gringada." When San Francisco
mayor Willie Brown orders the city's Human Rights Commission not to investigate complaints filed by Hispanics—effectively denying Hispanics equal
protection under the law—such racism is characterized as a "gringada." When
a white foreman cheats a Mexican day laborer, paying him $20 or $40 less
than was agreed to, knowing that Mexicans have few, if any, legal recourses,
such dishonesty is called a "gringada."

In fact, labor violations have always been a part of the Mexican migrant's
experience in the United States across the decades. "Thousands of Mexicans
brought to the United States as laborers during World War II say they have
never received money that was deducted from their paychecks for them, and
now many are seeking hundreds of millions of dollars in reparations," Pam
Belluck reported in April 2001. The plaintiffs, many older gentlemen in their
seventies, were bitterly disappointed when their case was thrown out of court
in August 2002.[41] "A federal judge in San Francisco has dismissed a lawsuit
by Mexican laborers seeking to recoup savings withheld from their wages

for work in the United States dating to the 1940s," Barbara Whitaker reported. "In his ruling, Judge Charles R. Breyer of Federal District Court wrote that he did 'not doubt that many braceros never received Savings Fund withholdings to which they were entitled,'" but that's life—at least in these United States.[42]

This is one reason Mexican immigrants are the least likely to become American citizens; they resist the idea that they are condemned to live their entire lives in a society where they are subjected to the daily humiliations of one gringada after another. In *Immigrant America: A Portrait*, Alejandro Portes and Ruben Rumbaut reported one statistic that stunned Americans: 97 percent of Mexican immigrants who were admitted legally in 1970 had, by 1979, decided *not* to become American citizens![43] This decision confirmed what Mexican immigrants said in poll after poll, but many non-Hispanics refused to believe: that Mexican immigrants fully expect to return to Mexico. The facts bear them out; more than 75 percent of Mexicans who immigrate to the United States *return* to Mexico in due course. This decision, then, is tantalizing, for it constitutes a complete *repudiation* of the idea that the United States is the land of opportunity, or that everyone who comes here wants to stay here.

No American wants to hear this, but Hispanics come to this country because they need a *job*, not because they are "yearning to breathe free." And when they get here, they despise "America's baggage of racism." They are ambivalent about American society, and they manifest their uneasiness by creating a *parallel* society—in Spanish, coexisting with the larger English-speaking one, creating a barrier that separates them from what they find distasteful. This may be a harsh assessment, but it explains why Hispanics have insisted on, and succeeded in, speaking Spanish.

A Brave *Nuevo Mundo* for Corporate America

Puerto Rican grandmothers and Mexican-American gringadas indicate the emergence of something never before seen in the United States, one that has breathtaking implications for corporate America: *parallel* consumer markets separated by *language*. Consider this: If learning about Puerto Rican grandmothers and Mexican gringadas came as news, it is a measure of how little corporate America understands the Hispanic marketplace.[44] Hispanics use Spanish as a buffer from the greater mainstream society, a refuge from "America's baggage of racism," a mechanism by which Hispanics self-segregate. Hispanics understand—and reject—the dehumanizing process that polarizes society when one is forced to live inside the racial box of American life. While Randall Robinson argues that racism "is a social disease that exempts no race from either of its two rosters: victims and victimizers," Hispanics take a stand against being forced to play this racist game by speaking in Spanish. (In the debate between blacks and whites in the United States over "Ebonics," for instance, Hispanics understand the reasons African-Americans want to differentiate themselves linguistically, as a defense mechanism against the inexplicable hatred directed at them throughout the centuries.) Hispanics thus register their own protest by self-segregating through language, and this is a fundamental fact of life that has sweeping consequences for corporate America for one simple reason: the Hispanic market exists as a consequence of America's racist past.[45]

Not unlike my British friend who defied South Africa's apartheid by insisting that his race was "human," in a bold affirmation of identity and a resounding repudiation of America's racist baggage, Hispanics will speak Spanish to one's face. If a company is to sell its goods and services to them, the company needs to have to deal with them in Spanish. In a single generation, spearheaded first by the stellar achievements of Cuban-Americans in south Florida and second by the unprecedented success of NAFTA, the United States has become a *bilingual* nation.

The reason the United States has become a bilingual nation is simple: No other immigrant group had two national television networks broadcasting in their language, making Spanish a consumer language from coast to coast, at a time when its members have been entering the American middle class. Hispanics have Univision and Telemundo, but French-Americans, Italian-Americans, Japanese-Americans, and all other hyphenated-Americans cannot boast full-fledged television networks.[46] The impact of this conscious choice to speak Spanish in public is about more than language; it is about *consumer marketing.*

Consider the changed landscape that corporate America must negotiate in the wake of Hispanic ascendancy. While Condé Nast is denounced for perceived bigotry, Procter & Gamble is hailed for its vision. "We are asking those who feel offended by this piece to forgive us for our insensitivity," the editor of *Vanity Fair*, a Condé Nast publication, said in February 2003. "The backward bigotry of (Edna's) statements was so far over the line that we felt it could only be taken as satire. In our judgment it was a politically incorrect but blatantly satirical barb directed against anyone who might be unaware of the great contributions Latin people have made and continue to make in every walk of life, here in the United States and around the world."[47]

The incident that prompted this apology was a comment published in the February issue of that publication, which featured Mexican actress Salma Hayek on the cover. "Forget Spanish . . . Who speaks Spanish that you are so desperate to talk to? The help? Your leaf blower," Dame Edna, an Australian cross-dressing humorist whose real name is Barry Humphries, advised a reader who wanted to know if learning Spanish as a second language was a good idea. "There's nothing in that language worth reading except Don Quixote, and a quick listen to the CD of Man of La Mancha will take care of that."[48]

Latino activists organized a letter-writing campaign, some picketed newsstands selling the magazine, hundreds of subscriptions were canceled, and the incident generated a backlash that, even after the apology was issued, confirmed the suspicion that the views expressed unwittingly reflected the biases of *Vanity Fair*'s editors. "When we hired Barry Humphries two years ago to write a satirical advice column in Dame Edna's name, we did so on the comedic premise that Dame Edna is the last person on Earth that anyone would go to for sound advice. Clearly this advice column should not be taken seriously," the magazine's editors said. That the magazine's apology required further elaboration suggested to many Latino activists that *Vanity Fair*'s statement should not be taken seriously either. (That so many Latinos subscribe to *Vanity Fair* was "a surprise," as one contributor said when asked to comment on the fracas, which itself is a curious observation. It should be noted here that the difference between "Latino" and "Hispanic" is one of class and politics. "Latino" denotes working-class Hispanics; "Hispanic" is preferred by middle-class Hispanics. "Latino" is also used, often condescendingly, by non-Hispanics when promoting a political agenda.)

Now consider Procter & Gamble's experience with Hispanics during the same month. Crest, P&G's oral care brand, became the first P&G consumer product to air a Spanish-language advertisement during a nationally broadcast television event, the 45th Grammy Awards on February 23, 2003. The commercial, aired in Spanish with no English-language subtitles, won kudos from Hispanics. "Procter & Gamble has been among the leading advertisers in the Spanish language since the sixties," Rob Steele, president–North America of Procter & Gamble, said. "This spot is just one example of the many ways we are connecting with Hispanic consumers including a variety of outreach programs addressing relevant concerns and issues facing Hispanic families."[49]

"This is a welcome validation of our importance as a community and a market," Teresa Rodriguez, a news anchor for Univision, said. "It speaks about how mainstream Hispanics and the Spanish language have become in the United States. To get Hispanic brand loyalty, companies have to speak to us in our language."[50] P&G's offices in Cincinnati were inundated with congratulatory calls from grateful Hispanic consumers around the country.

There are lessons in these anecdotes, and it speaks to the subtleties that suffuse the Hispanic market. There is the need to recognize that there are today two *parallel* consumer markets in the United States; Hispanics will learn English, to be sure, but out of self-respect, they *cannot* abandon Spanish. The United States in the twenty-first century will mature as a *bilingual* society, one in which these two languages will exist side by side, at times in conflict but more often seeking an accommodation. This is a *political* decision, one that has sweeping economic consequences.

After all, the case could be made that Condé Nast and P&G were engaged in different forms of the same thing: tongue-in-cheek *dalliance* with Hispanics. P&G's broadcasting a Crest commercial in Spanish on a nationally televised English-language awards ceremony could have been seen as a facetious send-up, no different from Dame Edna's ridicule of working-class Hispanics in her column. The careful reader, however, should have noticed that in the former incident, *Vanity Fair* outraged "Latinos," while in the latter, "Hispanics" showered accolades on Crest. Understanding these nuances, and their implications, is important, for this determines whether a company will incur the wrath of consumers who cancel subscriptions and picket, or whether a company will be hailed as an enlightened corporate citizen that is living up to the expectations that society sets.

When P&G hit a home run with its Spanish-language commercial on the CBS telecast of the Grammy Awards, it wasn't a fluke. It was part of a national advertising campaign to reach Hispanics. P&G's "Avanzando con tu Familia" ("Helping Your Family Succeed") is a decade-long marketing campaign that recognizes Hispanic ascendancy. "Procter & Gamble's 'Avanzando con tu Familia' is another long-term community outreach initiative created to provide Hispanic families with tools and information to help them get ahead and achieve their goals," P&G announced in a press release prior to the Grammy Awards. "It addresses four primary areas: education, health, traditions and home."[51] In contrast, when R.J. Reynolds spent a million dollars to "understand" the Hispanic market, some of the perplexing results they found—working-class Mexican-Americans in Texas feared being "taken advantage of" by mainstream Americans, upper-class Cuban-Americans resisted being "Americanized" despite their success—have their origins in the Hispanic refusal to live their entire lives inside the racial box.

Consider how surprised Hispanics are to learn of the racial box of American life. Marie Arana, the book editor for the *Washington Post*, was born in Peru of a Peruvian father and an American mother. As a young child, on her first visit to the United States to visit her maternal grandparents, then living in Wyoming, she was in for a rude awakening. After sailing from Peru to Miami, the family boarded a train bound for Denver, where they would then take a bus to Wyoming. This is how she describes her surprise arriving in Missouri:

In the St. Louis station, [her older sister] Vicki and I took off in search of a bathroom and came to a stop before two doors marked *Ladies*. One said *Colored*. The other said *Whites*. We puzzled over the words, wondering what they meant, but Mother came by, grabbed our hands, and pulled us through the second door.

"Why does the other one say *Colored*, Mother?" Vicki asked.

"Because only the colored are supposed to go through it," she replied.

"Colored?" my sister asked, revealing a rare lack of enlightenment.

"Yes. Haven't you noticed in the station, darling? Or on the train? The black people?"

"With black hair, you mean?" Vicki asked.

"No, dear." Mother answered on her way into a cubicle, latching the door behind her. "Not black hair. Black *skin*. You have black hair, but you're white. Your skin is white. So is mine."

I listened and looked down at my dark-olive knees dangling over the snowy commode. They were green. They were yellow. They were brown. They were colored. Never in a million years could they be called white. But when Vicki and I emerged from the bathroom and looked around the station, we saw what was meant. . . . Here in March of 1956, in the St. Louis train station, however, where black and white was spelled out so boldly—where colors were carved on doors with directives—I do believe that for the first time I feared a little for myself.[52]

This is how a six-year-old Hispanic girl is introduced to American life. It is thus this fear of being forced to live with racial labels and directives that Hispanics retaliate against by speaking Spanish. This fear has not subsided over the decades; those who would dismiss America of the 1950s with America of the 2000s need only recall how George P. Bush, grandson of president George H.W. Bush, nephew of president George W. Bush, and son of Florida governor Jeb Bush, told Hispanic interviewers at the Republican National Convention in 2000 how he had been "subjected" to racism his entire life, by virtue of his mother being Mexican and his "looking" like a person of color.

The demographic and economic numbers behind Hispanic ascendancy, however, are as impressive as they are undeniable: 38 million Hispanics in the United States and 101 million Mexicans constitute a formidable market in and of itself. P&G's campaign, moreover, is a superior approach for it reflects what this discussion has implied: Hispanic ascendancy in the United States represents an opportunity to serve a community that is struggling to make the transition from working class to middle class. The Hispanic market, as a consequence, is comprised of aspiring consumers, though the things to which they aspire are fundamentally different from the things to which non-Hispanic consumers aspire.

It can therefore be concluded that:

1. In the last quarter of the twentieth century, Hispanic ascendance has transformed the United States into a bilingual nation that, coupled with the economic integration of Mexico into the U.S.-Canada free trade bloc through NAFTA, has changed the linguistic consumer market of North America.
2. The Hispanization of the United States affects corporate America in how consumer goods and services are marketed and merchandised, how the question of language in the workplace is handled, and how bilingual education meets the needs of bilingual and parallel consumer markets.
3. Hispanics use language to self-segregate from mainstream society as an affirmation of identity, and as an act of resisting being forced to live their lives inside the racial box that defines American life.
4. Hispanic ascendancy means that in addition to the creation of parallel consumer markets divided by language, corporate America's understanding of "diversity"—in the marketplace, in the workplace, and in civic life—has undergone a sea change.

2

Management Realities of a Fragmented "North American" Market

Abstract

The dilemma confronting Nielsen Media Research is a harbinger for corporate America. If its reports divide a given television market by language, it will underreport the Hispanic market and overreport the number of English-language viewers. If, on the other hand, it does not make this division, its ratings will misrepresent the true cost of reaching television viewers for the entire spectrum of firms throughout corporate America that advertise on television. At stake in the battle being waged by executives at ABC, CBS, NBC, Telemundo, and Univision for the "soul" of how Nielsen measures its ratings are billions of dollars in advertising revenue. The resulting linguistic divide in how best to measure television ratings constitutes the opening salvo in a decade of seismic shifts, one that promises to accelerate as the medium-term impacts of NAFTA's success are felt in the decade ahead. The implications of the cultural-linguistic market segmentation are undeniable, for it contradicts the twentieth-century assumption that the U.S. consumer market would remain a monolingual one. The resulting fragmentation of the American consumer market furthermore implies that the influences that inform the Hispanic market must be considered, since these externalities produce distinct segments of economic consequence, creating one continental Hispanic market throughout the whole of North America. Fragmentation, finally, can fast become fractious when the political aspects of the Hispanization of the United States impact, with greater

49

vigor, corporate America, and firms throughout corporate America fulfill their obligations of being responsible corporate citizens.

The decision of U.S. Hispanics to speak in Spanish, coupled with the rapid integration of the Mexican economy after one decade of NAFTA, has created a fragmented linguistic market, in both the United States and throughout North America. This has impacted more directly the media and advertising industry, for how to reach Hispanic consumers has become more complicated, and oftentimes in unexpected ways. "On Wednesday, the chairman and chief executive of Univision Communications Inc.—a man who, in a city of avid self-promoters, is notoriously averse to publicity—filed to sell half his shares in the company, the nation's largest Spanish-language television network," Andrew Pollack reported in the *New York Times.* "That half alone is worth $700 million, many times the roughly $50 million he put up when he led the group that purchased the company in 1992."[1]

By 2001, "Noticiero Univision" was beating "The CBS Evening News with Dan Rather" and "ABC World News Tonight" in the New York metropolitan area. Turmoil erupted at ABC, CBS, and NBC when Nielsen Media Research indicated it wanted to revamp how it measures television news in the New York market, where it estimated it was undercounting almost 250,000 Hispanic households. The drama that has ensued is a measure of how ill-prepared corporate America is for the Hispanization of the U.S. and North American consumer market. Indeed, in the major metropolitan markets, including New York, Miami, Los Angeles, Houston, and San Antonio, more consumers get their news from Jorge Ramos—the Miami-based Mexican news anchor on Univision's evening news broadcast from Miami—than get their news from Dan Rather or Peter Jennings. More American homes in New York City, in fact, get their news from a "foreign" television network than they do from either CBS or ABC, making 2001 a defining moment in the cultural-linguistic revolution that has occurred in the U.S. consumer market. It is clear that the continued segmentation of the American consumer market poses challenges, one that stands to become more complicated as the United States, Mexico, and Canada continue to integrate, throwing French into the linguistic equation.

A Linguistically Fragmented North American Consumer Market

Corporate America is fast becoming aware that the growing presence of Hispanics in the United States is more than a question of language. As we saw in chapter 1, Hispanics refuse to assimilate as all other immigrant groups previously have done, and the United States consumer market is now a bilingual one. Furthermore, this fact discredits the widely held assumption that it is the English language that is fast becoming the *lingua franca* the world over. The belief that everyone in North America will speak English is not the reality of the twenty-first century.[2]

Mais non, as they say in Quebec. Rather than English becoming the language of North America, NAFTA itself has instigated the fragmentation of how the people in all three nations speak. There are now five linguistic markets in North America—Mexico, Hispanic United States, Anglophone United States, Anglophone Canada, and Francophone Canada—comprised of three languages. Two of these markets are Spanish and, by 2025, will comprise half the people who live in the entire continent.

"We argue that although some level of globalization is taking place, it tends to be overstated," Joseph Straubhaar, Consuelo Campbell, and Kristina Cahoon report in their analysis of the fragmentation of television markets in North America.

> [M.] Ferguson's excellent discussion of the myths of globalization raises several key problems: the idea that the world is becoming one homogeneous culture, largely fed by the U.S. culture industries; that big cultural industries, like those of the U.S., have an automatic advantage due to economies of scale and the polish of their products; and that differences of time, space and geography are eroded by technology. Within the formation of trans-national cultural-linguistic markets for television, we see several distinct markets within NAFTA. Anglophone Canada is very strongly tied to the U.S. within an Anglophone cultural area. Quebec is tied by language and history to the Francophone cultural-linguistic market, but more distant in both geography and extent of ongoing contact. The Hispanic U.S. is tied both to Mexico and to a larger Latin American or Latino cultural-linguistic market by language, shared history and ongoing immigration. Beyond their inclusion in these cultural-linguistic markets, the cultural sub-units of NAFTA (Mexico, Hispanic U.S., Anglophone U.S., Anglophone Canada, and Francophone Canada) show varying degrees of differentiation from their cultural-linguistic influences.[3]

The North American consumer marketplace is clearly a more complex one. Consider the proliferation of Mexican television programming in the United States, and its further fragmenting of the U.S. Hispanic market. While "U.S. programming has not really declined much in the NAFTA markets, as it has in some other parts of the world . . . other intra-NAFTA production and flow has grown: more from Mexico (and Puerto Rico) into the Hispanic U.S.; more production within Quebec coupled with a continuing presence of English-Canadian material; and a seemingly stable balance in broadcast television between English-Canadian and U.S. programs in Calgary," Straubhaar, Campbell, and Cahoon write. "This supports our argument that globalization is a complex phenomenon that needs to be examined at four separate levels: a largely U.S. global layer, varied cultural-linguistic markets (including Anglophone, Francophone and Latin American within NAFTA), continuing strong national-level production (particularly within the U.S. and Mexico within NAFTA); and, particularly in the cases of Quebec and, to lesser degree, U.S. Hispanics, a strong subnational layer, built upon language and cultural differences within the nation."[4]

As senior executives begin to grapple with the impact of the socioeconomic and cultural forces unleashed by Hispanic ascendancy, strategic implications abound. Indeed, for corporate executives, the implications are more than linguistic. "But speaking their language isn't necessarily about language at all, it's about being 'in-culture,' a term coined by Hispanic marketing strategist Isabel Valdés," Rebecca Gardyn writes. "Valdés identifies core values among Hispanic youth that set them apart from their general market counterparts, such as *Familismo*, or a strong family orientation, which influences how they use and respond to media. For instance, Hispanic teens are more likely to watch television with their parents than non-Hispanic teens. . . [But b]eing 'in-culture' with today's youth is something which most marketers and traditional Hispanics ad agencies have little experience."[5]

An integral aspect of the phenomenon of "in-culture" can be best understood in the context of *normas hispanas*. The historic processes that produced Hispanization throughout Latin America over the centuries are now found in the United States and, to a lesser extent, Canada. One demographic and marketing "megatrend" that represents a sea change is the disproportionate percentage of youth—consumers aged fifteen to twenty-five—who are Hispanic. The Hispanization of the United States in terms of culture is more than the visible success of Jennifer López or Gloria Estefan; it is seen in the nuances of popular consumer culture that reflect a different set of values and aesthetics. How these processes are being fueled by the business of NAFTA provides many insights into the differentiation and segmentation of the North American consumer market.

How NAFTA Fuels the Hispanization of the United States and the World

Americans are so confident that the world wants to become like us that we presume our culture is destined to dominate the modern world. We look at McDonald's, Mickey Mouse, and Coca-Cola as proof positive of our global reach. This, however, is an American ethnocentric conceit, one that mistakes our disproportionate influence as a "first adopter" and "innovator" with long-term dominance. In fact, there are some Americans who fear that our nation's "global reach" with our culture is a threat to other societies, at times even equating the efficiency of the American capitalist system with "imperialism" or "cultural domination." One example, of course, is the concern that the English language, through popular culture and technological innovations (such as the Internet), constitutes a threat.

The Hispanization of the United States—and NAFTA's stunning success—disprove this concern. It is clear that when other cultures employ the same efficiency of the American capitalist system, they can compete effectively, and they can secure greater market share. It is Japanese cultural values that dominate in the global video game market, for instance. Does this mean that when an American youngster plays a video game he or she is being subjected to "Japanese cultural imperialism"? The belief that, through popular culture, the United States dominates global entertainment media is likewise demonstrably false.

Although Hollywood films are shown all over the world, for instance, and the United States clearly dominates the movie-making industry, this is not the case when it comes to television programming. "Whereas American TV shows used to occupy prime-time slots, they are now more typically on cable or airing in late-night or weekend slots," Michael Grindon, president of Sony Pictures Television International, told the *New York Times*.[6] As consumers around the world tune in "domestic" programming, American television programs will continue to be displaced. Suzanne Kapner writes in the *New York Times:*

> First-run domestic fiction programs in the five largest European Union countries—Germany, Britain, Italy, Spain and France—increased 5.7 percent in 2001 and have grown 43 percent since 1996, the European Audiovisual Observatory recently reported. That pattern has played out in many countries around the world. A 2001 survey by Nielsen Media Research found that 71 percent of the top 10 programs in 60 countries were locally produced in 2001, representing a steady increase over previous years. American movies on television still drew big ratings, grabbing 9 percent of the top 10 slots, but American dramatic or comedic series typically rated much lower than local shows.[7]

In other words, as soon as other nations acquired the ability to create their own television programming, America's dominance in that industry—which reached its apogee in the 1960s—has continued to decline. Furthermore, as Hispanic ascendancy and NAFTA became a fact of life in North America, the Mexican television production industry, by leaps and bounds, gained significant market share—in both the United States and around the world. Indeed, to the surprise of corporate America, more television viewers around the world are familiar with Mexican television programming than they are with Hollywood movies. Araceli Ortiz de Urbina and Asbel López reported for UNESCO on the goings-on in the Ivory Coast in 1998:

> During Ramadan last January, some of the mosques in Abidjan decided to bring forward prayer time. This thoughtful gesture saved thousands of the faithful from a painful dilemma—whether to do their religious duty or miss the latest episode of Marimar, a Mexican TV melodrama which has turned the whole country into addicts of *telenovelas*, soap operas made in Latin America. Meanwhile, on the other side of the planet, hundreds of thousands of Yugoslavs hold their breath so as not to miss the tiniest detail of the Venezuelan soap opera Kassandra. "We know Kassandra's innocent and we want her trial stopped," the townspeople of Kucevo, in southeastern Serbia, wrote to the Venezuelan government, with a copy to Serbian President Slobodan Milosevic. This is just one of many examples of how fiction can invade real life and how far people come to identify with it.[8]

The Latin American soap opera is a multibillion-dollar export industry, with Mexico leading the way in terms of global sales. In 1998, *World Link* wrote: "Televisa, the Mexico-based Spanish language broadcaster, leverages the content of its *telenovela* brand of soap operas across the world. Jean Azcarraga, the young and dynamic president and CEO of Televisa, explains how the right balance of universal appeal and cultural specificity can make for a winning global export: 'Our *telenovelas* really travel well. They are produced for the Mexican market and our specialisation in this field of dramatising human experience gives us a competitive advantage. We do not need to change the content because it has universal appeal.'"[9]

In the same way that Mexican Hispanic culture has made itself felt in consumer markets around the world, it is now being felt within the United States. In fact, the success of Mexico in propelling "global" Hispanization through television programming is one reason that Spanish is becoming one of the two dominant languages in the Western world. Kevin Carton, of the media and communications group of PricewaterhouseCoopers, argues that English and Spanish will become the two principal languages of worldwide media this decade.[10] Televisa, whose programs are broadcast to spellbound audiences from Tokyo to Moscow, generates more than $120 million a year in *export earnings profits*, making Mexican *telenovelas* a major global cultural force, rivaling Hollywood in terms of people reached.[11]

Just as the United States has become a bilingual nation, around the world Spanish-language television programming rivals American television exports. To those who argue that the world is "destined" to speak in English, including misguided novelist Peter Schneider who welcomes "the specter of English"—but doesn't himself speak English—consider the following anecdote. When the Japanese media interviewed me in Costa Rica, our interview was conducted in English, since it made more sense to put Japanese subtitles over my spoken English.[12] Americans point to this as confirmation that, because the Japanese "default" to English when doing business in Costa Rica, English is becoming the world's *lingua franca*. But when I was interviewed in Germany by the Italian media, that interview, on the other hand, unfolded in Spanish: more Italians learn Spanish as their second language than learn English. What is one to make of that?[13]

In fact, the presumed proliferation of English has been both greatly exaggerated and proved to be presumptuous wishful thinking. In the nineteenth century, Mark Twain noted that reports of his death were greatly exaggerated. In the twenty-first century, reports of the domination of the English language have been similarly greatly exaggerated. Consider the humbling reversals the English language encountered in the late 1990s in Asia. "It is unclear whether there is a market for English language programming: the myth of panregional Asian TV in English has exploded," *WorldLink* reported in 1998. "This is underlined by ABN (Asia Business News) and CNBC (NBC's 24-hour business news channel) Asia's decision to join forces. ABN-CNBC shows that Asia is not big enough for two English language business broadcasters—and maybe not even for one. Instead, ABN-CNBC will target regional language audiences, such as Mandarin and Hindi."[14]

On this continent, rather than English becoming the "language" of NAFTA, NAFTA itself has empowered French and Spanish, as the emergence of Spanish-language markets throughout the United States attests. To understand these forces, one does not need a Harvard MBA. French anthropologist Claude Levi-Strauss anticipated all of this in his arguments espoused in Structuralist tenets: At the same time that there are forces bringing the world together (globalization), there are social factors creating differentiation (local market segmentation). What this means, then, is that while business elites around the world are proficient in English for commerce and science (technical know-how), at least in the Western world Spanish is emerging as the preferred spoken language in social and cultural settings. Most Italians do not wish to pursue careers in international commerce, and consequently prefer to learn Spanish as a second language, simply because so many other people in the Western world speak Spanish. And though English facilitates international business throughout Asia, English is not spoken widely when the workday is concluded.

Decline of English-Language Markets in the United States and Mexico

"In 1962 in Mexico, total programming was mostly national (59%), with a sizeable amount from the U.S. (38%), little (3%) international and no regional programming," Straubhaar et al. report. English, however, failed to dominate Mexico during the three decades that followed. In fact, thirty years later, one found that "by 1991, total television programming was 66.6% national, 24.4% U.S., 7% international, and 2% regional."[15] English-language television programming continues to decline in Mexico, and in California, the Southwest, Texas, Florida, and New York. As Univision and Telemundo increase their market share throughout the United States, these two Spanish-language television networks are changing how language and the media function.

One unintended consequence of Hispanic ascendancy has been a substantial decline in the exposure of American English in Mexican homes, and a remarkable increase in the Spanish spoken in the United States. In NAFTA's first decade, while American programming—particularly cable—has entered Mexico, it has been a two-way street. Consider the proliferation of Mexican television programming in the United States. "In Mexico, the amount of U.S. programming in prime time and in the total day declined sharply from 1992 to 2000. National programming increased correspondingly . . . Here we can see evidence of a new kind of cultural proximity, going beyond language and cultural tradition, which builds on trade ties between Mexico and the U.S., migration and family ties across the border, increasingly common consumption items and patterns, and geographic proximity to overcome to some degree language and cultural differences," Straubhaar et al. write. "This supports our argument that globalization is a complex phenomenon that needs to be examined at four separate levels: a largely U.S. global layer, varied cultural-linguistic markets (including Anglophone, Francophone and Latin American within NAFTA), continuing strong national-level production (particularly within the U.S. and Mexico within NAFTA); and, particularly in the cases of Quebec and, to lesser degree, U.S. Hispanics, a strong subnational layer, built upon language and cultural differences within the nation."[16]

The fragmentation of North America into five linguistic "markets," moreover, is not a new phenomenon. It can be argued that Hispanic ascendancy and the success of NAFTA together are the impetus for restoring a historical process interrupted by the Mexican-American War. Indeed, the forces that made NAFTA possible are the same forces that have unleashed a "democracy" of language, where French is affirmed in Quebec, and the North-South commerce from Mexico to the United States has been restored.

Recall how the Mexican-American War interrupted a centuries-old commercial and cultural route. In 1598 Juan de Onate formally claimed what is now the American Southwest for Spain. For more than two centuries, as we all learn in high school courses on American history, the trade routes that opened New Mexico and Arizona to the world came via Mexico City. With its ports in Manila and Acapulco, Spain's trans-Pacific routes brought the riches of Asia to the Southwest, borne on the backs of mules, from Mexico City. Everything from cilantro to Chinese porcelain journeyed north through the Camino Real to the Southwest. It was not until 1821, when Mexico declared its independence from Spain, and other areas of what had been New Spain scoffed at the ambitions of the young Mexican republic, that the North-South route was redirected. "Far removed from the center of Mexican political life, California took no direct part whatsoever in the events that resulted in Mexican independence," Manuel Gonzales writes in his superb history of Mexicans in what is now the United States. "The majority of Californios, some 3,200 people by 1821, had no special feelings about independence one way or the other, and they quickly resigned themselves to the new order."[17]

The Santa Fe Trail, running east to west, joined the outpost of New Mexico to the United States by linking Santa Fe to St. Louis, Missouri, a link that predominated, that is, until NAFTA. It is thus through NAFTA, then, that the historic "north-south" cultural routes are being restored, with the "east-west" corridor being relegated to an artificial construct associated with America's nineteenth-century nation-building. "At the beginning of a new century, there may be no country on earth with as much potential to destabilize the U.S.— and to preserve its standard of living. No wonder people can't decide how much the border should be a barrier, how much a bridge," Nancy Gibbs reported in *Time*.[18] The historic trade routes—of commerce and culture—are restoring familiar patterns in the settlement of the North American continent. The spread of the Spanish language is part of that primacy.

What does this mean for corporate America? Quite simply, that the pop culture and the mass media in the United States will continue to fragment, with Hispanic icons gaining currency. Consider one anecdote that proves instructive in what this means for the "restoration" of the cultural—and consumer—life of the United States. When Jorge Ramos, the Mexican news anchor on *Noticiero Univision* (and who commutes between Miami and Mexico City), was having lunch in New York, this is what happened. "Mr. Ramos, 44, chuckled when he remembered how last year he was eating at an outdoor café in Manhattan with several of his Univision colleagues when they noticed that the actress Sarah Jessica Parker was sitting at the next table," Mirta Ojito reported in the *New York Times*. "Yet the fans who walked by were stopping to ask not for her autograph but for Mr. Ramos's. Finally curiosity won, and Ms. Parker asked the waiter, 'Who are those people?' The waiter, a Latino, knew and told her."[19]

Though *Sex and the City* is high on the radar screens of Anglo-Americans, it is not high enough on the radar screens of *all* Americans. It is, in fact, a mere bleep in the life of the *majority* of the people who live in the *three* NAFTA nations. One reason the use of Spanish is growing at a phenomenal rate in the United States is that, under the auspices of the Spanish Institute for Foreign Commerce, or ICEX, in Madrid, Spanish cultural organizations are spending millions of dollars to promote proper Spanish language in the United States. The purpose is to encourage youngsters to celebrate their cultural heritage and delight in speaking the language and values of their family.[20]

To be sure, the emergence in the 1990s of positive role models—Jennifer López, Mario López, Christina Aguilera, Oscar de la Hoya, Salma Hayek, Jay Hernández—emboldens Hispanic youth into seeing that one does not have to forsake one culture to succeed in another. The American dream can be dreamt in Spanish as well as in English. "It was important as an affirmation to sing in Spanish," Rubén Albarrán of Mexico's pioneering rock band Café Tacuba, said. "We had to define ourselves."[21] Café Tacuba, which has toured with Beck in the United States, reaffirms the ability of Hispanic culture to transcend borders.

The seismic shift in demographics is not lost on television programmers. "Hispanics, it turns out, are driving the overall growth of the country's television audience, and according to the latest Nielsen research, account for 18 percent of viewers who are 18 to 24, and 15 percent of those 18 to 49, the most desirable group for advertisers," Mireya Navarro reported in the *New York Times*. "And with about half of Hispanic-American households thought to prefer watching programs in Spanish, English-language broadcast networks are trying different tactics and are making programming more friendly in an effort to reach a group that has been elusive but has become too important to ignore."[22]

That Spanish continues to be spoken by more and more consumers in the United States who are younger and younger has great cultural consequences. There is a backlash to this, of course. There is resentment among non-Hispanic Americans, oftentimes manifesting itself in subtle shades of bias. In a market economy, however, it is the customer who must be courted.

To court Hispanics—in the United States and throughout the whole of North America—corporate America has to accept certain facts of life. Hispanic culture, for instance, is characterized by a different set of aesthetics; Hispanics dismissed the cultural movement of the 1960s, where hippies and flower children informed the life and lifestyle of an entire generation of Americans. Differences in cultural values and aesthetics at times conflict with the American mainstream. Joan Didion, quoted earlier on the subject of the role of language in the emergence of the Hispanic market, also reflected on the social and cultural implications of Hispanic ascendancy.

"There was even in the way [Cuban and Hispanic] women dressed in Miami a definable Havana look, a more distinct emphasis on the hips and décolletage, more black, more veiling, a generalized flirtatiousness of style. . . . They wore Bruno Magli pumps, and silk and linen dresses of considerable expense. There seemed to be a preference for strictest gray or black, but the effect remained lush, tropical, like a room full of perfectly groomed mangoes," she writes.[23] In another section, she relates how we "were sitting at the kitchen counter, drinking the caffeine and sugar infusion that is Cuban coffee," while interviewing an exile of renown about the state of U.S.-Cuba relations, a superfluous and crass comment on her host's graciousness.[24]

What is one to make of this? Is it a compliment, considering that the "Havana" look in question refers to the world of the 1950s, when women were more concerned about their clothes than their careers? What is the point of disparaging espresso coffee?

Didion wrote *Miami* in 1987, a full decade before *Sex and the City* reintroduced American women to the idea that it is possible to be stylish and sexy and remain very much a feminist. It was published a decade before Starbucks inculcated in Americans an appreciation for coffee culture; Cuban coffee has its origins in Italian espresso. The clothes Cubans wore and the food they ate were out of step with the "assimilated" American mainstream. For Didion, the Cuban refusal to wear clothes from the Gap and eat McDonald's Big Macs was a way of rejecting an American identity.[25] So was, as Didion describes, the Cuban "disinclination to speak English" in public. The Cubans, in essence, were the first immigrants who, arriving in the United States, challenged the idea of assimilation. These Hispanics were not entirely American, Didion observed, for they "undermine" the historic American "conviction that assimilation was an ideal universally shared by those who were to be assimilated."

That is to say, America's social contract with immigrants implied that anyone—"the huddled masses yearning to breathe free"—was welcome, provided he or she assimilated, and that meant learning and speaking English. Those who did not assimilate would be relegated to an underclass—whether they originated in Italy or China, or anywhere else—and languish in ethnic neighborhoods, with diminished possibilities for advancement. To enter the mainstream, one had to speak English, lest he or she be destined to remain in a "Little Italy" here, or a "Chinatown" there, or any other ethnic ghetto of the working-class immigrant. Millions of immigrants signed on, changing their names upon arriving at Ellis Island to something that sounded more "American" and insisting that their American-born children speak only English, and worked years to assume an American identity.[26]

Didion correctly recognizes that the Cubans, since their exodus from Havana in the mid-1960s, tore up America's social contract and challenged the predominance of the English language. These Cubans, after all, were not "huddled masses" disembarking at Ellis Island, grateful for the chance to start a new life. They were educated, professional, and solidly middle-class people who sought to bide their time in south Florida until they could resume their comfortable lives in Havana. These immigrants—who insisted on calling themselves not immigrants but "refugees" and referred to the United States not as their new homeland but as a place of "exile"—were successful middle-class professionals. They expected to be afforded certain imperatives of a capitalist market economy: *the seller speaks the language of the buyer.*

Recognizing this Cuban attitude for the linguistic revolution that it was, Didion looks upon these successful foreigners—who can float bonds and attend black-tie charity galas in Spanish all over town—as a *foreign* middle class that refused to be assimilated. These so-called "immigrants" refused to live in the ghetto of Little Havana for more than a nanosecond and moved right into the grand homes of Coral Gables, patronized fine restaurants, shopped at chic boutiques, and drove fancy cars. The business community had to respond pronto, hiring bilingual staffs and reaching out to consumers who, regardless of their proficiency in English, would take their business to the more solicitous competitor down the block.[27]

What is one, then, to make of Hispanics? What is one to make of Cubans in Miami driving in BMWs with shopping bags filled with Bruno Magli pumps, who insist that the United States is an "exile"—a sort of Purgatory of indeterminate duration before going to a better place? (What is one to make of working-class Mexicans in New York that insist that no matter what, were they to die in the United States, their remains are to be shipped back to Mexico for a *proper* burial?) What is one to make of the fact that the largest minority in the United States looks upon the nation with such weariness that they drop out by creating a *parallel consumer market* that speaks *Spanish?*

Taken aback by the differences between the "sound of spoken Spanish . . . in Miami" and in other American cities, such as Los Angeles, Didion argues that while "Spanish remained a language only barely registered by the Anglo population" in these other cities as "part of the ambient noise," in Miami, Spanish was spoken "by the people who ate in the restaurants," people who "owned the [fancy] cars" and people who led professional, politically active, solidly middle-class lives, making a "considerable difference" in the city's "socioauditory scale."[28]

Didion, in other words, concludes that these are the first Hispanics to leave the linguistic working-class ethnic ghettos and enter the American middle-class speaking Spanish. Didion's *Miami* was the first book to examine what happens when an American city becomes Hispanic. The paragraph about language quoted in the first chapter has generated tremendous criticism of Didion among Hispanics. The nature of this criticism, however, is not apparent to non-Hispanics at first. Consider the paragraph in question again:

> This question of language was curious. The sound of spoken Spanish was common in Miami, but it was also common in Los Angeles, and Houston, and even in the cities of the northeast. What was unusual about Spanish in Miami was not that it was so often spoken, but that it was so often heard: in, say Los Angeles, Spanish remained a language only barely registered by the Anglo population, part of the ambient noise, the language spoken by the people who worked in the car wash and came to trim the trees and cleared the tables in restaurants. In Miami Spanish was spoken by the people who ate in the restaurants, the people who owned the cards and the trees, which made, on the socioauditory scale, a considerable difference.[29]

This paragraph makes many Hispanics angry. If it is not apparently obvious what Hispanics find objectionable about this description about the views expressed in this paragraph, consider the same paragraph with "blacks" substituted for "Spanish." It would read:

> This question of [race] was curious. The [sight] of [black people] was common in Miami, but it was also common in Los Angeles, and Houston, and even in the cities of the northeast. What was unusual about [black people] in Miami was not that [they were] so often [present], but that [they were] so often [visible]: in, say Los Angeles, [blacks] remained ... only barely registered by the Anglo population, part of the ambient [visuals], the [color of] the people who worked in the car wash and came to trim the trees and cleared the tables in the restaurants. In Miami [blacks were] the people who ate in the restaurants, the people who owned the cars and the trees, which made, on the socio[visual] scale, a considerable difference.

Are Hispanic objections now more understandable? Didion's characterizations of Miami are audacious. Indeed, the entire feeling conveyed throughout *Miami* is the prose of an English speaker's alarm—Didion obsesses about her personal safety in downtown Miami, is concerned that Spanish is being spoken by city officials, becomes appalled that televised election debates for the office of mayor unfold in Spanish, grows disoriented by the lay of the entire landscape of south Florida—which is like a mirage rising and falling with the ebbs of the tides where the sun rises and like the flows of the Everglades (a "river of grass") where the sun sets—and concludes with the reluctant epiphany that south Florida is no longer fully American.

Her fears about the meaning of Hispanic ascendancy, however, are unfounded. More than a decade later, with Americans adopting a more flirtatious sense of style (analyzed by college students taking feminist studies courses where the hot and spicy clothes worn by the characters in *Sex and the City* are deconstructed in a postmodern Marxist sense); standing in line at Starbucks for the café lattes and double espressos (hyper-caffeinated, sugar-infused); where action heroes bid their opponents farewell in Spanish ("Hasta la vista, baby!"); and American youth seeking to live it up by living *la vida loca*, the realities of the emergence of a bilingual consumer culture in the United States is less threatening than Didion feared in her disconcerting book. Didion, to her credit, correctly identified the profound consumer and cultural implications that Miami, as a Hispanic city, represents: Miami Cubans pioneered a revolution in which Hispanics rewrote the American social contract in terms of language by making the United States a bilingual consumer nation—*Press 1 to continue in English, por favor.*

Rather than recognizing that, in terms of cultural trends, Hispanic aesthetics are closer to those of Europeans, she comments upon precisely the manner of dressing and the preference for coffee that would become all the rage in the United States a decade later. The image glamorized by Sarah Jessica Parker sipping a double espresso from Starbucks while dishing flirtatiously with her friends is what was happening in Cuban Miami a decade ahead of the American mass consumer market! "Every man calls barbarous anything he is not accustomed to; we have no other criterion of truth or right-reason than the example and form of the opinions and customs of our own country," Michel de Montaigne gently reminds us. "There we always find the perfect religion, the perfect polity, the most developed and perfect way of doing anything!"[30]

Didion is not alone in her struggle to understand Hispanics, to be sure. The R.J. Reynolds market research astounds in the simple fact that it has no qualms about littering its consumer profiles with disparaging remarks. That social critics such as Didion and corporate giants such as R.J. Reynolds alike see Hispanics through the eyes of prejudice is a sustained and continuing problem in the face of Hispanic ascendancy.

The intermingling of both languages and cultural aesthetics in the U.S. marketplace, as if America were speaking in parallel tongues and viewing consumer products in parallel aesthetics, changes marketing and merchandising in unexpected ways. One example of the rise of Spanish is that *Noticiero Univision* is a brighter bleep on the whole of the continent of North America, so it is only natural that more New Yorkers want Jorge Ramos's autograph than Sarah Jessica Parker's. Another example of the consumer consequences of Spanish ascendancy, which itself is a revealing fact of life in New York City in 2001, was the critical "shortage" of mariachis in the Big Apple. With more than 300,000

Mexican migrants rippling through the greater New York metropolitan area, the social, cultural, and economic consequences of these demographic changes are making themselves felt in unexpected ways, whether it is a shortage of Spanish-speaking 911 operators, or mariachi bands to play at weddings.[31]

The careful reader no doubt noticed the parallels between language and culture. In Canada we saw how French has spread through legislation. In the United States Spanish has spread because of economics. Because the business of America is business, economics always trumps politics. Thus the politics that ended the Mexican-American War and created the Santa Fe Trail, establishing cultural and economic trade between the East and West coasts, has now been trumped. Hispanic ascendancy, and NAFTA's success, has restored the Camino Real economic and cultural thoroughfare, and in so doing, transformed the environment in which consumer marketing takes place. Specifically:

1. The Santa Fe Trail was an aberration, a political construct that interrupted the centuries-old Camino Real flow of goods, culture, and immigration.
2. Hispanic ascendancy is fueling the emergence of a different set of aesthetics, more in tune with European sensibilities than with Anglo-Saxon or Puritan ones.
3. Corporate America must overcome the subtle biases against Hispanics, an impediment to successful marketing.
4. Economics will continue to drive the development of the United States, not legislation; in the twenty-first century the United States will become a bicultural marketplace.
5. The restoration of the north-south cultural exchange between Spanish America and English America is one of the most important socioeconomic development that will shape the United States this century.

These observations make more sense than comparing Cuban women to mangoes, or commenting that California Hispanics are to be commended for their "relative lack of hostility toward the White race."

Hispanization and Marketing in the United States

Hispanization, naturally, impacts marketing programs in the greater continental Hispanic marketplace. "The fluctuating demographic trends in the United States over the last three decades have inspired the initiation of entirely new kinds of business and services created to reach a culturally diverse consumer base," Marilyn Halter explains in her book on marketing to ethnic groups.

"More and more, consumers themselves are expressing culturally distinctive desires, needs and wants in their shopping habits, and these demands as well as patterns of product loyalty prompted consulting, research and communications firms to begin specializing in multiethnic niche marketing."[32]

The cumulative size of the various market segments within the greater Hispanic markets, time and again, proves to be larger than anticipated and characterized by fluid, undefined parameters. Understanding the results of the 2000 census is crucial in approximating the size of the market, a market that defies precise measurement by the ability of most Hispanics to understand English, and how the meaning of the terms themselves are defined. Consider one example: Soledad O'Brien, the anchorwoman of "American Morning" on CNN, is the daughter of an Australian immigrant of Irish decent and a Cuban refugee, who is black. O'Brien, who speaks "Spanglish" at home, is thus a member of the National Association of Black Journalists, the National Association of Hispanic Journalists, and was named one of the Top 100 Irish-Americans in 1998 by *Irish American* magazine.[33] O'Brien, technically, is "Hispanic, Black" according to the census bureau, but that her ethnicity warrants an article in the *New York Times* is itself a sad commentary on race in America. "The Anglos hegemony was only an intermittent phase in California's arc of identity, extending from the arrival of the Spanish," Kevin Starr, state librarian and author of cultural histories of California, has been quoted as saying. "The Hispanic nature of California has been there all along, and it was temporarily swamped between the 1880s and the 1960s. But that was an aberration. This [Census 2000 report] is a reassertion of the intrinsic demographic DNA of the longer pattern, which is part of a California-Mexico continuum."[34] California's "DNA" foreshadows further fragmentation of the consumer market in the United States, with each fragment being further segmented, much like the Camino Real has asserted its dominant position over the Santa Fe Trail.[35]

"The term Latino is itself a recent construct, born on American soil, to define its members as something other than mainstream Americans," Susan Sachs writes in the *New York Times*. "But relying on a classic view of minority to understand this robust, diverse and politically fickle group is risky."[36] Though NAFTA is accelerating the process by which diversity unfolds, producing an infinitely more diverse consumer market, in the United States, Canada, and Mexico, it is not overwhelming. It is as simple as walking up to the nearest ATM machine in a major urban city to see, firsthand, how market segmentation is rippling across the landscape.

"Roughly one quarter of Latinos living in the United States are noncitizens," Lynette Clemetson reports. "And while there has been a significant migration of Hispanics to cities in the South, Midwest, and central plains, more than 50 percent of the Latino population remains concentrated in Texas, California and New York."[37] The proliferation of language options reflects both the banks' business need to provide services in the language of their customers and the demographics of American cities neighborhood by neighborhood.

At times the pace of change can be overwhelming, so much so that one forgets historical processes. For instance, in San Francisco there is concern that the Fillmore district, a predominantly black neighborhood, is losing its character, falling victim to the forces of "gentrification." Not a few neighborhood activists, in fact, demonstrate against what they decry as the "destruction" of a "traditional" black neighborhood. What is lost, however, is that the Fillmore being a black community is a relatively new phenomenon, one that dates back only to the 1940s; from the 1860s until the 1940s, what is now known as the "Fillmore" was a Japanese neighborhood.

It was only the result of a racial injustice against the Japanese who were vilified and targeted that changed this neighborhood from Asian to black. "In the early months of World War II, San Francisco's Fillmore district, or the Western Addition, experienced a visible revolution," Maya Angelou writes, describing her experience in San Francisco in the 1940s. "On the surface it appeared to be a totally peaceful and almost a refutation of the term 'revolution.' The Yakamoto Sea Food Market quietly became Sammy's Shoe Shine Parlor and Smoke Shop. Yashigira's Hardware metamorphosed into La Salon de Beauté owned by Miss Clorinda Jackson. The Japanese shops which sold products to Nisei customers were taken over by enterprising Negro businessmen, and in less than a year became permanent homes away from home for the newly arrived Southern Blacks. Where the odors of tempura, raw fish and *cha* had dominated, the aroma of chitlings, greens and ham hocks now prevailed. The Asian population dwindled before my eyes."[38]

Likewise, those who decry the spread of Spanish in the United States forget that what we are living through as the twenty-first century unfolds is the "cultural gentrification" by which Hispanic culture reclaims its rightful place in a geography from which it was wrongfully excluded. The matter of Spanish in the United States is interesting, for the paradox is that it is a complete reversal of the circumstances surrounding the question of the spread of French in Canada. It is the marketplace that is dictating where and how Spanish spreads, the natural process of corporate America competing to provide sound customer services to their customers.

The reason American Airlines, for instance, has customer service numbers for Spanish speakers is that its business depends on transporting Latin Americans and Hispanics on its airplanes. The reason State Farm has telephone banks manned by bilingual operators is that it depends on selling insurance to Hispanics to prosper. The reason each and every one of the Fortune

500 do business in Spanish is that to fail to do so would put them at a competitive disadvantage. Here, then, one sees the fundamental paradox in which the business community, in pursuit of market share and profits, stands at odds with reactionary political movements seeking to establish "English Only" legislation. A political stance that might be appropriate in Canada, in other words, is doomed to fail in the American marketplace.

As Didion reports, English-speaking Americans often express "dismay" that Spanish is heard more and more on the socioauditory scale. Its reach is inescapable in daily life in most major cities; at checkout lines in supermarkets, there is a proliferation of bilingual publications. *People* and *People en Español*, for instance, are displayed side by side, to be picked up by shoppers waiting their turn to check out. The economic power of Hispanics is disconcerting in both its visibility and its economic size. The *Miami Herald* sells fewer copies than *El Herald*, both published by Knight-Ridder for the south Florida market, a measure of how, in some consumer markets, the Spanish-speaking consumer market is larger than the English-speaking one. Hispanic ascendancy astounds in how relentlessly it is entering the mainstream consciousness of American society and the market segmentation these processes, including an accompanying resentment among "mainstream" consumers, entail.[39]

Externalities in the North American Hispanic Market

What this higher social and economic profile demonstrates, then, is that the Hispanic market responds to certain externalities, as much economic as cultural in nature. Externalities, as Thomas Schelling argued in the 1960s at Harvard, form an integral part of

> activities in which people's behavior is influenced by the behavior of others, or people care about the behavior of others, or they both care and are influenced. Most of these activities are substantially free of centralized management in many societies, including our own, or subject to sanctions and proscriptions that work indirectly. . . . And though people may care how it all comes out in the aggregate, their *own* decisions and their *own* behavior are typically motivated by their *own* interests, and often impinged on by only a local fragment of the overall pattern.[40]

In the continuing quest for status vis-à-vis other consumers, and where "reasonableness" is a cultural value, one finds that among Hispanic consumers, their choices reflect cultural values that become the defining "externality."

Hispanics' economic choices take into account the choices made by other

Hispanics within the context of what is "reasonable." Whereas non-Hispanic consumers respond to demonstration effects—when one neighbor builds a swimming pool, other neighbors follow suit in due course—Hispanics hinge their individual choices after assessing the "reasonableness" of that decision. The cultural imperative to resist being seen as "unreasonable," therefore, regulates consumption decision. Such consumer externalities, as Schelling noted, "are either-or situations . . . [in which] you care about my choice or my choice affects yours. You may not care but need to know: whether to pass on left or right when we meet. Or you may not need to know but care: you will drive whether or not I drive, but prefer that I keep off the road."[41]

In keeping with the cultural predisposition to identify with John Kenneth Galbraith, it is not surprising to realize that Hispanic consumer behavior favors self-restraining coalitions, which are a form of paternalistic intervention by government. This may guarantee a superior social outcome for all, but the cost is limiting an individual's choices. Cornell economist Robert Frank summarizes the social logic behind this strategy through an analysis of how hockey players resolve the dilemma of one specific externality:

> Hockey players, as a group, would not freely choose to live in a society that prevented them from imposing helmet rules. The libertarian who insists that the right not to be restricted cannot, as a matter of principle, ever be negotiated away, shows contempt for the rights of people to resolve such issues for themselves.
>
> Once the issue of collective restriction of individual behavior is recognized as no more a moral than a practical one, policymakers are led to focus on the task of assessing their constituents' preferences concerning the available choices.[42]

Hispanics appreciate the paradox that, in this world, there are times when having a choice is no choice at all.

The Hispanic market, then, is segmented by more than language. It is clear that the cultural legacy of "paternalism" manifests itself in one startling revelation: Hispanic consumer behavior revisits the twentieth-century debate between John Kenneth Galbraith and Milton Friedman. Both economists pondered the proper role of government in a society's economic life. Friedman argued that a "social consensus" regarding the "rules" that govern over a marketplace work effectively only when "most participants most of the time conform to them without external sanctions; unless that is, there is a broad underlying social consensus."[43] In Friedman's opinion, then, the proper role of government is "to provide a means whereby we can modify the rules, to mediate differences among us on the meaning of the rules, and to enforce compliance with the rules on the part of those few who would otherwise not play the game."[44]

Galbraith, in contrast, gives weight to the moral questions raised by what society produces and what consumers want. Galbraith, in essence, argues that the moral value of the material goods we're playing *for* is just as important as the economic rules by which we play. After all, is a game worth playing if the prize is false? Galbraith unequivocally says no. Hispanic consumers agree with Galbraith's argument that the danger of living in a society that is filled with abundance is that there are many things that tempt us but few that fulfill us. This is the same idea that proponents of the "Ecosystem Model" attempt to convey, but Galbraith expressed it first, and in a far less convoluted way. Galbraith challenges consumers to ask if their wants are misguided, which is to say, unreasonable. Galbraith argues that there is an

> even more direct link between production and wants [which is] provided by the institutions of modern advertising and salesmanship. These cannot be reconciled with the notion of independently determined desires, for their central function is to create desires—to bring into being wants that previously did not exist. . . . [Indeed], as a society becomes increasingly affluent, wants are increasingly created by the process by which they are satisfied. Wants thus come to depend on output.[45]

Will consumers be duped into wanting the unreasonable simply because companies produce the unreasonable?

These philosophical musings are encouraged by the frustrations of Hispanics in their countries of origin. Unlike the United States, where material abundance is a given, the nations of Latin America continue to struggle with the formidable task of enfranchising multitudes who languish in poverty. This socioeconomic challenge is something that is publicly discussed and debated. In societies where social progress has entailed expanding "paternalism," consumer behavior is informed by the fluid ebb and flow of what constitutes real "progress."

This is an exasperating process. As Hernando de Soto, the Peruvian economist, says of "development" campaigns that attempt to lift people from poverty, there are continuing challenges:

> Few had anticipated this enormous transformation in the way people lived and worked. The fashionable theories of the day about "development" sought to bring modernity to the countryside. Peasants were not supposed to come to the cities looking [for] the twentieth century. But tens of millions came anyway, despite a backlash of mounting hostility. They faced an impen-

etrable wall of rules that barred them from legally established social and economic activities. It was tremendously difficult for the new city people to acquire legal housing, enter formal business, or find a legal job.[46]

The influx of "unreasonable" farmers and "peasants" from the country to the city undermined the establishment of "rational" market economies.

What Friedman advocated proved elusive: a government that allowed for "the organization of economic activity through voluntary exchange presumes that we have provided, through government, for the maintenance of law and order to prevent coercion of one individual by another, the enforcement of contracts voluntarily entered into, the definition of the meaning of property rights, the interpretation and enforcement of such rights, and the provision of a monetary framework."[47] None of this convinced Galbraith, of course. For him, the "final problem of the productive society is what it produces. This manifests itself in an implacable tendency to provide an opulent supply of some things and a niggardly yield of others. This disparity carries to the point where it is a cause of social discomfort and social unhealth."[48]

Hispanic consumer behavior is thus the product of conflicted decisions. One remedy to overcome this peculiar set of circumstances is to make consumer decisions easier for Hispanics through strong branding. This entails, of course, strategies to penetrate various market segments through the deliberate use of branded "evoked sets." Hispanic consumers respond favorably to brands that are differentiated through visibility. As for "evoked sets," consumer behavior in supermarkets illustrates the phenomenon. "The way this information is recorded in memory can influence consumers' preference for brands, and whether the brand will be considered for purchase," Barbara Kahn and Leigh McAlister argue in *Grocery Revolution.*

The way products are presented influences how consumers make their decisions. Consider, for instance, how yogurt is displayed in supermarkets. If a store displays yogurts by brand—Dannon in one place, Yoplait in another, and so forth—consumers will gravitate toward the brands more familiar to them, then choose the flavor they prefer. "If," Kahn and McAlister argue, "the products had been displayed with all the strawberry yogurts together, then all the lemon-lime yogurts, and so forth, consumers would most likely choose which flavors they wanted first, and then choose which brand name they would most like for that particular flavor."[49]

This is a decades-old marketing strategy. Andre Schiffrin, who founded the New Press, recalls how two brands displaced independent bakeries in the mid-twentieth century this way:

C. Wright Mills originally organized the inquiry that showed how national brands such as Tip Top and Wonder had replaced the small bakeries that used to be in every town. The large industrial outfits initially offered bread at prices that greatly undercut local bakeries. They also encouraged local grocery stores to give more shelf space to their bread by hiking up discounts. Price differentials were at first sufficiently attractive to drive the smaller producers into bankruptcy. Having eliminated the competition, the companies raised their prices in predictable monopolistic succession and Americans were left with plastic-wrapped and plastic-tasting bread that was more expensive than the locally produced loaves it replaced. Only many decades later did specialist bakeries begin to flourish again in the large cities, selling excellent but very expensive loaves to the small numbers that can afford them.[50]

Hispanic consumers have a higher brand loyalty than non-Hispanic consumers do, suggesting that familiar merchandising strategies can be updated for the current generation of Hispanic consumer.

The reason for this Hispanic loyalty, furthermore, has its origins in the "social flux" in which one's "reasonableness" is subject to be judged along a social continuum. Brand recognition and brand loyalty are social markers of "reasonability." In societies where racial characteristics hold far less currency than in American society, Hispanics resort to the age-old distinctions between "gente *sin* razón" and "gente *de* razón." The Hispanic concepts of "gente *sin* razón" and "gente *de* razón," and how they affect the Hispanic consumer market, are fully examined in chapter 5.

For now, suffice it to understand that in Hispanic society, being a person "de razón"—"of reason"—is a sign of social sophistication, but it has nothing to do with one's income. Social intercourse in American society often depends on distinguishing between those who are considered to have "taste" and those who are deemed to be "vulgar," at times disregarding a person's actual income. Of a childhood friend's mother, Maya Angelou writes that she "lived in reduced circumstances, but she was genteel, and though she worked as a maid I decided she should be called a governess."[51] Now recall how Jethro on *The Beverly Hillbillies* would, in the process of becoming acculturated to city life, signal his sophistication by emulating how he believed city bachelors behaved and what they consumed, all in order to impress young city women.

Social snubs to those considered "nouveau" or "gaudy" in American society are used to send the message that simply because one has acquired money doesn't mean one has "arrived" at an acceptable level of "reasonableness." Coming from societies that were convulsed in rapid urbanization, Hispanics are sensitive to distancing themselves from being perceived as unsophisticated country folk. Economist De Soto describes the social and political forces that transformed human societies throughout much of the twentieth century:

> After 1950, there began in the Third World an economic revolution similar to the social and economic disruptions in Europe in 1800. New machines were reducing the demand for rural labor just as new medicines and public-health methods were cutting the rate of infant mortality and extending life spans. Soon hundreds of thousands of people were trundling down the newly built highways to the cities so alluringly described in the new radio programs.[52]

Hispanics have more recent experiences with the processes of urbanization and, as more recent immigrants themselves, are more sensitive to the socioeconomic implications of this phenomenon. One mechanism for this is to identify "world class" brands for consumer products that, through conspicuous consumption, can signal their sophistication—and their reasonableness. More than non-Hispanic consumers, Hispanics in the United States are prepared to pay a premium for brands considered prestigious, and are more loyal to the consumer brands that they favor.

Since World War II, economists have offered various explanations for the contradictions in consumer behavior, contradictions that are called "stated" versus "revealed" preference in the literature. These contradictions and conflicts reflect the continuing attempt of the market economy to reconcile what consumers say they want, and what they actually consume. For Hispanic consumers, the cultural externalities that inform consumption decisions constitute a force that results in ever greater segmentation of the marketplace, one in which familiar strategies must be updated to the specifications of these consumers' aspirations. "The economist does not enter into the dubious moral arguments about the importance or virtue of the wants to be satisfied," Galbraith argued. "He doesn't pretend to compare mental states of the same or different people at different times and to suggest that one is less urgent than the other."[53]

Hispanic consumers in the United States, however, in fact do.

The Growing Market for Educational Services to Hispanics

Hispanics, as a demographic group, remain undereducated. The overwhelming immigrants of Mexican and Central American ancestry were, in their native lands, disenfranchised, afforded few privileges or opportunities to pursue a formal education. Critics have often charged that these immigrants—particularly illegal aliens—are in fact "economic" refugees, arriving in the United States to sell their manual labor. "Give me your tired, your poor, your huddled masses yearning to breathe free, the wretched refuse of your teeming shores," Emma Lazarus wrote. "Send them, the homeless, the tempest-tost to me."

Here they are, in desperate need of formal education. Indeed, we have already briefly seen how California's bilingual education is in disarray, simply because so many of these immigrant children are "indigenous" people—Mexican Native Americans—who do not even speak Spanish. To be sure, as Hispanic consumers enter the ranks of the middle class, they will follow the Cuban model: become fluent in both English and Spanish, and pursue higher education. As a result, the college, adult, and continuing education industry enjoys tremendous opportunities for sustained growth as the number of Hispanics living and working in the United States continues to increase. To their credit, Hispanics, particularly those from Mexico, Puerto Rico, and Central America, are self-conscious about educational shortcomings.

This quality contrasts sharply with the self-confident Hispanics from most South American countries and the initial waves of Cuban exiles, many of whom arrive in the United States with college, graduate, and professional degrees. This acknowledgement of inadequacy is also different from non-Hispanic Americans. In the course of interviewing scores of applicants in Mexico, Spain, and the United States over almost two decades, for instance, I can attest to the cultural differences that one finds. Hispanic candidates for non-management positions almost invariably offer that one of their goals is to improve themselves—"superarme." Non-Hispanic candidates, on the other hand, suggest that they know everything they need to know. There is comfort in the honesty of people who acknowledge their educational deficiencies, compared with so many others who are know-nothing know-it-alls.

While one group underestimates their skills, the other overstates them.[54]

To be sure, most Hispanics do not have a first-rate education or superior management skills, unlike Luis Alvarez, the American-born scientist who was awarded the Nobel Prize in 1968 in physics, or Roberto Goizueta, the Cuban-born executive under whose management the Coca-Cola company enjoyed a period of sustained growth. As a demographic group, Hispanics' educational level falls well below the level of the non-Hispanic population at large. What John Kenneth Galbraith observed of America's native-born poor also holds true for underprivileged Hispanics. "The poor in the United States, while none could doubt their degradation and misery, were once largely invisible—poor blacks were hidden away on the farms and plantations of the rural South with primitive food, clothing and shelter, little in the way of education and no civil rights," he wrote in *The Good Society*. "Many poor whites were unseen on the hills and in the hollows of Appalachia. Poverty was not a problem when distant, out of sight. Only as economic, political and social change brought the needy to the cities did welfare become a public concern, the poor now living next to and in deep contrast with the relatively affluent."[55]

To understand why educational levels are lagging, one has to revisit the social development of Mexico for much of the twentieth century, decades before NAFTA, because U.S. Hispanics of Mexican ancestry share these social values, ideas, and worldview of the importance of education and the need for public education. From the late 1920s through 1988, Mexico implemented an economic development program largely based on the classical economics formula advocated in import substitution. Domestic producers were protected from foreign competition by the state, either through taxes and tariffs or through direct subsidies to industry. The result was a closed economy in which government—and an array of government agencies—played a significant role in guiding the economy. "Mexican paternalism" thus defined the parameters within which private enterprise itself developed and contributed to the economy. With the natural interplay of supply and demand familiar in capitalist economies, where the *laissez faire* that contributes to sound efficiencies across industries was thus interrupted and undermined, two phenomena developed.

First, the Mexican economy became inefficient, with bloated state enterprises, from oil industry where Pemex attained legendary status as an inefficient and corrupt oil producer, to Aeroméxico, which was once an inefficient carrier before it was privatized more than a decade ago. Mexican industry, unable to compete in international markets and dependent on trade and nontrade barriers to ensure its market share and profitability, played a marginal role on the world stage. A parallel development was the explosive growth of a far-reaching but underfinanced social welfare system. This system included an education secretariat with an ambitious mandate of providing free public education to every Mexican child, millions of whom speak little Spanish, for there are nearly sixty native languages still spoken by the 11 million Mexican citizens classified as "indigenous."

The social aspects of these social programs nurtured a dependence on the state. The proliferation of social welfare programs designed along socialist principles and modeled along the familiar communal social organizations of Mexican Native American societies, more commonly referred to as "indigenous" people, were very popular.[56] It required very little from the Mexican public, for the government promised to "recycle" the nation's oil wealth. The idea that Mexico's oil could be used to subsidize a welfare state—free education, free national health care, subsidized housing—held the promise that Mexico's ruling party, the Institutional Revolutionary Party, or PRI, would be able to dispense patronage, similar to the way the Saudi royal family secures the loyalty of its subjects through a benevolence.

These promises were not entirely fulfilled, particularly providing universal education to all children. There were inadequate schools, poorly trained teachers, insufficient funding, for everything from school lunch programs to classroom materials. Mexico's situation was complicated by the simple fact that for many indigenous people, Spanish itself was a "foreign" language. "Bilingual" instruction in, say, Nahautl-Spanish or Zapotec-Spanish meant that many communities were disenfranchised by virtue of the lack of properly trained teachers. (The National Indigenous Institute, unable to educate its polyglot constituency of indigenous children, was criticized, for under the guise of respecting a native community's "sovereignty," it had in fact washed its hands of its responsibilities.) It is from these communities at the margins of Mexico's mainstream society that the bulk of illegal immigration to the United States originates.

The importance of knowing this, however, is that this history has informed the social expectations of U.S. Hispanics of Mexican ancestry. Their Spanish-language skills are oftentimes rudimentary, and they may not even be able to read or write in Spanish, let alone English. Recall how Feliz Martínez described to the *New York Times* her journey from her village to New York in search of her husband, who perished when the World Trade Center was destroyed in the terrorist attack of September 11. She said, "My husband José worked in one of [the towers]. Two days later [on September 13], I left my four children and went to look for José . . . I don't even understand how I did it; I can't read or write [Spanish]."[57]

The nature of the education Mexicans received was limited in certain fundamental ways. That Mexico was a one-party state for much of the twentieth century meant that it was in the interest of the Mexican state to teach its people enough to be literate (and be able to contribute to the economy by being gainfully employed), but not enough to be critical (of the government). Thus Mexican schools sought to teach the basics: reading, writing, and arithmetic. But they did not want to encourage critical, independent thought. Mexicans were taught instead the basics, of course, and what was deemed important. Mexican students, as a consequence, excelled at memorization, for example. In the same way that American students compete in a National Spelling Bee, similar educational achievements were encouraged. Mexican students, for instance, could name the capital of each state, know by heart historical facts, recite literary tracts, and so on.

But there would be a blank stare if one were to ask a Mexican student, "Did Antigone do right by challenging Creon to reclaim her slain brother's body?"

If Mexican students were taught how to debate the merits of breaking an immoral law in order to uphold a higher morality, that would invite the kind of independent thought that any authoritarian regime wishes to avoid. Mexicans' education, therefore, sought to reassure the government that criticism would not be encouraged, while producing workers and professionals that could perform their duties without causing problems for the state. After all, one can be an accountant or architect, a physician or an engineer without having to reflect upon the moral dilemmas that have been debated throughout the West since the ancient Greeks.

There is an inevitable downside to this kind of education, to be sure. When people have not been taught to think for themselves and to be critical about the world around them, then there is a stifling impact on innovation and creativity, and it undermines active civil involvement in public affairs. For a nation of 100 million people, Mexicans have, as a consequence of the education imposed upon them by the PRI since the 1950s, not been able to contribute to the world community as they did, say, during the Edwardian Age. Since the "Golden Age" of Mexican cinema and the great muralist movement, in fact, in the first half of the twentieth century, Mexicans have been playing catch-up in the mid-1990s to take their rightful place in the world of culture.[58] The legacy of this miserly educational program is evident.

Consider something as simple as reading an in-flight magazine. For most of the 1990s I was a frequent flier on Aeroméxico. It was not uncommon to read an article in its in-flight magazine without noticing the limitations of the Mexican education of the contributors. An article on Cancún, for instance, would enumerate facts: "X" number of hotel rooms, "Y" number of takeoffs and landings at Cancún's international airport, and "Z" number of tourists last year. But was Cancún thrilling? What did such a dynamic resort mean for the entire community? What was the best part of a stay in Cancún?

On all these questions, there would be nothing. Instead, the reader would be overwhelmed—and bored—by statistics. This kind of rote education, where facts are remembered and then repeated, is one in which the meaning or interpretation of the facts enumerated would be absent. This kind of education—perfectly crafted sentences, accurate reporting of facts, a logical presentation of the facts—has its limitations, which are at odds with the demands of dynamic market economies that are subject to tremendous competition.[59] Indeed, American managers in Mexico often voiced frustration at the impoverished "problem-solving" skills and the "lack of initiative" of their Mexican employees.

Corporate America has, at times, used this "passive education" in dishonorable ways. "The accelerating immigration of Hispanics has meant massively downward pressure on their wages, negotiating power and ability to confront their employers over violations of their rights," Stephen Klineberg, a sociology professor at Rice University in Houston, who studies immigration, told reporters. "Whether you're legal or not, you need that job, and you don't want to raise problems because there are a lot of other people in line for that job."[60]

Klineberg's observations were made in a lawsuit filed by the Hispanic employees of Quietflex, of Houston. Hispanic employees complained that management segregated their departments by race, giving a preference to Asians over Hispanics, while managers were overwhelmingly "Anglo." "It was a classic case of pitting one racial or ethnic group against another," Richard Shaw, secretary-treasurer of the AFL-CIO in Houston, told *New York Times* reporter Steven Greenhouse of his union's position on the matter.[61]

Hispanics, particularly those of Mexican origin, encounter obstacles imposed by the natural limitations when critical thinking is not well-developed, which means they are less likely to stand up for their rights.[62] It proves instructive, then, to see how Mexicans living in the United States, or working for an American audience, make the transition from passive education to critical inquiry. Individuals such as Alma Guillermoprieto, who writes dispatches for the *New Yorker* magazine, and novelist Elena Poniatowska are the exceptions, of course, for these individuals are not the products of typical Mexican education. An example of a professional who exhibits the hallmark worldview of a Mexican education, and who has made the leap from passive to active intellectual inquiry, is Univision anchorman Jorge Ramos. In his acclaimed book, *The Other Face of America*, one can see the transition between his passive Mexican education and the active requirements of a post-NAFTA Mexico. The reason this is important is simple: The most important Hispanic news anchorman in the United States is a Mexican who commutes from Mexico City to Miami to deliver the news—and more American households get their news from him than they do from Dan Rather.

"I must confess that each time I thought I had put the final period on this book, another idea came to mind, another story to tell, another statistic," he writes in the introduction.[63] Ramos, an attractive, ambitious young Mexican, begins his book by enumerating eleven "statistics" that presumably justify his writing the book![64] And throughout his discussion, he vacillates between asserting his opinion and justifying it with statistics, as if the strength of his conviction or his opinion did not suffice. The book becomes a riveting portrait of a man in transition, particularly since in his subsequent one, *No Borders: A Journalist's Search for Home* (HarperRayo 2002), he no longer feels the need to "explain," with statistics, the reason for his opinion. This is a remarkable example of the personal growth and self-confidence that accompanies acquiring a different kind of education.

It is clear that there are tremendous opportunities as educators, community colleges, universities, and corporate training programs understand that a disproportionate number of Hispanics have never been taught critical thought. It is imperative for Americans involved in the education industry to understand that, historically, the process by which "gente *sin* razón" become "gente *de* razón" is by learning to think critically, solve problems, and take initiatives. These are not insurmountable obstacles, but it is simply a matter of addressing a compelling gap in the kind of education that Mexicans, and Hispanics, have received.

Here, then, one can appreciate fully the cultural challenges that Hispanics pose. The "culture shock" described earlier that *gente humilde* have historically demonstrated throughout Latin America as they arrive in the city also holds true of the Hispanics who arrive in the United States. Whereas it's an amusing *Beverly Hillbillies*-style anecdote to recall Rosario May's surprise at the existence of indoor plumbing when she first arrived to work in my grandmother's household as a maid, this ignorance is far less amusing in other areas, such as in the pursuit of an education. "Experts say that Hispanic students battle many of the problems that other minority students do—the lack of role models and practical college advice at home, as well as inadequate preparation from schools," Mireya Navarro reports. "But they also face additional barriers of language and culture, particularly an attachment to the extended family, the experts say. Latino teenagers often stay home while attending college, making it all the more likely that they get caught up in their families' financial needs."[65]

They also get caught up in the familiar worldview of poor immigrants: "gente humilde" who have "poca cultura" about the modern world. For educators, it is important to recognize the pressures Hispanics encounter. *Gente humilde* are, by definition, poor, and as a consequence put a greater premium on present, not future, income. There is also the "poca cultura" worldview that sees young adults as the primary caregivers for grandparents, immediate breadwinners, and where a young woman leaves her parent's house to enter her husband's. Navarro writes:

> Some students complained about parents who came to this country to work and want their children to do the same—as soon as possible. In some families, girls in particular are expected to marry young, or at least not leave home until they marry. "My mother at first said, 'You have to start working like everyone else,'" said Estrellita Garcia, 20, a Spanish major at California State University in Los Angeles. "I told her 'O.K., I'll start at McDonald's,'

but without an education you'd have a low-paying job all your life," said Ms. Garcia, who transferred from East Los Angeles Community College and is a full-time student. "Now she's more supportive, I guess."[66]

Once these cultural obstacles are overcome, Hispanics thrive. "Colleges have come up with a host of programs to entice and retain Hispanic students, from 'Latino floors' in freshman dormitories to orientation courses," Navarro reports. "Institutions like the University of California at Los Angeles are also aggressively working with community colleges to increase transfers, something many private schools are doing to increase diversity. With the right support, administrators at U.C.L.A. and other institutions noted, graduation rates for Latino students are comparable to those for other groups."[67]

This process of helping people of *poca cultura* learn about contemporary life, and of initiating *gente humilde* to the tradeoffs of modern life—sacrificing income today while going to school full-time for a professional career later on—is one of subtle acculturation, one in which public and private administrators throughout Latin America have ample experience. The process of personal evolution from irrational to rational thinking has distinguished "gente *sin* razón" from "gente *de* razón." A person who thinks one can get ahead in the world by dropping out of high school is a "persona *sin* razón." A person, on the other hand, who believes that making the sacrifices required to become a college graduate is deemed to be a "persona *de* razón." As anchorman Jorge Ramos himself demonstrates, this process is not one that takes years, but it is a skill that oftentimes accompanies the process of acculturation; learning English as a second language is more arduous than learning how to "superarme" by acquiring critical thought.

Now R.J. Reynolds' market research begins to make sense:

1. U.S. Hispanics of Mexican descent are people of color who were not afforded formal education.
2. In Mexico their lack of formal education subjected them to discrimination, with most people assuming they were "gente humilde," or even "gente sin razón."
3. They came to the United States primarily to work, prepared to take the most difficult jobs, simply to survive.
4. Their difficulties in this country are compounded by their lack of education, their inability to speak English, and the racial baggage of American life.
5. That the most humble of Mexicans, by virtue of living in the United States, acculturate to some degree means that their cultural illiteracy

of Mexico and their functional illiteracy in the United States, creates tensions between Mexican Hispanics and Mexicans.

6. If R.J. Reynolds finds that California Hispanics are "grateful" to be in the United States, what this means is that they are grateful for a job; Texas Hispanics who fear being "taken advantage of" are Hispanics who have been in the United States long enough to be subjected to American racism.

7. Tremendous opportunities are to be found in providing educational opportunities for Hispanics, who, as the present century unfolds, will comprise the largest educational market in the world.

3

Labor, Immigration, and Business

Abstract

The American labor force is being transformed by Hispanic ascendancy, with the greatest influence deriving from the presence of so many Mexican immigrants and Mexican Hispanics. It has already been shown that Hispanics of Mexican and Central American ancestry comprise three out of four U.S. Hispanics. In order to understand how these changes are impacting corporate America, it is necessary to understand Mexican labor. Mexican workers, in record numbers, are becoming U.S. Hispanics of Mexican ancestry. It is therefore necessary to understand how Mexican society informs the character of these 25 million U.S. Hispanic workers. It is impossible and irresponsible to speak of the U.S. Hispanic labor market without a discussion of the Mexican labor market. It is comprised of three categories: (1) highly skilled workers who have, over the course of the past half century, found employment in the growing urban centers; (2) semiskilled labor that has abandoned rural communities and moved to centers with significant maquiladoras, or in-bond factories in industrial parks near urban centers and along the U.S.-Mexico border; (3) unskilled labor that, unable to find sufficient employment in Mexican cities, has entered the United States illegally, with the vast majority of these illegal workers returning to Mexico permanently in due course. The economic growth engendered by NAFTA has accelerated these historical trends. Mexico's professional class is more experienced and sophisticated, and highly competitive in world labor markets. The technical expertise of semiskilled workers is increasing as Mexico moves to "second-stage" maquiladora facilities. Mexican unskilled labor is returning from the United States and Canada with signifi-

cant trade and craft skills. For its part, the American economy continues to benefit from the influx of Mexican workers, not only in being provided the raw labor that is in critical shortage across the United States, but in revitalizing urban centers whose decades-long population declines have, since NAFTA, been reversed. What has not changed to reflect these economic realities, however, are the politics surrounding immigration laws in the United States. Mexican President Vicente Fox's efforts to work on a comprehensive guest-worker program that would allow for the "regularization" of the millions of Mexican citizens currently living and working in the United States were abruptly derailed by the events of September 11. This is unfortunate for, not only do continental economic forces now require a more sophisticated approach to labor issues, but also the egregious civil and human rights violations that antiquated immigration laws produce diminish the credibility of the North American marketplace as it aspires to remain the world's leading trading bloc.

"The indictment of Tyson Foods Inc., the nation's largest meat processor, on charges that it conspired to smuggle illegal immigrants to work at its plants is a sign of how dependent the American food and agriculture system has become on foreign-born workers, many of them here illegally," David Barboza reported from Chicago. "Because of this heavy reliance, agriculture experts say, a major effort to crack down on the hiring of illegal workers could disrupt the nation's food industry. 'This would really cripple the system,' said William Heffernan, professor of rural sociology at the University of Missouri who has studied immigrant labor. 'In the communities where these plants are located there isn't an alternative work force. They'd have to raise wages and improve the conditions.'"[1]

The indictment alleged that six Tyson employees had conspired to smuggle illegal Mexican immigrants to work in a dozen of Tyson's poultry processing plants. This unprecedented 36-count indictment, furthermore, accused Tyson executives of conspiring to obtain counterfeit work papers for the illegal immigrants. Tyson employees were acquitted. Tyson, however, denying that a conspiracy took place, placed the indicted employees on administrative leave at that time. Tyson finally challenged prosecutors' and the government's charges that its corporate culture "condones" these practices, arguing that immigration laws were "irrational" and "absurd."

With all due respect to the Justice Department and Tyson management, it is clear that when corporate America has to go to such extremes to secure laborers for jobs that Americans do not want to perform, there are other, structural problems with the nation's immigration laws. There is something fundamentally amiss when corporate managers face indictment simply because they are desperate to find factory workers. Make no mistake, illegal workers from Mexico do the hardest, dirtiest jobs in the United States for low pay and few, if any, benefits. Consider *New York Times* journalist Charlie LeDuff's report from a North Carolina slaughterhouse. "Slaughtering swine is repetitive, brutish work, so grueling that three weeks on the factory floor leave no doubt in your mind about why the turnover is 100 percent," he explains. "Five thousand quit and five thousand are hired every year. You hear people say, They don't kill pigs in the plant, they kill people. So desperate is the company for workers, its recruiters comb the streets of New York's immigrant communities, personnel staff members say, and word of mouth has reached Mexico and beyond."[2]

LeDuff's story confirms in graphic detail what John Kenneth Galbraith observes about the work the poor perform in general. "Work also consigns men and women to the anonymity of the toiling masses," he observes. "Here it consists of repetitive, tiring, muscular effort replete with tedium. It has often been held that the good workman enjoys his work; this is said most frequently, most thoughtfully, by those with no experience of hard, physical, economically enforced toil."[3]

While the contributions of immigrant laborers have been recognized— "there would now be little fruit, few vegetables and fewer canned goods in our stores at affordable prices in the absence of migrant workers," Galbraith noted—the inhumane conditions under which they labor have gone largely without comment.[4] One of the few to document the conditions under which these workers labor is Eric Schlosser, author of *Fast Food Nation,* who, in an interview with Salon.com, explains that slaughterhouse workers have what he calls the worst jobs in America. "And these people do get hurt. They tend to be the lowest-paid meatpacking workers—they're the most likely to be illegal immigrants. And in the book I have a list of some of the injuries they've suffered in recent years, and some of them are literally ground up in the machinery. It's horrible. These are the ultimate in disposable workers."[5]

No human being is "disposable," of course, and it is an affront to human decency for any person to be treated as such.[6] Think of how Americans felt when Islamic extremists characterized those killed on September 11 as "infidels" who were "disposable" in an ongoing jihad against the West. Now consider the price exacted from "disposable" workers in the United States. "In effect, migrant workers, so necessary for the success of the labor-intensive U.S. agricultural system, subsidize that very system with their own and their families' indigence," the U.S. Department of Labor reported in 1994. "The system functions to transfer costs to workers who are left with income so marginal that, for the most part, only newcomers and those with no other options are willing to work on our nation's farms."[7]

Despite their contribution to the American economy, migrant workers remain woefully disenfranchised. "The U.S. and Mexican governments have never wanted to sit down and say, 'Here is the reality of immigration.' Instead they have let it grow into the chaos that it is," said Andres Rozental, who along with Mack McLarty headed the United States–Mexico Migration Panel.[8] As a result, even well-intentioned attempts to improve the lives of migrant workers are suffused with pathos. "Last spring, in a move some say is a national model, county residents approved Measure L, which loosened long-sacrosanct zoning restrictions against development on agricultural land to permit the building of farmworker housing," Patricia Leigh Brown reported from northern California. "The measure calls for up to five camps to provide temporary shelter for up to 300 farmworkers. This month, a majority of the valley's 1,900 vineyard owners, representing some 44,400 acres, voted to tax themselves $7.76 per acre to help pay for and operate the new housing. The demand for worker housing is in many ways a distinctly Napa problem. While 75 percent of California wine grapes are picked by machine, roughly the same percentage in the valley is picked by hand. Workers here brave porch floors [i.e., they sleep on porch floors in fields] for hourly wages that on average are 9 percent higher than elsewhere in the state: up to $100 on a good picking day."[9] If one were talking about horses working on a farm, there would be no need for a ballot measure to provide "adequate" stables, or housing, that was "humane," since the Humane Society would not allow such treatment, or mistreatment, of animals.

When Fox took office as Mexico's president, however, there was a concerted attempt to address these problems head on. "Mexico stands to gain equitable treatment of its citizens . . . and the United States gets control of its borders," Senator Phil Gramm said after meeting with Fox in Mexico City in January 2001. "It's clear that it's the kind of program that Mexico wants . . . and we think the American people can be sold."[10] These priorities were succinctly framed by Foreign Secretary Jorge Castañeda when President Bush arrived in Mexico in February 2001. As quoted in the *New York Times:* "We think the broad immigration and labor agenda includes humane, civil, and adequate treatment for Mexicans: Mexicans here, going there; Mexicans as they cross the border; Mexicans when they start work; and Mexicans who have already been in the United States for a long time," Castañeda said at the time. "The best way to ensure this is for them to have papers. There is no better way for Mexicans to defend themselves than for them to be legal."[11]

This is how U.S.-Mexican relations were envisioned, with Fox anticipating reaching an "agreement" by the end of 2001. A week after he addressed a joint session of Congress on Capitol Hill, these plans were derailed by the events of September 11. In fact, it took a year after September 11 before immigration reform and the need to establish a fair, manageable, and sustainable guest-worker program captured the attention of American officials and appeared once again on Washington's political radar screen. Tamar Jacoby commented in the *New York Times:*

> The nation needs to think again about the changes under consideration a year ago: a package of reforms that would have increased the number of visas for Mexican workers and legalized the status of many of the undocumented migrants already here in the United States. The plan may sound unwise today—after all, many Americans are more suspicious now than ever of new immigrants. But the truth is, a more liberal policy is not antithetical to greater security. On the contrary, creating legal channels for migrant workers and registering the millions already here offers the best hope for homing in on the few foreigners who have indeed come to this country to do us harm.[12]

There is, of greater importance, the matter of human decency and civil rights. In Alexandria, Virginia, for instance, this is the plight of one Mexican woman as reported by the *Washington Post.* "No, the Mexican immigrant cannot rent an apartment. No, she cannot open a bank account. No, her husband, an electrician, has no guarantee he will be paid fairly, if at all," Mary Jordan and Mary Beth Sheridan wrote. "And no, there is no escaping the fear that she or her husband could be deported at any moment by immigration officials."[13] There is something fundamentally wrong when people working hard to earn an honest living are prevented from opening a bank account, while terrorists can do so freely.[14] In order to make sense of the immigration quagmire in which the NAFTA nations are engulfed, let us examine the origins, challenges, and solutions that are credible, and meet the needs of the people of North America.

The Nature of Illegal Immigration

The first "illegal" aliens in North America were Americans from the East Coast who ventured west of the Mississippi in the nineteenth century. It was none other than American settlers who violated Mexican immigration laws when they first moved into Texas, and then into California and the Southwest. "More and more Yankee illegal aliens filled California, and their disregard for Mexican passport regulations convinced the locals of their general disrespect for Mexican law," Douglas Monroy writes. ". . . As had happened in New Mexico, Mexico had lost the allegiance of its frontier citizens. Disorganized and unable to defend the locals against Indian depradations, yet meddling in local affairs and trying to collect taxes and tariffs, the Mexican government brought down [Spanish] Californio hostility against it. . . . Thus, many Californios began to consider withdrawing from Mexican sovereignty and forming some other allegiance."[15]

Time passes, and the tables are turned, not without irony. John Steinbeck acknowledged American disenfranchisement of Mexicans from what once had been their territory in *Grapes of Wrath*. He wrote:

> Once California belonged to Mexico and its lands to Mexicans; and a horde of tattered feverish Americans poured in. And such was their hunger for land that they took the land—stole Sutter's land, Guerrero's land, took the grants and broke them up and growled and quarreled over them, those frantic hungry men; and they guarded with guns the land they had stolen. They put up houses and barns, they turned the earth and planted crops. And these things were possession, and possession was ownership.
>
> The Mexicans were weak and fled. They could not resist, because they wanted nothing in the world as frantically as Americans wanted land.
>
> Then, with time, the squatters were no longer squatters, but owners; and their children grew up and had children on the land. And the hunger was gone from them, the feral hunger, the gnawing, tearing hunger for land, for water and earth and the good sky over it, for the green thrusting grass, for the swelling roots. They had these things so completely that they did not know about them any more.[16]

Historical amnesia served the United States well for most of the twentieth century.

It won't, however, get anyone anywhere in a Hispanicized America. There are certain hard realities, hard realities that must now be addressed. As David Barboza reported in the *New York Times:*

> About one million farm laborers are on the job at any one time, according to the United States Department of Agriculture. And a government study estimated that nearly 40 percent are illegal. A few years ago, the Immigration and Naturalization Service estimated that about 25 percent of meatpacking workers in the Midwest were probably illegal. The government, though, has had little success in stemming the flow of illegal immigrants to food and agriculture companies. Federal raids on meatpacking plants sent many illegal workers back to their countries. But it outraged food companies, who complained of disruptions. Civil rights officials accused the government of harassing Mexicans and others from Central America. And Midwestern politicians sometimes complained that slowing down the work at meatpacking plants increased the supply of livestock and thereby harmed hog and cattle farmers, who had already been suffering from low prices for their goods.[17]

However they are ill-treated, the promise of American jobs keeps workers coming; nothing can keep them out. "All that Gatekeeper and its counterparts in Arizona and Texas have accomplished since they were launched six years ago is to move the undocumented foot traffic out of the urban areas and—not coincidentally—out of the public eye. In the process, these operations have made smugglers indispensible," Claudia Smith, of the California Rural Legal Assistance Foundation, wrote. "Meanwhile, a migrant a day dies on our southwest border."[18]

That humanitarian crisis and the post–September 11 need to implement a viable North American Security Perimeter (NASP) program to protect the United States requires that a new immigration and border control policy must be developed. "The battle for the border is largely symbolic," Karl Eschbach of the Center for Immigration Research at the University of Houston is on record as saying. "No matter how much control you have, it doesn't appear to stop the flow of immigrants. It only controls how much it costs them, where they do it and how they will die."[19]

Illegal immigration touches all of our lives, whether we buy produce in supermarkets or eat in fine restaurants or depend on caregivers for our children. The absurdity of current immigration laws is nowhere better demonstrated than in the fact that immigration-reform opponents themselves rely on illegal immigrants. "I go to dinner at restaurants and probably have come into contact with people who are here illegally," Representative Tom Tancredo, a Colorado Republican, said after he was accused of having illegal aliens remodel the basement of his home in Littleton. "I do not ask, of course."[20]

"So long as they stay out of trouble once they're here, most Americans ignore illegal aliens. I've yet to see a customer walk out of a restaurant because his dishes were being washed by an illegal alien," said Linda Chávez, who was forced to withdraw her nomination for secretary of labor in January 2001 when it was revealed she had hired an illegal alien as a nanny.[21]

Corporate Complicity in Illegal Immigration

"Every day, on many streets across this city, immigrant day laborers wait in the hope that they will be selected to perform construction work," Judge Doris Ling-Cohan wrote in *Fernando v. Vasquez*. "Some are here legally; some are here illegally. Nevertheless, having performed the work, they then wait and hope that they will actually be paid for their services."[22]

That many migrants are unable to open checking accounts means, naturally, that they prefer to be paid in cash. That itself has given rise to another way of exploiting laborers: workers who opt to be paid by cash vouchers are illegally charged transaction fees. In *Flynn v. Labor Ready, Inc.*, Lowell

Peterson, an attorney for the plaintiffs, argued that New York State's Labor Law Section 193 prohibits involuntary deductions. "The law does not permit one to avoid liability for an unlawful act by offering the victim the opportunity to accept lawful treatment," he said. Peterson argued that it was illegal for Labor Ready Inc. to deduct as much as $1.99 from the wages of laborers who requested to be paid in cash.[23] Imagine the moral depravity of a company that charges its workers a fee to receive their wages, when the firm itself refuses to provide the necessary documentation necessary for these workers to open bank accounts.

Not unlike unscrupulous executives at Enron, WorldCom and Tyco, too many people in corporate America have used the illegal status of their workers as a weapon against them. "For more than four months, they worked without pay and lived in squalid conditions. When they finally demanded their back wages, they were dismissed," Michael Janofsky reports in the *New York Times*. "Now, virtually broke and living in immigrant quarters in Longmont, Colo., as guests of Boulder County, 14 Mexican quarry workers who entered the United States legally with temporary work visas have hired lawyers to help them fight for what they say they are owed and for the right to remain in this country to work. 'These guys did everything right,' said Mario Hernández, the spokesman for the Mexican consulate in Denver. 'They followed the rules but had only a very bad experience to show for it.'"[24] This experience is repeated around the country without end. "Thousands of Mexican workers have been dismissed from airport restaurants and parking lots and from companies that prepare inflight meals," Sam Dillon reported from the Northwest. "Others have had full-time jobs cut to part-time."[25]

America's current immigration laws, in fact, suggest that upward mobility requires a permanent underclass comprised of new immigrants who are economically exploited and politically disenfranchised. Indeed, even those Mexicans who are legal and work full-time jobs are not ensured fair treatment. Reporting on the plight of laborers planting trees, who number 15,000 and are in the United States on temporary visas, Steven Greenhouse describes the pattern of exploitation that alarms federal officials. "These modern-day Johnny Appleseeds, whose numbers have more than doubled in the last three years, journey north in the hope of earning more than $5 a day they earn back home. Federal officials say these migrants are often paid far less than they are due because of widespread violations of wage and hour laws. . . . Traditionally, poor whites have done the work of replanting American forests. In the last 10 years, however, the forestry business, like other industries that depend on unskilled labor, has turned largely to immigrants on temporary visas to do the arduous work."[26]

These labor violations have been a part of the Mexican migrant's experience in the United States across the decades. "So until Mexico is willing and able to del with the 'push' factors that force millions of its citizens to seek a better life in the United States, and until the United States is willing to deal with the 'pull' factors that lure millions of poor people here from around the world, we should expect that deaths among immigrants will continue to occur," Peter Nunez testified before Congress on June 24, 2003, describing the perils and abuses these migrants face.[27] "We are farther away from the horrors of Sept. 11, and we've had a chance to digest it," said John F. Gay, co-chairman of the Essential Worker Immigration Coalition, a business group that supports granting legal status to millions of illegal immigrants. "People inside and outside of Congress are beginning to understand that immigration reform makes you more secure."[28]

"This is a court of law, young man," Oliver Wendell Holmes famously said, summarizing the essence of the American legal system that far too many people fail to grasp, "not a court of justice."

And so it is.[29] In the face of the inherent injustice and disjunction of the American legal system, the Mexican government has long complained to U.S. officials. That Mexico under the PRI was anything but democratic itself, of course, undermined its credibility. That, however, has changed. "Mexico's new government can speak with particular credibility in the defense of democracy and human rights. I am confident that you will claim your rightful place as an advocate of these values—particularly in the Americas," Jesse Helms told Vicente Fox upon making a visit to Mexico City.[30] "I have always said the good people of this great country deserve an honest government of their own choosing," he told reporters. "Apparently the Mexican people felt the same way."[31]

Mexican democracy has given Fox's officials new credibility, and this means that the legitimate concerns of the migrant workers can no longer be ignored. This begs the obvious question: If the American economy requires a steady supply of cheap immigrant labor to perform the unpleasant tasks others will not do, who will scrub the floors, mind the children, and pick the produce once today's immigrants move up the economic ladder? Whether they remain in the United States, or more likely, when they return to Mexico, who will do the nation's dirty work?

The Advantages of "Regularizing" the Labor Force Across North America

The security risk of having a shadow population of 5–6 million "floating" people in the United States is a concern for all three NAFTA nations. That people come and go and move about is inevitable. "If it becomes harder for people to enter countries legally, they will do it illegally, and indeed some die in the attempt," Diane Coyle writes in *Paradoxes of Prosperity.* "If governments were to succeed in stopping the movement of people, it would also mark the diversion of the benefits of globalization to serve only the interests of the rich countries. There is already enough uneasiness about whether globalization is as good as it's cracked up to be. The economic benefits can only emerge if it is politically acceptable, and that means it must work for poor countries, too. Migration is what human beings do; they always have."[32]

The debate over what to do—if the American government deported all the illegal aliens in the United States, produce would rot in the fields, factories would stand idle, restaurants would be hard-pressed to serve up meals—continues to rage, with a heightened post–September 11 urgency.[33] "We wanted to make as strong a statement as we could that our mutual agenda has not been lost in the aftermath of the disaster of September 11," Senate Democratic leader Tom Daschle is quoted as saying, when he and Representative Richard A. Gephardt, then House minority leader from Missouri, traveled to Puebla, Mexico. "Our agenda regarding our mutual relationship is every bit as important, and our commitment every bit as strong."[34]

The chorus calling for immigration reform increased as 2002 became 2003, from coast to coast. "Not only would legalization eliminate a vast population of second-class noncitizens—the existence of such a population is an affront to our democratic values—it would also allow us to identify and keep track of these millions of undocumented immigrants without resort to law enforcement," Tamar Jacoby wrote in the *New York Times.*[35]

"Among the specific proposals," James F. Smith reported in the *Los Angeles Times,* "[is to] create more opportunities for legal temporary work in the United States, legalize more Mexicans who have lived without permission in the U.S., crack down on organized-crime syndicates that smuggle migrants, and work jointly to reduce the number of migrants who die trying to cross the 2,100-mile border."[36]

"Our proposal will bring undocumented immigrants out of the shadows and into the light of accountability and greater cooperation in our fight against terrorism," Gephardt told attendees at the annual meeting of the National Council of La Raza in the summer of 2002.[37] Rafael Fernández de Castro, one of the authors of a study recommending an immigration plan commissioned by the Carnegie Endowment for International Peace in Washington and the Autonomous Technological Institute of Mexico, told the *Los Angeles Times,* "This is a window of opportunity to seize the moment and start building a long-term solution."[38]

"There are very good reasons for crafting a special immigration relationship with Mexico, given its propinquity, its historical ties and NAFTA," said T. Alexander Aleinikoff, a former general counsel of the Immigration and Naturalization Service who is now a senior associate at the Migration Policy Institute. "That said, when it comes to the legalization proposal, it's very hard to distinguish long-term undocumented immigrants from Mexico in the United States from long-term undocumented immigrants here from other countries."[39]

And yet, there remains resistance. There are two reasons for this hesitancy over legalization, one rational and the other not. There is foremost the matter of race. The United States has the baggage of racism that still poisons its civic life. This is a factual assessment of the hostility immigrants face. In fact, consider how politics defines the incredibly disparate "rights" that different Hispanics find in the United States. A (white) Cuban who washes up in front of the Delano Hotel in Miami Beach is granted asylum—and is entitled to Social Security, Medicare, and welfare benefits immediately. A (brown) Mexican in the United States is deported, even if he has a job, pays taxes, is married to a legal resident, and has an American-born child.

"United States immigration policy is not fair. Never has been. Probably never will be," journalist Eric Schmitt concedes. "Ever since the Chinese Exclusion Act of 1882 barred Chinese laborers from the country, American immigration history has been littered with laws and policies that have favored some countries and discriminated against others."[40] What accounts for this disparity in American immigration policy? Whereas Cubans were almost exclusively whites of direct European immigrants to Latin America—and are therefore as "white" as any Anglo-American, Mexican migrants in question are short, stocky, dark-skinned—and are more readily subjected to "racism" and "lookism." Thus (white) Hispanics, such as actress Cameron Díaz, are "invisible" in the American mainstream, but (dark-skinned) Hispanics, such as labor organizer César Chávez, are easily identified as "minorities."

Apart from the inherent lack of fairness, however, the other reason is the mistaken belief that Mexican immigrants want to settle permanently in the United States. The numbers of illegal Mexicans in the United States—3–4 million—have remained stable over a generation. "Most Mexican immigrants work in the United States to save money, and return to Mexico to improve their lives with the money they saved while working here," Douglas Massey of the University of Pennsylvania's Mexican Migration Project said. "There is a pattern, in which fathers or older brothers come work in the United States for a few years, then their sons or younger brothers do. It's uncommon for an entire family to migrate, and only when migrant workers in the U.S. marry here and have children do they 'settle' in and put down roots."[41]

"Face the facts: Temporary workers are rarely 'temporary' and never just 'workers,'" Paul Donnelly wrote in the *Los Angeles Times,* arguing for making green cards the real "payoff" for guest workers. "They are people with families building a better future."[42] The "facts," however, are different from the way Donnelly presents them. Mexican migration patterns have remained consistent for more than a century. "Roughly two-thirds of the migrants were single men, and most assumed that they would go back to Mexico some day," Douglas Monroy writes of historical trends. "Virtually no Mexican immigrants initiated and completed naturalization procedures in the United States; it is unlikely that it even occurred to them to do so. Their social and political aspirations and consciousness remained oriented toward Mexico even after the journey north. . . . Remaining north of the border was an unintended consequence of their effort to survive in Mexico."[43]

Indeed, Mexicans remaining in the United States permanently are seen as failures back home.[44] There is no embarrassment in having to go to the United States for an opportunity to make money, to pursue an education, to get a break. But there is the social understanding that the United States is not one's home, and that one is expected to return home after a few years working there. "For generations, Mexico regarded people who left for the United States as turncoats who would sell their patrimony for a fistful of dollars," Tim Weiner writes bluntly, though this is not entirely accurate.[45]

The Mexican migrant's familiar saying succinctly belies this idea: "I will come back rich, or I will send for you."

This goal, scoffed at by American cynics who dismiss an ignorant migrant's naïveté, is actually feasible. "Wealth," after all, is relative. To start one's own family-run business in Mexico can be done for about $6,000–$10,000. A working-class Mexican who can save this amount in a few years considers himself "rich," insofar as he has saved the necessary capital to start a small business that will provide a livelihood for himself and lifetime employment for at least his male children. By comparison, as measured in loans made by the Small Business Administration and the fees to buy into a franchise business, to start a modest small business in the United States costs $30,000–$60,000. Those who, for whatever reason, do not manage to save their start-up capital often resort to bringing other family members to the United States and settling here.

Consider the implications of these patterns. It is important to realize that in the same way that generations of disenfranchised Americans— underprivileged minorities, poor whites—found the opportunity for advancement through military service, millions of Mexicans have seized the opportunity to better themselves by spending a few years in the United States. The chance to work and learn about the world is the foundation upon which one can build a future. These "facts" are accurately reflected in recent studies that recommend a "migration plan." "Among the specific proposals," James Smith reported of the Carnegie Endowment for International Peace and the Autonomous Technological Institute of Mexico report, "create more opportunities for legal temporary work in the United States, legalize more Mexicans who have lived without permission for years in the U.S., crack down on organized-crime syndicates that smuggle migrants, and work jointly to reduce the number of migrants who die trying to cross the 2,100-mile frontier."[46]

A decades-old guest-worker program that has proved successful and can be used as a model is the one between Mexico and Canada. "The documents they carried guaranteed they would be treated fairly," Anthony DePalma writes of Mexican migrant workers in Canada. "They did not mind living in old farmhouses, with sheets draped across the windows and greasy stoves in the kitchen. They did not complain about being almost totally isolated on the farms with only minimal contact with surrounding communities or, occasionally, a representative from the office of the Mexican consulate in Toronto. They had no delusions about settling in Canada permanently; they were strictly forbidden to stay, and besides, most planned to return home with the $3,000 to $4,000 they'd be able to save during a single season to build a house, buy a satellite television dish, pay for a child's education, or otherwise get ahead."[47]

American officials act as if they are being asked to invent the wheel, and even well-intentioned plans are, too often, counterproductive.[48] The result, then, is the creation of a shadowy world, where millions of Mexicans live on the margins of American society. How Mexicans in the United States cope with these peculiar circumstances—political disenfranchisement, taxation without representation, racial discrimination, and being disproportionately targeted by criminals—is instructive in understanding their place in American society and their contributions to the economies of both the United States and Mexico in unexpected ways.[49]

Consider, for instance, the mass migration of the Mixtec, a Mexican Native American people from Puebla and Oaxaca, to the metropolitan New York area. "Puebla residents, or *poblanos,* make up more than half the Mexican population in New York. Analysts are unclear exactly why the phenomenon began, but since the mid-1980s and 1990s, *poblanos* have been coming in record numbers," Paloma Dallas reported. "Before them, a small influx of Mexicans from the Yucatán Peninsula came in the 1920s, and others from Jalisco and Michoacán came in the 1950s and 1960s. However, the population began to take off in the 1980s with the arrival of *poblanos* and others from the Mixteca region, which includes parts of Puebla, Guerrero, and Oaxaca, and is home to some two-thirds of the Mexican community in New York."[50]

How important is the migration of Mexican Native Americans to the American Northeast in political, economic, social, and anthropological terms?

No one knows, but there are surely future doctoral theses to be written examining the unprecedented migration of indigenous peoples from central Mexico to the New York metropolitan area during the 1990s and 2000s. Regardless what cultural anthropologists will discover, at present the *political* impact is already known. "Thousands of miles away from their own constituents, the two top Democrats from the United States took a morning ride today through a rural stretch of central Mexico that had all the trappings of a campaign," Ginger Thompson reported from Puebla, Mexico. "Senator Tom Daschle, the majority leader from South Dakota, and Representative Richard A. Gephardt, the minority leader from Missouri, visited villages in Puebla State that are connected to the United States by the blood and money of immigrants."[51]

The contributions of these reticent, disenfranchised constituency cannot be underestimated; their economic contributions are significant. Illegal aliens helped New York City's population increase to a record 8 million, according to the 2000 census. What is true in New York is also true across the country, where many decaying urban centers are being revitalized (if not gentrified) by the massive influx of Mexican immigrants.[52] "After half a century of seeing its population dwindle as people abandoned the core of the city and moved to the suburbs, Chicago has finally rebounded," Pam Belluck reported. "For the first time since 1950, the city's population grew, and by a larger number than demographers and historians had been expecting. . . . The growth is primarily the result of an influx of immigrants, especially Mexicans and other Hispanics."[53]

Farther out West, the results are the same. "The battle over [the San Fernando] Valley secession [from Los Angeles] would transform the country's second largest city, slicing off roughly a third of its residents and some of its most solidly middle-class neighborhoods," James Sterngold reported of Latino efforts to break away from Los Angeles and incorporate their own city. "It would energize other secession movements (Hollywood is also trying to separate itself) and could divide the city further into an array of competing municipalities."[54] The result of this political activism is that, through sheer numbers, California society has changed in unintended ways. "What this means is that, at least in Southern California, we have reached that critical mass where Latinos are no longer an isolated interest group protecting one way of seeing their interest," Harry Pachon, a professor at the Claremont Graduate University and president of the Tomas Rivera Policy Institute, was quoted as saying.[55]

California, where minorities are now the majority, foreshadows the entire

Southwest. "The new illegal workers [in Arizona] have helped sustain the state's buoyant economy, and economists and demographers acknowledge that without them, that economy and those of many other states could not have grown so fast," Michael Janofsky reported. "At the same time, their growing numbers—and their work in a shadow economy that earns them cash income on which they pay no taxes—have exerted pressures on county agencies. Many schools, hospitals and libraries are struggling to accommodate rising need."[56]

This leads to the question of race and how racism impacts American immigration policies. The distinctions between "racism" and "lookism" will be discussed at length in chapter 6, but for now, suffice it to acknowledge that discrimination plays an important role in the obstacles that are thrust in the path of Mexicans who come to the United States to work and live temporarily. Let us not kid ourselves: if these immigrants looked like other "attractive" Hispanics—Antonio Banderas, Cameron Díaz, Jennifer López, Ricky Martin—there is little doubt that some kind of guest-worker or amnesty program would have been put in place decades ago.

Racism, of course, is a factor insofar as there are historical prohibitions against miscegenation among America's Puritan founders.[57] That "Anglo" Americans can find people of color physically attractive, however, was seldom openly discussed.[58] This has changed over the past decade. Interracial attraction is now a mainstay of television entertainment, from MTV to PBS to HBO. Openly portrayed, this, quite naturally, affects youngsters, whose world is now comprised of greater freedoms and possibilities. In the teenage film, *Crazy/Beautiful,* for instance, the history between the Californios and the first American settlers, who married the Californios' daughters, is revisited, albeit in reverse. " 'Crazy/Beautiful' has its flaws, but it's elementally entertaining, and believable enough to transport us completely into its world for an hour and a half," Stephanie Zacharek wrote in Salon.com. "Nicole (Kirsten Dunst) is a 17-year-old troublemaker who's careering toward disaster: She has been picked up on DUI charges, and . . . her emotional problems are knotty and deep-rooted; still, Nicole barely acknowledges the privileges her social status affords her. . . . She couldn't care less that she's able to attend a top-flight school—a school that one of her less-privileged classmates, Carlos (Jay Hernández), has to travel two hours by bus to reach. Carlos [in contrast] is blazingly bright and ambitious; he hopes to escape his barrio background to become a naval pilot."[59]

The question of class is more important than that of race, even when the film portrays the lives of deprivation of struggling Hispanics accurately. "This is a classic love story, but one that's not afraid to take a few jabs at the cluelessness of goodhearted liberals who, despite their admirable intentions, can never quite grasp how the other half lives."[60]

Cognizant of how different appearances encourage racism in the "real" world, civic and law enforcement officials are equally concerned about community relations, and how to ameliorate the perception among minorities that they are unfairly targeted by the police. "A possible perverse side effect [of illegal immigration from Mexico]," Robert Samuelson warned in the *Washington Post,* "is a rise in prejudice against Hispanic Americans, who are confused for immigrants, even though they've often lived here for generations."[61] Samuel P. Huntington, however, is less than sympathetic, and, in terms of advocating public policy, his position has disturbingly racist overtones, one in which Hispanics are categorically defined as "problems" that "Anglos" must address. Huntington presents the "problem" in this way:

> Mexico thus represents a very distinct problem as far as the United States is concerned. Without Mexican immigration, the overall level of immigration to this country would be perhaps two-thirds of what it has been. . . . Illegal entries would be relatively minor. The average level of the skill and education of immigrants would be undoubtedly the highest in American history. The much debated balance of the relative economic benefits and costs of immigration would tilt heavily toward the former, and the wage levels of less skilled Americans would rise. The bilingual education issue would disappear from our agenda. A major potential challenge to the cultural and conceivably the political integrity of the United States would also fade away.
>
> Mexico and Mexican immigration, however, will not disappear, and Americans must learn to live with both. That may become more and more difficult. . . . In almost every recent year, the Border Patrol has stopped over one million people attempting to come into the United States illegally from Mexico. It is generally estimated that each year about 300,000 do make it across illegally. If over one million Mexican soldiers crossed the border Americans would treat it as a major threat to their national security and react accordingly. The invasion of over one million Mexican civilians [is] . . . a comparable threat to American societal security, and Americans should react against it with comparable vigor.
>
> Mexican immigration is a unique, disturbing, and looming challenge to our cultural integrity, our national identity, and potentially to our future as a country.[62]

With all the melodrama of a Victorian hysteric, Dr. Huntington thus sounds the alarm bell—a decade too late.

R.J. Reynolds spent a million dollars to find out that some Hispanics were timid and others assertive. American intellectuals arrived at the similarly peculiar conclusion, but at far less expense: first, it was Didion's conclusion that Hispanic women in Miami resembled "mangoes," and then it was Huntington's assessment of Hispanics in Los Angeles as being a "societal security threat."

Where, one wonders, does a vegetarian member of Al Qaeda fit in?

"All of us who are not racists—liberals and conservatives alike—have an instinctive tic against explicit racial classifications, which is understandable given our nation's history of racial injustice," Ronald Dworkin wrote in defense of affirmative action. "But if we really want a more just society, we must be prepared to re-examine this instinct with an important distinction in mind: we must distinguish between policies whose premises deny equal citizenship and those whose premises affirm it."[63]

Inherent in this attitude, of course, is the sensible application of the law. "Government efforts to enforce immigration laws strictly since last year's terrorist attacks will bar thousands of Canadian and Mexican college students from returning to school in the fall and cost colleges and universities near the borders millions of dollars, college officials say," Danny Hakim reported in the *New York Times*. "Obviously the teachers are concerned, because that's their livelihood. The students are concerned because they want to go to school," Daryl Hendry, admissions director at El Paso Community College, is quoted as saying.[64]

American college officials reported that it was "too mind-boggling" to figure out how many millions of dollars would be lost in tuition paid by students—and in state and federal funding for programs that depend on the total number of school enrollment.[65] When federal officials learned that American colleges and universities stood to lose hundreds of millions of dollars in tuition from Canadian and Mexican students who commuted to attend institutions of higher learning along the border, "homeland security" and INS officials relented.[66] It is clear that the cumulative impact of piecemeal immigration legislation, often politicized, and seldom long-term in scope, has created a nightmare, one in which honest immigrants are turned away, and enemies of our nation are granted free entry as they please.[67]

It is in these absurd realities of American life that Mexican migrants resort to "improvise" as they go in order to survive while in the United States. Another place where this is as widespread as a strategy in the New World is, of all places, Cuba. "The fact that a writer like myself," Daniel Chavarría said, "whose works sell well in Europe and Latin America, should choose to live in Havana is, for many people, as if I had chosen to live on Mars: beyond explanation. . . . Here there are a lot of problems . . . there are injustices, but the country has survived. This is the kingdom of improvisation. Everything has to be invented."[68] This sums up the sentiment that many of the Mexicans express when they speak of their experiences in the United States: almost always grateful for the opportunity to work and save some money, but equally pleased to be back in Mexico, where they are welcome and safe.

Toward a Viable Guest-Worker Program

"Our thinking," Ricardo Morales told the *New York Times,* "is that we will make sacrifices now so that our families can live better and so that one day we will live better back home."[69]

Their thinking, which also reveals their motives, has not changed over the decades: work in the United States, save money, and return. "Normally, the migrant men who work illegally on Long Island's East End would be making travel plans. The summer construction and landscaping jobs are drying up, and the holidays are approaching. This is the time they begin drifting back to Mexico with money orders in their wallets and chocolates for their women," Charlie LeDuff reports. "'I want to go home,' Mr. [Lorenzo] Castillo said. 'But I can't go home. I haven't made enough money. And if I go, will they arrest me? Or if I come back, will they arrest me then? I can't take the chance. I'm staying here for the winter.'"[70]

At the other end of the country, the situation is the same. "In past years, [the migrants] said, they had even gone home to see their families for the winter or, perhaps, traveled to Florida or Texas, where farm work could be found. But many said they were remaining in Seattle, because they could not afford to go elsewhere or because they were worried about security crackdowns along the border and in the United States," Sam Howe Verhovek reported in the *New York Times.* Feeling stranded because of the dramatic economic slowdown of 2002, some migrants were joining the ranks of the homeless, who, because of their immigration status, were especially vulnerable. "'Now I would do anything to just be able to go home,' Raúl [a Honduran national who declined to give his last name] said about the city where his wife and his son and daughter, both 6, live."[71]

As Rubén Martínez chronicles in his book on Mexican migrants, migrants do return to Mexico:

> They come with the new clothes or still in the dirty jeans in which they picked the last of the crops or washed the last pile of restaurant dishes. They come back with billfolds thick with dollars or as poor as they left, perhaps even deeper in debt to the local loan sharks. Often they come in a car they just bought with cash, because most migrants don't have checking accounts or credit cards and hardly ever apply for bank loans. They have

gassed up the car at fluorescent-lit pit stops on all-nighters down I-5, I-19, I-25, or I-35, the interstates that lead to San Diego, Nogales, El Paso, and Laredo. . . . This time no Border Patrol jeep will chase them. The [Border Patrol] does not patrol the highways' southbound lanes, because they know the migrants are heading home and thus deportation is unnecessary.[72]

This passage is reminiscent of a description of the enthusiasm that college-aged young adults have when they are going home after the semester is over.

There is also a sense of relief that comes from leaving a place that is alien, and judgmental. In the case of American society, obsessed by race and traumatized by racism, the pressures of living in a world where race is foremost can be daunting; African-American men complain of the stress that comes by virtue of being a black male in America.[73] "Children of Native American and African-American intermarriages, for example, typically could not get others to accept their 'Indianness' and almost always were defined as African-Americans. . . . . [In such a case], individuals may choose one identity for themselves, but others in society may make another choice for them," Russell Thorton writes of American Social Darwinism gone mad. "The black-Indian child may think of himself as Indian, but if no one around him does, then he has run up against the limit of his own power to choose a racial identity."[74] American credibility is undermined by such racism, but this absurd position is not uncommon.[75]

For Mexicans, who are subjected to discrimination, there are certain factors for policymakers in both countries to consider. Foremost is creating a guest-worker program, based on Canada's successful model, which would allow Mexican laborers to find employment and American companies to fill the positions they have without either party being forced to break the law. The issuance of a "Declaration in Defense of Migrants in 2002" by the University of Texas—Pan American's Center for Border Economics, a think tank on NAFTA commerce, established principles that offer the framework for a viable guest-worker program between the United States and Mexico.

Facilitating simple matters—something as ordinary as securing a driver's license or opening a bank account—would help Hispanics working legally in the United States from being victimized. Rachel Swarns reported in the *New York Times:*

Across the United States, state and federal officials acting out of concern for national security are applying post–9/11 measures in a way that affects a broad cross-section of illegal and legal immigrants. West Virginia and Utah have recently enacted laws that will prevent or make it difficult for illegal immigrants to get licenses, according to the National Conference of State Legislatures. Legislators in Georgia blocked a measure that would have eased such rules. All told, more than a dozen states have considered such legislation this year, sending waves of anxiety coursing through Hispanic and Asian communities. In Texas, social service agencies say some Mexican and Asian illegal immigrants have responded to the pressure by burrowing deeper underground—closing bank accounts and declining to report incidents of domestic violence. People are said to be increasingly fearful of attracting attention from the local police, whose powers in some jurisdictions are being increased by the new measures.[76]

The failure to help immigrants solve ordinary problems undermines their economic success. Often simple matters, such as opening a bank account or purchasing real estate, are made difficult by misguided laws and policies. Mary Beth Sheridan reported in the *Washington Post:*

So far this year, the Mexican government has distributed about a half-million of the cards, known as *matriculas consulares.* In recent months, the cards have been recognized as official identification by nearly 200 U.S. police departments in such cities as Los Angeles, Chicago and Houston, according to the Mexican Embassy. Dozens of banks and city governments accept them. Now the cards are starting to appear in the Washington area. Supporters say the cards help hardworking immigrants who must present an official photo ID for basic necessities, from cashing a check to registering a child for school. Obtaining such an ID has become much more difficult since Virginia and other states, reacting to the Sept. 11 terrorist attacks, stiffened requirements for issuing driver's licenses and other identification.[77]

What is clear, however, is that American banks are pushing to adopt any form of identification that will allow them to reach this community.[78] "If we're to be successful and continue to grow, we're going to have to become the bank of choice for the Hispanic community," Jeffrey Bierer, a spokesman for Bank of America, said on the matter.[79] "Right now it's like a landslide— the bankers come to us," Enrique Berruga, under secretary for foreign affairs in Mexico's foreign ministry, said. "It's very good news for the American banking industry that all that money that was under the mattress is now in their arteries and their financial system."[80]

Obstacles in opening bank accounts and getting driver's licenses and the other mundane things of life, such as securing a telephone line or paying an electric bill, extend to other areas of life. Consider the obstacles they encounter. Reyna Guzmán, a Mexican migrant in northern California, wanted to achieve the "American dream" by purchasing a home for herself and her family. "She wanted the family under one roof and arrived at the realtor's with some $30,000 in the bank. She remembers the look of shock on the agent's face; she ignored it. Show me some houses, she demanded. When she saw the house on the hill, Reyna swore to make it hers," Rubén Martínez writes. "The realtor announced an asking price of $300,000—the going rate in neighborhoods like this one, full of big houses occupied, strangely, by small families, mostly Anglos. The owners rejected Reyna's initial offer. . . . The economy was on Reyna's side . . . the realtor called back. Would she care to reinstate the offer, since the owners hadn't been successful in selling to another party? She offered $200,000. They accepted. She put $30,000 down, took on a large mortgage, and the house was hers."[81]

These concerns are more urgent now that, consistent with the settlement pattern of the prairie lands of the Midwest in the nineteenth century, Mexican immigrants are arriving in smaller towns. North Carolina, for instance, led the nation in Hispanic growth at the end of the twentieth century, with the Hispanic population rising by 394 percent from 1991 to 2000. After North Carolina, the other states with the highest percentage increases, in descending order, were Arkansas, Georgia, Tennessee, Nevada, Minnesota, Nebraska, and Iowa.[82] As they move to rural communities, it is easy to see how the two disadvantages—an illegal presence and being people of color—converge. That Mexicans remain disenfranchised results in their being more vulnerable.[83] This makes it more likely that Mexican migrant families will become burdens on the social welfare system, which in turn fuels resentment and discrimination against them.[84] There is an undeniable inconsistency to American immigration law that cannot be sustained as NAFTA moves into its second decade.

"Americans have long seen Mexico as a river of illegal drugs and immigrants flowing north," Tim Weiner succinctly wrote of American misperceptions of their minor NAFTA partner.[85] Latin Americans have long seen the United States as a place where they can make money, but where it is impossible to make a life. Of the millions of illegal aliens—mostly men—who come, many are overcome by the loneliness of living in the shadows, where they are discriminated against and where they are not welcome. "There are many ways to prey on the weak and the lonely. But one of the most profitable is to peddle love," Chris Hedges reported. "Many of the estimated 100,000 Salvadoran, Honduran and Guatemalan pot washers, construction workers or landscapers on Long Island [in New York State] frequent these seedy hostess bars just as legions of male immigrants, from the Chinese to Eastern Europeans, did in earlier eras. The deafening blasts of music, gyrating women and booze-soaked conversations have been repeated long before in other tongues."[86]

Then the longing is revealed. "We live a life for others, for those at home," Ivan Escalante, 24, who, lacking proper documents, cannot even open a bank account, told a reporter. "We have no lives here. As soon as we are paid we become vulnerable. We cannot keep money in our room; someone will steal it. None of us have cars, so we must walk. And on the streets of Hempstead there are a lot of assaults from the Salvadoran street gangs. The only distraction we have are the bars, but once you get there it is hard to stop. The cash is in your pocket. It is so nice to talk and dance with a woman."[87]

It is a mistake to dismiss people as unsuspecting dupes—as if there were any other kind—which is how Mexicans perceive themselves to be treated by Americans. "The United States has agreed to expand some kind of temporary worker program that brings more Mexicans in on a legal basis, and it acknowledges a need to deal with a legalization program for the illegal Mexicans already here," said Pamela Falk, a professor of international law at City University of New York and a former top House Democratic aide on Latin American issues. "The program will rest on a carefully worked-out partnership between the sending and receiving countries, one that recognizes also the contributions that undocumented Mexicans are making in the United States and that brings together willing workers and willing employers," Secretary of State Colin Powell said in August 2002, signaling that despite Homeland Security concerns, progress was being made on immigration questions.[88]

Almost a year later, the absence of a comprehensive agreement for "regularizing" the labor force across North America was noticeable after spectacular deaths. "An accord would drive many smugglers out of business and end the persistent hypocrisy of America's attitude toward illegal immigration," the *New York Times* wrote in May 2003. "Our nation as we have said before, virtually posts two signs on its southern border—'Help Wanted: Inquire Within' and 'Do Not Trespass.'"[89] The sense of growing lawlessness along the southern border—a lawlessness created by the absence of a temporary guest worker program—cast a dark cloud over America's conscience as gruesome deaths made front-page news.[90] "Illicit rings of coyotes, as the smugglers are known, are so common in the border area that immigrants often regard them as services rather than criminal syndicates," Kate Zernike and Ginger Thompson reported in the *New York Times*. "It is precisely their informality that makes them especially difficult for United States authorities to track, and potentially very dangerous for those who put themselves in the smugglers' hands."[91]

"Some look at the south and see problems," President George W. Bush said on his first state visit to Mexico, reflecting on the integration of both

nations' economic and social lives. "Not me. I look south and see opportunities and potential."[92] One way of seizing those opportunities and nurturing
that potential is to treat others as we would like to be treated: honestly, de-
cently, charitably, all of which are missing from America's immigration laws.

The Emerging Conflict Between African Americans and Hispanics

The greatest political impact of the Hispanization of the United States is how
it colors the cultural and social landscape. "There is something called *black*
in America and there is something called *white* in America and I know them
when I see them, but I will forever be unable to explain the meaning of them,
because they are not real even though they have a very real place in my daily
way of seeing, a fundamental relationship to my ever-evolving critical place
in my interactive relationship to humanity," Carl Hancock Rux writes in
"Eminem: The New White Negro."[93]

This essay appears in *Everything But the Burden: What White People Are
Taking from Black Culture,* a collection of essays edited by Greg Tate, a
writer for the *Village Voice* in New York. The unintended irony of its publication was that, overshadowed by the census figures indicating the ascendancy
of Hispanics, America is no longer a question of *black* and *white,* but *black*
and *white* and *brown* (which is to say, *neither*). When this book first came
out, I sent a copy to a Mexican diplomat in New York. Weeks later, we had
the opportunity to get together for dinner, and I asked him what he thought.
The civil rights movement in the United States had long intrigued him, particularly given the continuing civil rights violations Hispanics suffer in this
country. "These essays," he offered, are "so pre-Census 2000" as to render
them "almost irrelevant to the new realities" of American demographics. "It
speaks to an American reality that no longer exists, even if it left dismal
unfinished business [reparations and black-white relations]. It is an embarrassing relic from the 20th century."

There is something called *black* in America, to be sure, but there is something called *Hispanic,* and whatever Hispanic is, it describes and affects more
Americans than does that other something called black. That is to say, there
is something called "reasonable" and something called "unreasonable"
throughout the Hispanic world, where differentiating between Reason and
Passion replaces distinguishing between black and white in American society. For centuries, that which has defied logic has been deemed unreasonable, and those deemed unreasonable have been encouraged, through
persuasion and through life's knocks, to evolve into a more reasonable approach to life. In Hispanic societies, this is a distinction that defies America's

social Darwinist legacy. Reasonable people come in all shades of color, as do unreasonable ones.

The stratification of people by their reasonableness is something that has baffled race-obsessed Americans for decades. This approach to the world proves exasperating, for it undermines how Americans divide the world into "black" and "white." If Hispanic societies accept that their citizens are not black and white—and therefore refuse to see the world in terms of race, how can Hispanics be assimilated, when Hispanics refuse to step inside the racial box of American life? One of the greatest conflicts between Hispanic and non-Hispanic America is when Hispanics, say from Cuba, simply say, "There was no racism in Cuba." Americans answer by accusing Hispanics of being in denial when it comes to matters of race. But if this is so, how can Americans explain the nonchalance of sweeping diversity of Hispanic societies, and the ease with which Asians (Fujimori in Peru), blacks (Trujillo in the Dominican Republic), Arabs (Menem in Argentina), women (Chamorro in Nicaragua), mixed-race (Chávez in Venezuela) or Native Americans (Juárez in Mexico) have all served as heads of state without fanfare? If society can be fluid, and one is judged by the content of his reasonableness, then one finds the kind of diversity throughout Latin American that race-obsessed Americans find impossible.

By comparison, in the United States, the most mundane development—the first woman secretary of state, the first black Supreme Court justice, the first divorcee to be elected president—is heralded as a "milestone." This is a powerful commentary on the limitations of American society, where even the *idea* of, say, electing an Arab-American or a Native-American president is sensational, but in Latin America it has, for more than a century, been a *reality*.[94] What this suggests is that America handled the abolition of slavery in the United States in an inferior way; a century of segregation after the Civil War served to oppress a group of people because of the color of their skin, creating a society in which millions were denied the right to their lives, liberty, and pursuit of happiness. More alarming still, an observer can be taken aback by how traumatized America remains by its history of black-white relations. "Pimping in the twenty-first century reflects a porous relationship between an illegal or at least illicit commodity and the hot glow of publicity," Beth Coleman writes in "Pimp Notes on Autonomy," one of the essays in Greg Tate's book. "The fame of black people possesses the retro glamour of a Marlene Dietrich."[95]

The purpose of dragging twentieth-century trauma into the twenty-first century is questionable at best.[96] As Hispanic ascendancy unfolds in the decade ahead, therefore, the greatest challenge for corporate America is to avoid repeating the mistakes it made in its dealings with the African-American community now displaced by Hispanics as the largest minority. The conflict in black-white relations in the United States arises for the "unfinished" business between white America and black America, which centers on the contention by African-Americans that the United States has not compensated their community for the suffering they and their ancestors endured through the institution of slavery. "No race, no ethnic or religious group, has suffered so much over so long a span as blacks have, and do still, at the hands of those who benefited, with the connivance of the United States government, from slavery and the century of legalized American racial hostility that followed it," Randall Robinson writes in *The Debt: What America Owes to Blacks.*[97]

Where do Hispanics fit in this grievance?

In fact, America has moved beyond a "black and white" reality, sadly without an honorable resolution to its legacy of racism and the burden of slavery, and the public debate over black-white relations is overshadowed by the consequences of Hispanic ascendancy. African-American leaders and academics will struggle for decades to understand what this means. "This conference [on the state of black studies held in Harlem in January 2003] looks at where the field has gone and where it's returning to, because people like Carter G. Woodson and DuBois understood it was not just about African-Americans in urban centers," Adrian Burgos Jr, a historian, is quoted in Felicia Lee's report in the *New York Times.* "We don't need to think about Latinos replacing African-Americans but how alliances in the past were built. The future politics in the U.S. will be centered around questions of how Latinos fit in."[98]

When it comes to the legacy of slavery and how American society has been polarized into a black-white dichotomy, Latinos do not "fit in" anywhere, simply because this form of racism is not a Hispanic cultural trauma. In the wake of the 2000 census, the more pertinent question is this: "Where does America's unresolved trauma over slavery 'fit in' as America is Hispanicized?" The answer is succinct: The unfinished business from the American Civil War is neither Hispanics' baggage nor their burden.

That Hispanics can be bamboozled into this black-white legacy is a political threat, one in which Democrats and Republicans, seeking the elusive Latino vote, will pander to with the promise of patronage. This kind of paternalism has seduced Puerto Ricans into the Democratic bloc and has swayed Cubans into the Republican fold. But paternalism is best left to the "unreasonable." The political danger that Hispanics face is that opportunists will use their relative disenfranchisement to use them, much the same way that Democrats have promised much more than they have delivered to African-Americans.

Consider, for instance, how in 1995 New York governor George Pataki shut down the Harlem Urban Development Corporation, which was a source of Representative Charles Rangel's power base in New York City. "The [Pataki] administration said the agency had not produced a single major commercial project despite having received $100 million to help rebuild Harlem," Raymond Hernández reported. "It also described the agency as a place with little oversight and controls as well as one where state money changed hands freely with little regard for contracting procedures or documentation."[99]

Does anyone believe that the residents of Harlem have seen the "benefits" of that $100 million at work in their community?

The use of government monies to dispense patronage to party loyalists is one way the Democrats have, for decades, exploited African-Americans. To their credit and for their sake, Hispanics recognize these tactics; Mexico's PRI undermined the democratic aspirations of the Mexican people for decades simply by handing out money to "gente humilde" who were bused in from the countryside to fill the plazas for political rallies, or by providing "phantom" jobs at Pemex, the state-owned oil company. In the United States, a far wealthier nation, it is possible for one person—Charles Rangel—to distribute more than $100 million over the course of two decades to the residents of his impoverished district in Harlem without being held accountable. Where did this "development" money go? Was it used to bring business to Harlem? If so, which businesses? Was it used for social or education programs? If so, which social services and which after school or vocational programs? Was it, as Rangel's critics in Albany suggest, used to benefit his supporters by creating phantom jobs and funding the activities of his cronies? If not, then where is the documentation for disbursements that would answer critics?

For corporate America, the danger, then, is this: it must guard against shakedowns by self-appointed Hispanic "leaders." A strong argument can be made that African-Americans have been poorly served by the self-serving. One need only recall the disgraceful misrepresentations of his role in the aftermath of the assassination of Martin Luther King Jr. to see how Jesse Jackson advanced his own personal interests. One can recall the audacious fraud upon the public that Al Sharpton perpetrated in the Tawana Brawley case to see how he used this episode to advance his own personal interests. One can see the millions of dollars that corporate America has handed over to these kinds of African-American leaders since the 1960s in what is, in fact, a disingenuous shakedown of corporate America by African-American Democrats.

What Hispanics need is a generation of leaders of impeccable integrity. The same, of course, is true of African-Americans, who are better served by the leadership of individuals like Colin Powell and Randall Robinson and role models like Oprah Winfrey and Maya Angelou. Hispanics cannot afford decades of opportunists who use "development" funds to be used to dispense patronage, and they cannot afford charlatans who, in their name, extort monies from the ranks of corporate America. It would be detrimental to the development of the American economy if the Hispanic community "politicized" itself by adopting the race-based identity that has created such sharp divisions throughout U.S. history. Corporate America has an obligation to guard against such a development, lest it allow itself to be used by a new generation of charlatans and opportunists to duplicate the very paternalism that has driven so many Hispanics from their homelands in search of job opportunities.

Of equal concern is the emerging rivalry between African-Americans and Hispanics. When Harvard's Henry Louis Gates Jr. speaks of the Hispanic threat to African-Americans' "privileged position," what does this mean?[100] What is the state of black-Hispanic relations, and how does it inform corporate America?

The reality is that Hispanics resist embracing the African-American struggle for civil rights, though Hispanics are the beneficiaries of the achievements blacks have achieved. The reason lies in the historic reluctance of African-Americans to champion the civil rights of nonblack minorities. Consider how blacks turned a blind eye to the plight of the Japanese in San Francisco during World War II. "As the Japanese disappeared, soundlessly and without protest, the Negroes entered with their loud jukeboxes, their just-released animosities and the relief of escape from Southern bonds," Maya Angelou writes of how blacks remained silent while the Japanese were stripped of their rights and shipped to internment camps. "The Japanese area became San Francisco's Harlem in a matter of months. A person unaware of all the factors that make up oppression might have expected sympathy or even support from the Negro newcomers for the dislodged Japanese. Especially in view of the fact that they (the Blacks) had themselves undergone concentration-camp living for centuries in slavery's plantations and later in sharecropper cabins. But the sensations of common relationship were missing. . . . No member of my family and none of the family friends ever mentioned the absent Japanese. It was as if they had never owned or lived in the houses we inhabited."[101]

Hispanics believe it is this legacy that is the real threat to blacks' "privileged position." Hispanic ascendancy has transformed the labor market in the United States and throughout North America, with far-reaching social implications that African-American and Hispanic leaders have not begun to consider. How corporate America responds to the socioeconomic repercussions that are rippling through the American economic and political landscape will take center stage as the role and expectations that a bilingual and bicultural nation expects of responsible corporate citizens are redefined.

Part II

The Emergence of the Hispanic Market in North America

How has NAFTA changed North America's demographics?

Why are Americans the fast-growing demographic group in Mexico?

Are Mexicans and U.S. Hispanics of Mexican ancestry changing because of their increased exposure to Americans, in the United States and in Mexico?

Why is there such a strong bond between Mexicans and Canadians?

Why is there animosity between Mexicans in Mexico and Mexicans in the United States?

What cultural ideas inform the worldview of all Hispanics?

What do Hispanics mean by "gente *sin* razón" and "gente *de* razón"?

What do Hispanics mean by *poca cultura* and *gente humilde*?

Why do Hispanics claim they transcend racism, but admit they struggle with discrimination?

Let's find out.

4

Americans in Mexico

"Demonstration Effects" of a Flourishing Demographic

Abstract

Not since the American Civil War have as many Americans ventured into Mexico as they have since the implementation of NAFTA. Officials at the American Embassy estimate that there were almost 800,000 American citizens living year-round in Mexico as of 2003. An additional 1,400,000 live in Mexico for some portion of the year, usually "snow birds" that spend several months during the winter. There are an additional 5 million Americans of Mexican ancestry who divide their time between both countries, where they have a legal right to reside. To this mix, consider that an estimated 225,000 Canadians—particularly Quebecois—live in Mexico at least part of the year. These demographic changes, which reflect the intermingling of the people of North America as never before, portend fundamental changes in the economies of all three nations. If African-Americans being displaced by Hispanics as the largest minority in the United States is eye-opening, there is in Mexico a parallel social upheaval. Consider the new generation of Mexicans born of either American immigrants to Mexico, or more commonly, of marriages between American and Mexican citizens. (These are Mexicans who migrate to the United States for a time, marry an American—often from another Hispanic group—and then return to Mexico with their American-born children.) The result is an exciting opportunity, one that parallels the dynamics of demographics last seen in Mexico during World War II, when a generation of Europeans fleeing the Nazis found refuge in Mexico. As this constitutes the "third" wave of American settlement in Mexico, the first

*in Texas and then in California, NAFTA's second decade stands to be shaped
profoundly by the socioeconomic consequences of the new "Hispanic" demographics across all borders.*

In 2003, one out of three consumers in North America is Hispanic. By
2025, one out of two is expected to be Hispanic. Hispanic ascendancy in the
United States is complemented by an astounding surge of Hispanics throughout the entire continent. But there are other factors in the demographic changes
sweeping across the landscape of North America as well, including this fact
that American immigration to Mexico is rising to record numbers, not only
affecting Mexican demographics, but also influencing Mexican society. With
hundreds of thousands of Americans retiring to Mexico, for example, Mexico's
healthcare industry is fast adapting to an influx of older individuals who
have long-term, chronic medical conditions, and Mexico's insurance companies are fast working to establish reciprocal agreements for Americans who
have U.S. health insurance, or U.S.-government coverage (Medicaid and
Medicare). The discovery of Mexico as a place where Americans can live
comfortably is growing as NAFTA integration accelerates and fuels the growth
of the North American Culture Area (NACA).

"Enticed by sweet weather and less expensive living—taxes on a $150,000
house here are $60 a year, and the same house would cost double in Wash-
ington—year-round residents from the United States have filled the towns
around Lake Chapala, trading life up North for the easy rhythms of central
Mexico and making up one of the world's most concentrated colonies of
U.S. citizens living abroad," Mary Jordan writes. Frank Cunzio, a 75-year-old
New Yorker, told the *Washington Post* reporter, "A lot of Americans think it's
sophisticated to go to Europe, that Mexico is their poor neighbor; they are
wrong. For one thing, there are a lot of rich Mexicans. There are a lot of
misconceptions in the States about Mexico. People here are cordial, family-
oriented. They smile more. . . . I don't miss anything—except you can't get
decent prosciutto or salami."[1]

Almost a thousand miles away, there are other American retirement communities drawing thousands of Americans. "Forget Miami," Margot Roosevelt
declared in *Time*. "Gringos are retiring in Mexico because it's sunny, sandy
and cheap." She says of one such community: "San Felipe is one of a handful
of Mexican towns that have become magnets for gringo retirees, and another
reason why it's often hard to tell where one country stops and the other begins."[2] A substantial number of American retirees choose Mexico because of
the health care. "We're acutely aware of the fact that about one-third of the
elderly in [the United States] don't have access to reliable prescription drug
coverage," Representative James C. Greenwood is quoted as saying. "In this

day and age, if you don't have access to prescription drugs, you don't have adequate health care. Some people are in desperate straits."[3]

Americans in Mexico, however, are not like traditional "ex-pats," living in a foreign country to enjoy benefits but unwilling to give back by becoming locally engaged. On the contrary, Americans are becoming agents of change through their active involvement. This is taking on place on several levels. My grandmother's contemporary, E. Wyllys Andrews, settled down a block away in the 1940s, and the Andrewses have been there ever since. Joann Andrews, not content with living a quiet life in a tropical "paradise," has, over the course of four decades, been a pioneer in Mexican environmentalism and conservation. As a founder of Pronatura, which now works extensively with the Mexican government and foreign nonprofit organizations, including the Nature Conservancy, she has done more than anyone else to protect the Yucatán peninsula's habitats.[4]

There are other kinds of cooperation now unfolding with astonishing speed. In the neighborhoods one finds Americans of all sorts marrying Mexicans. On the mile-long drive from a family home to our offices in Mérida, for instance, I pass by the homes of five couples, all with children, who consist of Americans married to Mexicans.[5] This intermingling of Americans and Mexicans represents opportunities, for as more Americans live in Mexico at least part of the year, a deeper understanding that is possible only through intimacy is possible. We have already discussed the Mexican experience in the United States, so it is only now appropriate to discuss the Americans in Mexico in order to appreciate more fully how both Mexico and the United States are changing as this century unfolds. These demographic changes inform the nature and character of Hispanic ascendancy in both the United States and across North America.

Americans' Ethnocentric Assumptions of Mexico Revisited

To understand how Americans and Canadians in Mexico influence the character of the U.S. Hispanic market, it is necessary to understand how Americans and Canadians are perceived by Mexicans in Mexico. Perceptions, or stereotypes, often endure because they offer simple and convenient answers to complicated questions, relieving us of the burden of having to exert much effort or time in thinking things through on our own. With so many demands in our lives, the prospect of neat and tidy solutions is comforting, and disarming. "We woke up this morning to another fabulous Mexico City morning, complete with the blue skies that no one in America believes exist here. The pollution and crime that are synonymous with Mexico City are certainly here, we just haven't seen much evidence of them yet. Instead, what we see is color," Mary Jordan and Kevin Sullivan, co-bureau chiefs for the *Washington Post*, wrote in Slate.com.[6]

American and Canadian managers who arrive in Mexico are often surprised by how their preconceptions are mistaken, and by the sophistication of the cosmopolitan lives they are afforded throughout the country. This reaction, of course, is the same on every side of every border. When I first moved to San Francisco in the mid-1980s, I understood that it would be impossible to live in what was an "Asian" city without learning an Asian language at some point. My ability to understand the city—and to enjoy its diversity—would be diminished if I did not make an effort to participate in the cultural and social lives of the people who lived there. The family living next to the rented house where I lived was Japanese-American. I enjoyed sashimi, found myself drawn to Japantown on weekends, participated in tea ceremonies, and grew fond of my neighbors.[7] Over the course of several months, I found myself gravitating toward understanding the culture of Japan. My own perception about Japan, that it was a homogenous society, appealed to me for it suggested that it would be an uncomplicated proposition to become familiar with it.

Throughout the West the perception of Japan, in fact, is that it is a homogenous society characterized by definite xenophobic tendencies. Upon becoming familiar with Japan, however, one sees a more complex culture emerging, contradicting the easy stereotypes Westerners hold.

That the four main islands of Japan are steeply mountainous also strongly affected Japanese cultural history, encouraging a heterogeneous evolution of what we denote collectively as "Japanese." That geography complicated communication and travel, in fact, resulted in the development of distinct local patterns. The traditions of one region are different from those of the other three main islands. While Japanese society appears to be a homogenous society from a distance, the more familiar one becomes with it, the easier it is to see the subtleties that suffuse the Japanese nation. From a distance, however, Westerners insist on seeing Japan through the myopic lenses of stereotypes.

Now consider the ethnocentric limitations that exist *within* a nation as immense and diverse as the United States. On the East Coast it is a cliché that there are no seasons in California. The spectacular autumn days when the forest foliage turns to brilliant reds, oranges, and yellows are absent along the California coast, where most of the state's people live. Whereas the cities along the East Coast endure harsh winter cold and months of snowfalls, the West Coast cities enjoy mild, sunny days. But anyone who has lived in California understands that there are seasons nonetheless. Foliage responds to the arrival of fall in subtle ways, evident in how the landscape changes around the fishing town of Pescadero in October, or how winter is evident in the afternoon light throughout the Napa region in January. The changes from one season to the next may be subtle, but they are there.

To someone from New York, whose point of reference is the East Coast, a blanket statement about the absence of seasons in California suffices. To a Californian who is confident of his more refined sensibilities, on the other hand, the absence of two feet of snow on the streets does not mean that winter is not different from summer. It is instructive to see how blanket assumptions have effects that range from the innocuous (misunderstanding the change from summer to fall in California) to the egregious (stereotyping the Japanese as homogeneous).

Another reason stereotypes endure is that there is a perverse comfort in being convinced that our notions about the world are true, even if they are not. Imagine how unsettling and upsetting Galileo's arguments proved to be to the people living at that time. Tony Cohan, an American writer dividing his time between Los Angeles and San Miguel, describes his epiphany about Mexico. "It dawns upon me that, arriving as tourist, I've blundered into a civilization," he writes. "How could I have lived so close by all my life and neglected to realize? . . . Had I been oblivious to the great territories to the south, my own hemisphere?"[8] If one blunders into enlightenment in a manner that is reminiscent of Plato's allegory, it is because in the course of our daily lives there it is easier to validate stereotypes.

In America's dealings with Mexico, it is so much easier to fall back on historical clichés. Let us say the tables were turned and Mexican perceptions of the United States were presented in a manner that was self-validating. Let us say, for instance, that a leading Spanish-language newspaper sent me to report, from Washington, D.C., on the American political scene. Let us further say that I was expected to reflect upon American culture and society and dash off a dispatch or two. Let us finally say that one Sunday morning I happened to walk by the White House where the annual Easter egg hunt was under way. Recalling from history lessons that eggs and rabbits feature prominently in ancient fertility rites among many European pagan peoples before the advent of Christianity, I decide to compose an article commenting on the pagan elements that dominate American celebrations of Easter—Sunday dinners, egg hunts, chocolate bunnies, parades. What would an American in Mexico City make of an article that read, in part:

> In a sign of the coexistence that often has marked Protestant America and early European pagan beliefs, American children eagerly hunt for brightly colored eggs and devour chocolate bunnies, both ancient symbols of European pagan fertility rites of spring. Americans have managed an easy merger

between European fertility rites and the observance of Good Friday and Easter Sunday—formal religious feast days commemorating and celebrating the resurrection of Christ—and pagan lore that makes these springtime festivities such an unusual part of American ways.

Anyone familiar with American culture would be astounded by such an interpretation of the how and why of Easter celebrations in the United States.

Now consider a real-life example of an equally misguided manner in which the American media too often presents Mexico to Americans. Edward Cody, on assignment for the *Washington Post*, sent the following article, titled "Shades of Mexico Past," which included the following passage:

> In a sign of the coexistence that often has marked Roman Catholic and pre-Hispanic beliefs in Latin America, great puffs of incense also rose from the roof of the church. Mexican Catholics have managed an easy merger between the observance of All Saints' Day on November 1 and All Souls' Day on November 2—formal religious feast days honoring the dead—and the indigenous lore that makes Day of the Dead such an unusual part of Mexico's ancient ways.[9]

This simple-minded way is how Mexico is presented to Americans every day, and how Americans see U.S. Hispanics of Mexican ancestry, as exemplified by the R. J. Reynolds research cited at the beginning of this book.

It is little wonder that seemingly innocuous cultural differences can often perplex. Now consider an incident that occurred when my paternal grandmother, a rather conservative Spanish lady, first came to spend an extended time with us in the United States. Our neighbors, Mr. and Mrs. Kavanoff, quickly befriended her; they were of the same generation and had similar interests. When I returned from school the Thursday before Easter, my grandmother showed me the Easter basket—filled with chocolate bunnies and candy eggs—that the Kavanoffs had given her earlier that day. She was touched by their thoughtfulness, but she didn't know what to make of the distinctly pre-Christian symbolism represented in that Easter basket, her first. "Maybe they think we're pagans," I offered, shrugging my shoulders, leaving her confused further, which is consistent with the tendency of teenage boys to try to get a rise out of the adults in their lives.[10]

To understand the nuances that have characterized relations between Mexicans and Americans of Mexican ancestry and to see the hostility that suffuses the dialogue between Mexicans on both sides of the border, it is necessary to consider the emotional baggage that Mexican-Americans so often bring to the table. As a study in contrast, first consider how non-His-panics Tony Cohan and his wife Masako Takahashi, a Japanese-American artist, describe their own approach to Mexico. Upon arriving in San Miguel for the first time, this is how they "discover" the community:

> We eat everything we see on the street. . . . We sip fresh juices through straws from plastic bags tied with rubber bands. . . . With the passing days I note the gradual departure of the frozen, strained glare in the mirror. Some vaguely human apparition gazes back.[11]

Tony Cohan and Masako Takahashi are not naïve tourists deluded by ro-mantic ideals, but rather, they are humbled navigating the everyday realities of everyday life as they embark on a journey of discovery. After they pur-chase a home in San Miguel, for instance, work requires that they commute between Los Angeles and San Miguel.

During a stretch when he was in the United States and she remained in Mexico setting up the house, the frustrations of figuring out how to make things work was felt on both sides of the border. "The simplest tasks seemed to take forever," Cohen writes, describing one of his telephone calls from Los Angeles to Masako Takahashi in San Miguel. He reports trying to be sympathetic to her plight. "'Just tell the water heater guy to bring the tanks over. He's only three blocks away.' Steely silence on the other end."[12]

The decision to let go of their preconceived ideas and have faith in life ultimately proved to be right. Patience and perseverance, they learn, is the more successful approach to succeeding in Mexico. In the ensuing months, after they had made their house into a home, they had a small dinner party to celebrate the string of small victories they have enjoyed:

> We take candles and wander out into the fresh night among jasmine smell, the sounds of dripping on the stones.
> "*Luna llena*," Vicente says. "Full moon."
> Holding our candles, we walk back across the patio, drawn irresistibly toward the garden. . . .
> "This is like *La Dolce Vita*," Carlos says.
> "Or Buñuel, his Mexican period," says Colette.
> "Susana and I will bring dessert," Masako calls.
> We find our way to the far corner of the garden and dry off the old stone seats. Setting our candles on ledges, we sit in the moonlight.
> Susana and Masako arrive with trays. . . . The custard, blended with thick cream, gelatin, and lime, dissolves on the tongue. The manila mangoes . . . combined with cactus berries, fuse into something unspeakably ambrosial. . . .

Slowly the electricity seeps on—a yellow-orange color not unlike the mangoes. As if the house were laboring to give birth to light. From the dark garden we watch Masako's studio come to life, a theater set. Then my studio and the main house light up. . . .

"Mango mousse in moonlight garden," Arnaud says.

"Tonight, Susana," Felipe says, "you have created a legend."[13]

Contrast this approach to life in Mexico with that of Richard Rodriguez, who proceeds to argue that Tijuana is Bombay on California's southern border:

I am chaperoned through the city by an official from the Comite de Turismo y Convenciones. Her English is about as bad as my Spanish. We stroll Avenida Revolucion, recently beautified—wider sidewalks, new blighted trees. There, says my hostess, where the Woolworth's now stands (where disinterested hag beggars squat, palms extended over their heads), used to be the longest bar in the world. And over there, beyond the blue tourist bus (which is being decanted by a smiling guide with a very wide tie), is the restaurant where two Italian brothers named Cardini created the Caesar salad back in the twenties. . . .

Gingerly I am steered through the inedible city by my hostess from the Comite de Turismo y Convenciones. Street vendors offer unclean enchantments, whirling platters of melon and pineapple, translucent candies, brilliant syrups, charcoaled meats, black and red. All are tempting, all inedible. I begin to feel myself a Jamesian naif who puzzles and perspires but will not dare.

"The usual visit, then, three or four hours?"

I notice my hostess is surreptitiously consulting her wristwatch. I'm spending a week, I tell her. I admit to her that I am visiting Tijuana by day, sleeping in San Diego at night.

Ah.

We stop at a café. She offers me something to drink. A soft drink, perhaps?

No, I say.

Cerveza?

But suddenly I fear giving offense. I notice apothecary jars full of improbably colored juices, the colors of calcified paint.

Maybe some *jugo*, please.

Offense to whom? That I fear drinking Mexico?

A waiter appears from stage left with a tall glass of canary yellow.

Ah.

We are all very pleased. It's a lovely day. I put the glass to my lips. But I do not drink.[14]

Whom would you rather have over? The American writer and his Japanese-American wife, or the affected San Franciscan whose lips are sealed?

This is an important distinction that Mexicans understand: Anglo-Americans are more generous in spirit—and less arrogant—than Hispanic Americans, for whom, in an often misguided attempt to be accepted by "mainstream" American society, prejudices about Mexico are currency. The nature of the tension between Mexicans in Mexico and Mexicans in the United States is fully examined in chapter 6. That there is an "intra-Mexican" rivalry, however, is one of the subtleties that informs the continental Hispanic market. "Listen, he says. I went back to my mother's village in Mexico last summer and there was nothing mestizo about it," Richard Rodriguez quotes a friend of his as saying, succinctly describing the Mexican-American's contempt for Mexico. "Dust, dogs, and Indians. People there don't even speak Spanish."[15]

Hispanic Views of Americans, from Latin America and Within the United States

How Americans are perceived throughout Latin America and within the United States informs the growing Hispanic view of life in the United States. Hispanics in Latin America have been deeply disappointed by the second Bush administration, fearing that the American president's preoccupation with the "War on Terror" and the events of September 11 have relegated the rest of this continent to the sidelines. Hispanics living in the United States, for their part, have encountered a disturbing "reality check"; their frustrations are born from the gap between the "land of opportunity" and the realities of economic and social life in this country.

Viewpoints of Hispanics in Latin America

Consider a summary of complaints this decade. Argentina, after defaulting on a $140 billion foreign debt in December 2001, floundered throughout 2002 with little sympathy, and less assistance, from Washington. Brazil, accusing Bush of turning his back on free trade by imposing tariffs on steel imports and refusing to reduce Washington subsidies to American farmers, is pulled back from freer trade, galvanizing the opponents of globalization.[16] Chile, promised a "fast track" to joining NAFTA, signed a free-trade agreement with the European Union in May 2002, while Washington's overtures grew cold and distant.[17] Colombia, confronting a sustained insurgency, elected a hard-line candidate, polarizing a society that is exhausted from being the "ground zero" of America's "War on Drugs."[18] Cuba, frustrated by the Bush administration's refusal to consider the growing bipartisan support for lifting the decades-long trade embargo, is dissatisfied with the White House's failure to follow through on Jimmy Carter's visit. Mexico's Fox, frustrated by the failure to expand the guest-worker program and reform America's immigration laws to reflect the realities of NAFTA, is undermined at home by his inability to deliver on Bush's promises.[19] Venezuela, convulsed by civil unrest that included the brief ouster of Hugo Chávez, remains alarmed at American complicity in the foiled coup and is under siege at home. Central Americans reluctantly began negotiations with Washington to establish a "free trade" zone, mindful of the experience of Chile.[20]

Viewpoints of Hispanics in the United States

"I expected to see dead bodies everywhere and drug dealers on every corner," Sister Lucila, one of the Roman Catholic nuns sent from Puebla to serve the Hispanic community in the Mott Haven section of the Bronx, told reporters. "They told me the South Bronx was the worst of society."[21] No dead bodies, but there are lots of good intentions with rigor mortis about.

Not all Hispanic perceptions are this extreme, but there is a certain hue that stains how the United States is seen south of the border. Consider how a grand-uncle dealt with his rebellious teenage son years ago. One day in late spring in the late 1990s, he asked his son to sit down for a discussion. He handed him an airline ticket, from Mexico City to Denver, connecting to Cheyenne, Wyoming. Then his father enumerated a laundry list of complaints. He was disrespectful, smoked, drank. He was doing drugs and spending too much money. He was lying to his mother, mocking his father, abusing his siblings, and being rude to the household staff. He was a child in a man's body, and it was time this ended. He was being "exiled" to a ranch, to work as a common cowhand. The son protested, and asked how long it would be before he could come home. "You can come back whenever you please," his father replied. "But when you return, you will show me your hands. And if you do not have calluses, then you are going back. Because you will not return to stay unless you have calluses on your hands. Having to live in the United States is your punishment. And it will make you a man."[22]

Most Hispanic immigrants who acquire calluses in the United States do so not because they are being punished, but because they have no other choice than to do punishing manual work. This is how a reporter for the *New York Times* describes Mexicans who simply started to show up in North Carolina seeking work in a slaughterhouse, and how their presence inadvertently upset the South's black-white racial hierarchy:

Standing in the hiring hall that morning, two women chatted in Spanish about their pregnancies. A young black man had heard enough. His small town the next county over was crowded with Mexicans. They just started showing up three years ago—drawn to rural Robeson County by the plant— and never left. They stood in groups on the street corners, and the young black man never knew what they were saying. They took the jobs and did them for less. Some had houses in Mexico, while he lived in a trailer with his mother.

Now here he was, trying for the only job around, and he had to listen to Spanish, had to compete with peasants. The world was going to hell.

"This is America and I want to start hearing some English, now!" he screamed.

One of the women told him where to stick his head and listen for the echo. "Then you'll hear some English," she said.

An old white man with a face as pinched and lined as a pot roast complained, "The tacos are worse than the niggers," and the Indian leaned against the wall and laughed. In the doorway, the prisoners [on a work release program at the factory] shifted from foot to foot, watching the spectacle unfold from behind a cloud of cigarette smoke.

The [white] hiring manager came out of his office and broke it up just before things degenerated into a brawl. Then he handed out the employment stubs. "I don't want no problems," he warned. He told them to report to the plant on Monday morning to collect their carving knives.[23]

To some Hispanics, the United States is a dangerous society, where violence lurks on every corner, especially when coworkers have company-issued knives. To other Hispanics, the United States is a form of punishment, a place to which strict disciplinarians banish their unruly children.[24] To most, however, it is the only economic opportunity that they have, given their circumstances.

For corporate America, it is important to understand the emerging cultural opinions Hispanics have about their Anglo, or English-speaking, neighbors and compatriots. These opinions inform Hispanic thought and feeling, offering rational explanation for the "reservations" the R.J. Reynolds market research uncovered about Hispanics—whether they live in California, Florida, New York, or Texas. These views center on two broad generalizations. Anglophone Americans seek to exploit Hispanics, and they refuse to apologize when they are mistaken. Hispanics view Anglophones as people who are blind, or insensitive, to the privileged position they enjoy in this country, and who are indifferent to behaving properly and excusing themselves when they are mistaken.

Specifically:

The Exploitation of Mexicans/Hispanics

Thoreau, in his wisdom, pointed out that if someone were coming to his home with the express intention of doing good, he would run for his life. Over the decades many Americans have come to Mexico expressing their intentions to "help," but with hidden agendas. This, of course, is not unusual. It is a modern conceit to appear to care more than one actually does.

Let us examine what happened when the world's attention focused on the plight of rain forests at the end of the 1980s. Deforestation, and the role that international lending bodies, Third World governments, and international conglomerates were playing in this environmental catastrophe, made headlines around the world at the time. Randy Hayes, a San Francisco activist, founded the Rainforest Action Network, or RAN, in response to this crisis. But apart from trespassing at the World Bank's offices in Washington, D.C., to drape banners over the side of the building, Hayes embarked on a self-aggrandizing crusade.

Not far from Cancún, the Vulcan Materials Company of Birmingham, Alabama, had begun to develop a limestone quarry. When concerns were raised about any perceived threat to the tropical habitat, E. Starke Sydnor, an officer at the firm, invited RAN to come from San Francisco and inspect the facilities. The Vulcan Materials site, operated with a Mexican partner, was known as Calica, and its operations were entirely in an area comprised of "scrub" vegetation, far from any "tropical" or "rain" forest habitat. "We paid to fly these activists to Cancún, put them up and gave them a tour," Sydnor said. "They even spent a few days on vacation when it was done, and then they flew back to the States."[25]

Hayes then returned to California and then denounced Calica–Vulcan Materials and the Mexican government. Publishing photographs of "displaced" Maya "peasants" who were posed in front of bulldozers, RAN accused Calica–Vulcan Materials and the Mexican government of "destroying" the rain forests of the "ancient" Maya, threatening the traditional lifestyles of these indigenous people. It was, however, all a fabrication. Hayes had to search for Maya "peasants" to pose in front of bulldozers being used in an expansion of Cancún's airport, which is located less than two miles from the beaches.

During its first years, in fact, RAN operated as the "Randy Hayes Fan Club, Randy Hayes President." Without any concern for integrity, RAN was prepared to do, say, and publish whatever it took to generate donations from a concerned, but duped, global public. That Americans would come to Mexico and exploit Mexican citizens by using them as props in a staged hoax designed to advance the domestic political agenda of an American organization is astounding, but it is representative of the kind of "ugly" Americans that Mexicans fear. With philanthropists like these, there is no need for misanthropes.[26]

American Hubris and the Refusal to Apologize

"Democratic institutions generally give men a grandiose opinion of their country and themselves," Alexis de Tocqueville observed. "The American leaves his country with a heart swollen with pride. He comes to Europe and at once discovers that we are not nearly so interested as he had supposed in the United States and the great nation that lives there. This begins to annoy him." [27] This annoyance leads to arrogance, which in turn results in hubris. Then there is the American legal system, one in which, because of a perverted tort system, courteous apologies are interpreted as admissions of liabilities, putting anyone who apologizes at legal jeopardy—and financial risk.

The American reluctance to apologize, however, has significant consequences. It might make sense under the American legal system to eschew apologizing, but others find fault with a society that discourages what basic human decency demands of civilized people: saying one is sorry when one is in error.

To understand how this attitude affects Americans' relationship with Canadians and Mexicans, first consider the psychology of language. "The *message* is the meaning of the words and sentences spoken, what anyone with a dictionary and a grammar book could figure out," linguist Deborah Tannen explains. "Two people in a conversation usually agree on what the message is. The *metamessage* is meaning that is not said—at least not in so many words—but we glean from every aspect of context: the way something is said, who is saying it, or the fact that it is said at all. . . . When we talk about messages, we are talking about the meanings of words. But when we talk about metamessages, we are talking about relationships. [28]

For almost a quarter century, foreigners have consistently asked questions about what they find confounding about the American society. Why, for instance, is the United States prepared to apologize for other people's mistakes, but not its own? Why does the United States raise a "national" museum about the Holocaust in Washington, D.C., when no Jew was ever sent to a concentration camp on American soil, but refuses to raise such a museum dedicated to slavery in the United States, which stands as America's most terrifying crime against humanity? [29]

Confessing another's sins does not result in absolution.

This, however, happens in all areas of American life. At times it is inexplicable, such as when the United States apologizes for the weather in other countries, or after it executes a foreign citizen. [30] What purpose do superfluous apologies serve?

Even in small matters, there is a reluctance to act with decency and apologize. In the aftermath of the attack on the World Trade Center, for instance, a small, nonprofit organization in Mexico wanted to help New Yorkers. Their contribution was, however, ridiculed by the *American Prospect* in Boston, when Garance Franke-Ruta dismissed their efforts, characterizing it as "a little money." As anyone who lives in New York and was there during the terrorist attack of September 11 can tell you, it is unwarranted to criticize anyone who helped out. Neither Franke-Ruta nor *American Prospect* editor Harold Meyerson, however, apologized to the Mexicans.[31] In trying to understand I am reminded of Ann Coulter's notorious phrase, "savagely cruel bigots who hate ordinary Americans and lie for sport," and I feel it also applies to how Mexicans are treated by some Americans.[32] I can think of no other satisfactory explanation for what motivated this disregard for Mexicans.

It is not a great leap to understand how this fault in the American character affects bilateral relations. As more Americans relocate to Mexico for professional or personal reasons, there are "concerns" that this is one thing neither Mexicans want to see "imported" into their country.

This is not to say that the benefits of an increased American presence in Mexico do not far outweigh other issues; the demonstration effects of Americans in Mexico are, on balance. Americans in Mexico, in fact, are contributing tremendously to nurturing Mexican self-confidence and optimism about the future. In some ways, then, Mexico is the opposite of Japan, for if Japan is, as former California governor Pete Wilson described, "a place of micro optimism and macro pessimism," then Mexico has become a place of micro pessimism and macro optimism, where individual self-doubts do not taint confidence about that nation's potential. American initiative and entrepreneurial spirit is suffusing the Mexican business climate. American are teaching by example, and the newfound Mexican professionalism and faith in the future displays a quintessentially American flavor.

The "American Confidence" Demonstration Effect on Hispanics

The term "demonstration effect" is used by economists to characterize consumer behavior that is influenced by the actions of other consumers [i.e., "keeping up with the Joneses"]. When one family on the block gets a pool, in short order, other homeowners get pools. During NAFTA, one powerful argument was that, by opening the economy, Mexicans would benefit from the "demonstration effects" of seeing efficient business models, whether it was a McDonald's franchise or an American Airlines nonstop service to Cancún. Today, advocates of a more engaging relationship with Cuba argue that if a million American tourists made their way through Havana each year, the "demonstration effects" of a capitalist system would be more evident among the Cubans.

With increased exposure to Americans, whether it is from Americans living and working in Mexico or the sheer number of Hispanics that now live in the United States, the Hispanic worldview is changing in fundamental ways. "When I first arrived in Mexico," Alain Giberstein, a Frenchman who moved from Paris to Mexico City more than a decade ago, said, "people were very, shall we say, informal. They arrived late, or canceled appointments. It was very difficult for them to make commitments. Shipments were late, or incorrect. Payments were not timely. It was a struggle, simply because there was a certain lack of professionalism about how business was conducted. It was very frustrating."[33]

As his business grew in the 1990s, however, changes were clearly noticeable in his dealings, both in Mexico and with American Hispanics. "Now, it is remarkable to see how attitudes have changed. People are so much more professional. There is a, shall we say, 'first world' approach to business. After the peso was devalued in December 1994, I seriously contemplated moving back to France. But I always believed in Mexico and the Mexican people and decided to remain. It wasn't easy, but I am glad I stayed. Throughout the 1990s, Mexico has changed in so many ways. The emergence of a business ethic is remarkable. Mexico before and after NAFTA is two different countries. It is night and day, it is that dramatic."[34] The dramatic changes in Mexico's "business culture" since NAFTA is but one result of the "demonstration effect" Americans are having on Hispanics. These changes can be characterized as the "Americanization" of Hispanic culture, in fact. Consider three that are in greater evidence among Hispanics, regardless of where they live. Specifically:

Demonstration Effect #1: Cultural Self-Confidence

There is tremendous optimism for the new generation of Hispanics. Not unlike Rick Marin, a reporter for the *New York Times* who belatedly embraced his cultural heritage in his father's clothes, the generation of Hispanics that is growing up with Christina Aguilera, Antonio Banderas, Penelope Cruz, Gloria Estefan, Salma Hayek, Enrique Iglesias, Jennifer López, and Ricky Martin realize they can have their cake and eat it too. "Hispanics under the age of 18 constitute one of the largest and most complex demographics in the nation. Unlike their parents and grandparents, who felt compelled to, at least publicly, melt into the American pot, this generation of consumers—representing 35 percent of all Hispanics—wants the best of both worlds," Rebecca Gardyn reported in *American Demographics*.[35]

Unlike Raquel *Tejada* who had to become Raquel *Welch* in order to make it in Hollywood, today's Hispanics can make it on their own terms, speaking in their native tongues, and with no apology.[36] "Marketers think that eventually they will only need to advertise in English in order to reach U.S. Hispanic youth," Olivia Llamas, project director of the Yankelovich Hispanic MONITOR, explains. "But what we are finding is the opposite, they're not losing that language or culture."[37]

Once Hispanic students were sent to detention for speaking Spanish in class, but with the advent of NAFTA, American teachers are taking crash courses in Spanish to maintain discipline in the classroom. "On the contrary, they are increasingly embracing [their language and culture]," Gardyn reports. "Fifty-four percent of U.S. Hispanic teens identify themselves as 'Hispanic Only' or 'More Hispanic than American.' Another 36 percent perceive themselves as being equally grounded in both cultures, according to TNS Market Development. Only 6 percent consider themselves 'more American than Hispanic,' and just 4 percent say they are 'American only.'"[38]

As Rick Marin found out to his surprise, there's more than one way to be fly and stylin' in your father's *guayabera*. It is Americans in Mexico who are allowing Mexicans to see their own country—and potential—with new eyes. Where the despairing and disparaging Richard Rodriguez only sees the past— "We stroll Avenida Revolucion, recently beautified—wider sidewalks, new blighted trees"—other Americans see the future. "I've seen this stuff all my life, and I've never grabbed the concept that we're surrounded by all this incredibly interesting, even beautiful, stuff," Jorge Verdin said of the "Nortec" art movement, based in Tijuana. "A gringo had to show this to me!"[39]

If "Nortec" art, which *Time* described as "Pop Art, and like most Pop Art it contains an abundance of energy and irony," it is in no small measure a result of an American presence.[40] "Graphic artists, fashion designers and filmmakers have been inspired to shrug off Tijuana's reputation as a cultural void and address the contrary realities of a place that's neither First World nor Third World; a culture that is neither Mexican nor American; an economy propelled by the dual engines of drug traffic and high-tech maquiladoras; a large, stable middle class sandwiched between grotesque poverty and excess narco wealth," Josh Tyrangiel reported. "The goal, simply, is to transform the strangeness of Tijuana into art."[41]

Thus Tijuana is on the cutting edge of "camp" as the twenty-first century begins. For Rodriguez to be escorted for a week by the Convention and Visitors Bureau and not to see the energy and vitality of North America's *first* "Warholian" city in the twenty-first century takes a special kind of blindness—or refusal to see beyond one's own prejudices. One is reminded of Miss Kilman in Virginia Woolf's *Mrs. Dalloway:* "[S]he was never in the room five minutes without making you feel her superiority, your inferiority; how poor she was, how rich you were; how she lived in a slum without a cushion or a bed or a rug or whatever it might be, all her soul rusted with that grievance sticking in it . . . —poor embittered unfortunate creature."[42] This is understandable. Immigrants, mindful of their status in their adopted countries, tend to eschew their ethnic heritage. "Americans at the end of the nineteenth century were divided by class, ethnicity, and race, much as we are today, although today's dividing lines differ in detail from those of a century ago (as Asians and Hispanics, for example, have replaced Jews and Italians as targets of discrimination)," Robert Putnam writes, by way of explaining the natural backlash that Asians and Hispanics encounter, even from the more insecure members of their own groups.[43]

American strength was first made evident in nineteenth-century California, with their skills "in the manipulation of capital and goods" and their determination to accumulate "wealth to gain status and power" and is now present in *Baja* California.[44] Indeed, S. Frederick Starr, a historian at Johns Hopkins University, described the PRI's regime in Mexico as one in which a "hierarchy of taste . . . was enshrined in the [state] funding, and was heavily skewed to the highbrow." Then, with democratic reforms and the changes ushered in by NAFTA, "one of the things that has occurred is that it has become more democratic. Culture . . . was a producer good; now increasingly it is a consumer good."[45] The images and aesthetics shaping American pop culture reflect the visual energy and vitality of Mexico. Mexico's producer goods are being transformed, through the marketing, packaging, and merchandising prowess of the United States, into consumer goods for global consumption.

That "American" ingenuity increasingly reflects the vision of people of all the Americas. "The border is a very painful place for me because it reminds me of all that Mexico has been unable to achieve," Mexican writer and social critic Guadalupe Loaeza, who shows her disdain for ignorance, told an interviewer. "Driving from one side to the other [Tijuana to San Diego], in a space that is geographically only a few miles wide, you feel as though you have traveled between two different worlds. And for me it is very painful that the world where there is most of the misery and poverty and corruption is Mexico."[46]

Though not evident to everyone, Tijuana's camp aesthetics are influencing American pop culture. Consider how that, in turn, is reverberating through the world of the hyper-hip of southern California. In the heart of Hollywood, *Flaunt*, which is described as "an envelope-stretching monthly dedicated to covering all that is hip, or wants to be hip," was founded by Luis Barajas, a Venezuelan-born editor who previously had spent a decade transforming *Detour* into "a Los Angeles-based hipster rag."[47]

It is through Hispanic eyes that Los Angeles hipsters now create the "hipness" in their lives. Nancy Gibbs, describing the intermingling of cultures along the border, reported:

It is often said the border is its own country, "Amexica," neither Mexican
nor American. Both sides regard their sovereign governments as distant
and dysfunctional. They are proud of their ability to take care of themselves, solve their own problems faster and cheaper than any faraway bu-
reaucrat. The Brownsville, Texas, fire trucks answer sirens on the other
side; in Tijuana, Mexico, health clinics send shuttle buses every morning
to meet people coming over for everything from dentistry to dialysis. The
school district in Mission, Texas, among the state's poorest, sends its old
furniture over the border to help Mexican schools that are lucky to have a
roof, much less desks and chairs. El Paso is redesigning the kilns of Juárez
brickmakers to cut the soot from burning old tires; the twin cities have
signed more treaties than their national governments can keep track of, let
alone ratify.[48]

Cultural changes are best seen in what is heard. It is through music that
youths express their spirituality, their emotions, and their ideas. It is American know-how, moreover, that facilitates the infusion of ideas and the fusion
of cultures, a process now accelerated as NAFTA's impact is felt on the music industry across the continent. "MTV Latino and CNN en Español have
been fundamental in spreading rock en español," Chilean Beto Cuevas is
quoted as saying. "They not only showed us what was happening in the United
States at the same time it was happening, but also allowed us to see what was
going on in Argentina or Colombia, countries that had their own rock tradition but hadn't been heard elsewhere because of a lack of communication,"
he told journalist Larry Rohter.[49]

The singular history of rock 'n' roll is illustrative of how economics, technology, and culture create business opportunities. Recall that Alan Freed,
now considered the "father" of rock 'n' roll, was one of the first disc jockeys
to play music by black artists on the radio. Denounced by his critics for
playing "race music" at WJW in Cleveland in the 1950s, Freed became the
greatest impresario of what, by the end of that decade, became known as
rock 'n' roll. As the rock 'n' roll revolution continued throughout the 1960s,
south of the border Mexican intellectuals decried the "bourgeois" and "decadent" nature of what, they argued, was a self-indulgent musical form. "At the
time that Latin rockers, most of whom are in their 30s, were growing up,
cultural discourse in Latin America was dominated by doctrinaire leftists
who argued that rock was a decadent manifestation of American imperialism
and that only folk-based indigenous music could be a valid form of expres-
sion," Rohter reported.[50]

There were several problems with this interpretation, of course, foremost
being that it was an argument advanced by misguided Latin Americans who

rejected anything and everything that was American to conform to the political ideology they embraced. Of greater importance, of course, is that rock itself is the cultural fusion between black and white musical traditions; it is indigenous to the cultural miscegenation of European and African traditions that unfolded in the United States. Not unlike Latin American cultural influences evident throughout California, across the Southwest, and inherent in the Texan identity, Latin American music reflects an American presence. "Rock may have been born as American music, but at middle age it is also the music of the Americas," Rohter contends.[51]

As surely as "rock en español" is becoming a cultural force south of the border, Mexican folk music is moving northward. "Members of Embajadores de la Frontera (Ambassadors of the Border) stroll from park to park to play traditional Mexican sounds in exchange for donations," the *New York Times* captioned a photograph of Mexican musicians walking to a park. "Yesterday, they went to St. Mary's Park in the South Bronx."[52]

Iconic signposts of Mexican cultural sensibilities are entering the United States in the Trojan horse of the American imagination. Here Mexico embraces the American democratic impulse for the vernacular. This, again, is a quintessentially American characteristic: America took Europe's opera and invented the musical; America took the Old World's ballet and invented figure skating.[53] "Such a dramatic shift in the mind-set required a thorough rethinking of well-entrenched business practices. In essence, a company that turns its customers into innovators is outsourcing a valuable service that was once proprietary, and the change can be traumatic if that capability has long been a major source of competitive advantage," Stefan Thomke and Eric von Hippel write in the *Harvard Business Review*.[54] One sees, in fact, the coolest of the cool, the blindest of the blind, the hippest of the fly, and the future of our continent in the emergence of SoCal's Nortec culture. Indeed, it is in the pages of *Flaunt* and the proliferation of "rock en español" that one sees glimpses of North America's acculturation foretold in the path first blazed by Juan de Onate in the sixteenth century, the first European to explore north from Mexico City to what is now the American Southwest.

Demonstration Effect #2: Mexican and Mexican-Hispanic Embrace of Americans' "Protestant Work Ethic"

There is also another kind of demonstration effect unfolding in Mexico. It is the example set by Americans living in Mexico; by Mexicans who, having worked in the United States, have been "Americanized"; and by the dashed hopes that Mexicans had placed in Latino leaders in the United States. Each offers lessons, both good and bad, about the social forces NAFTA has unleashed—and the sobering lesson about the disheartening persistence of "paternalism" in Hispanic thought.

There have always been Americans in Mexico, as there have always been Mexicans in the United States. There has always been intermarriage, linking both peoples in intimate ways, with the blood of one nation running through the veins of the other. The most obvious example, of course, is Vicente Fox: if the Irish-American immigrant from Ohio had been his grandmother and not his grandfather, Vicente Fox would be Vicente Quesada.[55] There are Mexicans in America's first family and there are Americans in Mexico's first family. This, however, is not new: it is the restoration of a trend interrupted by World War I and the Great Depression. At the beginning of this chapter, I mentioned that the last time Americans had "discovered" Mexico with as much enthusiasm as they have under NAFTA was during the American Civil War. For illustrative purposes, recall the story of the founding of La Consolidada, Mexico's first steel mill.

Harry Wright lost his father during the Civil War while still a teenager. Thrust into the position of being the "man" of his family, he took his mother, his three brothers, and four sisters to Ohio, where, in short order, he found employment with the Joseph Scrap Iron Company. Before long, he was sent to Mexico, where he decided to settle. With assistance from the administration of Porfirio Díaz, he founded La Consolidada, which prospered through world wars, civil wars, recessions, and depressions. The Wrights—Harry and his three brothers—lived their lives in Mexico, becoming, like thousands of other Americans, part of Mexico's fabric, economically, politically, and socially. In the nineteenth century, Mexico and the United States were frontiers for each other's entrepreneurs, with Americans the more ambitious, whether they were in Texas, Mexico, or California. A century later, this ambitiousness was on display after NAFTA was enacted. Mexicans were, at first, apprehensive about this American ambition. Indeed, what was true of the American presence in California—"Californio society was hesitant to welcome those whose purpose in life was to make money"—was also true during NAFTA's first years, but not any longer.[56] American attitudes toward Mexico have been reminiscent of Greta Garbo's portrayal of the depressed ballerina Grusinskaya in *Grand Hotel*. Garbo, upon discovering a jewel thief in her room, delivered what would become her signature line: I vant to be alone. At the conclusion of the Civil War, however, many Americans emigrated to Mexico, and many soon realized that their best bet for achieving the "American" dream was to be found south of the border. The "American-Mexican" descendants of these pioneering Americans are now being joined by the NAFTA generation of Americans who are expanding the borders of their lives, business and professional. Recall *Grand Hotel* once more. After

Garbo expressed her desire for solitude, the jewel thief, portrayed by John Barrymore, replied, "Let me stay for a little while." Garbo then murmured, "Just for a minute, then." He did, and in a minute, he seduced her.

Americans' legendary self-confidence is also seen in Mexican initiatives, now invigorated by democracy and economic opportunity. "As President Vicente Fox of Mexico stepped off the plane in Buenos Aires . . . with a high-powered delegation in tow, shares of Telecom Argentina shot up 20 percent when rumors spread that Carlos Slim Helú, the chairman of Teléfonos de Mexico, was interested in buying the company but was balking at its $3.2 billion of debt," Tony Smith observed, noting that Brazilian companies had been buying Argentine assets on the "cheap."[57] Mexican companies had also been expanding in other South American markets. In 2002, Alsea, the franchisee that owns more than 400 Domino's Pizza takeout restaurants in Mexico, acquired controlling interests in Domino's Pizza's Brazilian operations. "This is a tremendous opportunity for us to expand our operations in a promising market," Alberto Torrado, chairman of Alsea, said at that time.[58]

It is clear that the one demonstration effect of NAFTA on the Mexican business community is greater confidence. The arrival of American executives throughout the 1990s imparted unintended lessons about how to succeed in a market economy. These lessons are reverberating throughout Latin America, where more astute and sophisticated business leadership, as Brazilian investments in Argentina demonstrate, is replacing the traditional role corporate America played. In the give-and-take of life, these changes in Hispanic culture are felt on both sides of the border, where U.S. Hispanics now enjoy a higher profile, one that is commensurate with Hispanics' growing purchasing power.

The other "Americans" who are welcome are Mexicans who have worked in the United States. In the process of coming and going for several seasons while they save enough money to improve their lot in Mexico, however, changes occurred—through acculturation. Not unlike college students who return from their college towns more mature and more learned, so, too, Mexicans who live in the United States become more worldly and—some say—more sensible. This process of acculturation is aptly described by Richard Rodriguez in *Mother Jones:*

> The latest chapter of the Columbus saga may be taking place right now, as Latin American teenagers with Indian faces violate the U.S. border. The Mexican kids standing on the line tonight between Tijuana and San Diego—if you ask them why they are coming to the United States of America, they will not say anything about Thomas Jefferson or *The Federalist Papers.* They have only heard that there is a job in a Glendale dry cleaner's or that some farmer is hiring near Fresno.

They insist: They will be returning to Mexico in a few months. They are only going to the United States for the dollars. They certainly don't intend to become gringos. They don't want anything to do with the United States, except the dollars.

But the months will pass, and the teenagers will be changed in the United States. When they go back to their Mexican village, they will no longer be easy. They will expect an independence and an authority that the village cannot give them. Much to their surprise, they will have been Americanized by the job in Glendale.[59]

Sure enough, Mexicans do return to Mexico, in consistent numbers, and like clockwork. "There is a flow that comes and goes, with most Mexican immigrants not interested in settling down in the United States," Douglas Massey, of the University of Pennsylvania's Mexican Migration Project, said. "They want to the opportunity to come work in the United States, save their money, and then return to Mexico to improve their lot there, usually by opening their own small business."[60]

In the same way that the professionalism of Mexican workers—whether it is a teenager working at a McDonald's in Mexico City or a middle-aged software engineer working for a Microsoft contractor in Guadalajara—Mexican migrants returning from the United States do so with a higher level of skill that they can put to use at once. Anyone who lives in Mexico is familiar with the frustrations associated with getting things done, whether it is masonry work in a building or gardening to be performed adequately.

For years, whenever I visited my grandmother in her rambling home, there was always some project under way, projects that took twice as long as they should have under normal circumstances. At times the mason would disappear for months on end. He would reappear, explaining that he had gone back to his village, or hadn't felt like working, or whatever. Soon after NAFTA went into effect, he mentioned that he was thinking of going to Texas, and weeks later, he was gone. Six months later, he was back. Then a few months later, he was gone again. Months became years, and this pattern was repeated time and again.

Then in the winter of 2000, I was surprised by the quality of work done in my grandmother's garden; the brick paths and masonry were exceptional. My initial thought was that she had contracted a "real" mason. I was proved wrong when I later learned what happened. The mason had gone to Texas, but had continued on to Long Island. There he worked as a day laborer for several contractors, one of whom insisted that he work as if he were an apprentice. In due course, he found himself learning the techniques for bricklaying, plumbing, masonry, and the basics of construction work. He described working at some very exclusive addresses in the Hamptons, describing correctly some homes with which I was familiar.[61]

There is something to be said about the value of this kind of discipline in Latin America. On September 7, 2000, the Cuban government announced that the *Chicago Tribune* and the *Dallas Morning News* would be permitted to open bureaus in Havana. These two newspapers beat out the *New York Times* and the *Washington Post.* "They were the first papers to ask for bureaus. We played no favorites," Luis Fernández, press officer at the Cuban Interests Section in Washington, D.C., said. Noting that CNN and the Associated Press already had bureaus in Havana, the politics behind the decision demonstrate that perseverance is a sound strategy in Latin America.[62] Mexico, likewise, is fast benefiting from the perseverance of Mexican workers in the United States. It is when these "Americanized" workers return that the structural changes envisioned by NAFTA unfold in unexpected ways. The importance, then, is that the United States is making its influence felt vicariously through the skills acquired by Mexico's unskilled labor.

Demonstration Effect #3: Political Apathy and Cynicism

Not every influence is encouraging, however. It could be argued that Hispanics have nothing to learn about political cynicism from Americans, given the history of Latin America. But this rampant cynicism among Latin Americans has always been based on one assumption: that their political systems have undermined the development of democratic institutions and the rule of law. For Hispanics living in the United States, the realization that American democracy is so unjust and flawed comes as a crushing blow. Their idealism and expectations are shattered, and they are inclined to turn away from politics and civic engagement, further exacerbating democracy's shortcomings.

Take the curious case of Juan Hernández, an American citizen whom Fox tapped to head the Office of Mexicans Living Abroad. That initiative—designed to reach out to Mexicans living in the United States and Canada—has been called "Fox's Folly" by some of the more cynical elements in Mexican society. The celebrated agency created by Fox in December 2000 was closed in July 2002, and its responsibilities were taken over by the Ministry of Foreign Relations. What went wrong, moreover, is instructive, for it sheds light on the conflicts among Mexicans that will take decades to be resolved. Hernández, a Texan Hispanic with a grand vision for the future of Mexicans and Mexican-Americans, started with tremendous optimism. In a series of meetings of unprecedented nature, Mexican officials courted Mexican-Americans officially recognizing their community leaders and advocating the need to address their political interests.[63] Fox flew to Texas and California to speak before groups such as the Mexican-American Legal Defense and Education Fund (MALDEF) and to labor organizers in Bakersfield, in the heart of the Imperial Valley, and courted Hispanic business leaders from Houston to Chicago, Los Angeles to New York. The Mexican government flew hundreds of Hispanic leaders from all over the United States to meet with officials in Mexico City.

In this whirlwind courting of Hispanic leaders, however, several problems soon emerged that speak volumes about both Mexicans and Mexican-Americans. "It isn't as if we quizzed them on the books they had *written*," one aide to Jorge Castañeda, then Mexico's foreign secretary, confided. "We just wanted to know what books they had *read*."[64]

Mexican intellectuals, baffled by how uninformed and misinformed "Latinos" are—culturally illiterate in both cultures, at ease in neither—concluded that "Latino" leaders in the United States are not "ready for prime time" with their Mexican counterparts. This is a persistent indication that there is a culture clash that remains to be resolved. There is, after all, a class in Mexico of the privileged and pampered who affect a social conscience but have not advanced to the point of social action. The cafés and bistros of tony neighborhoods throughout major cities are frequented by "enlightened" young Mexicans who espouse the liberal views found in the bleeding-heart but uninspired editorials of *Proceso*, of course. But these mostly young men, dressed in Egyptian cotton shirts, donning cashmere cardigans from Brooks Brothers and wearing Gucci loafers, happily denounce "American economic imperialism" engendered by NAFTA, while enjoying the abundance that market economies provide. And apart from honing the outrage *du jour* promoted by the antiglobalization zealots, these pampered youth, apart from acquiring nicotine and caffeine addictions, have done little else on their own. It is easy to see the shallow nature of their social consciences when one shakes their hands: theirs are hands that have never known manual labor. Theirs are hands that have never held a firm grip on anything, whether it was spending a season in the countryside teaching a peasant to read and write, or by wielding a hammer at a Habitat for Humanity project.

"Fox's Folly," as critics within and without have termed the administration's efforts to reach out to Mexican-Americans, however, have a basis in fact. "These people lack complete 'seriousness,'" one Mexican diplomat in Washington, D.C., said, referring to the leadership of Latino civil rights organizations, not without some measure of alacrity. Some Mexican officials argue that Hispanic organizations are beholden to the Democratic Party; Fox wanted to remain distanced from the appallingly blatant partisan politics that characterize Hispanic organizations. "It is almost genetic," one Mexican commentator argued. "You can vote the PRI out of power, but you can't take the impulse of 'Chicanos' to latch on to the paternalism of the Democratic Party in the United States."[65]

One official handed me a clipping by Shelby Steele from the *Wall Street Journal:* "What black America deserves is leadership that ignites our energies with the idea that personal responsibility—despite past or even present suffering—is the only power that can truly deliver us to full parity with others. But today's black leadership only rallies blacks with a sense of their victimization into a voting campaign that promises nothing more than a little exceptionalism."[66] I was then told, "Steele could very well have been speaking about the Hispanic struggle to find leadership with integrity."

That conclusion, that Hispanic leaders are *gente humilde* and of *poca cultura* and who are not ready to deal with their Mexican counterparts, proved persuasive to Fox, who had to reverse course, recognizing the unexpected confrontations his Office for Mexicans Living Abroad had created. This controversy, then, is the essence of the great, whispered debate raging in Mexico in 2003: How to engage Hispanic leaders in the United States?

The consensus among Mexican intellectuals is that if the lingering and unfortunate Mexican paternalism *within* the United States were to be addressed, Mexicans in the United States would need more than an *Office* for Mexicans Abroad; they would need an *Institute* for Mexicans Abroad.

This institute, the plans for which were announced on August 7, 2002, signaled that, while Fox may have changed his approach, his goal is steadfast. On September 19, 2002, Fox named Candido Morales to direct the Institute for Mexicans Abroad, underscoring the thinking that suffuses Mexico's leadership. Morales, fifty-seven, was born in Oaxaca of Mixtec descent, and moved with his family to Sonoma County in California when he was thirteen years old. "The United States is the land of opportunity," he said upon his appointment. Reflecting on the land of his birth, but mindful of his heritage, he expressed his connection to the Mixtec people: "I always had an appreciation for the rich Mixteca culture and made trips to my village, which I love dearly because part of my family is still there."[67] Whereas U.S. Hispanics of Mexican ancestry see "dust, dogs, and Indians" in Mexican villages, Morales sees a vibrant, rich, and living civilization, suggesting that Hispanic cynicism may very well be arrested at an early stage.

Paternalism's Influence on Hispanic Consumer Behavior

The Hispanic mindset has been shaped by more than half a century of social democratic thought. It has shaped, to varying degrees, most Latin American societies and Hispanic thought. The development model followed by many Latin American countries, particularly Mexico and some South American nations, was based on a social welfare system in which the state played a central role. Mexican paternalism, for instance, became an ever more important instrument for trying to lift people out of poverty by providing them with health care, education, and employment opportunities.

"For the poor, the government can be central to their well-being, and for some even to survival. For the rich and the comfortable, it is a burden save when, as in the case of military expenditure, Social Security and the rescue of failed financial institutions, it serves their particular interest," John Kenneth Galbraith observed.[68] As the Mexican economy grew throughout the 1940s, 1950s, and 1960s, there were significant social dislocations—rural poor moving to the cities in search for better lives—that further taxed government institutions. The initial success of the PRI in providing fundamental social services, however, undermined its long-term viability, simply because there were insufficient resources available to the government to provide everyone with everything.

Unlike the nations of Scandinavia, which have a large, professional middle class, Mexico confronted the monumental task of integrating multitudes of poorly educated people, many of whom were indigenous peoples whose traditional lives were at odds with the modern aspirations of modern market economies. Unlike Saudi Arabia, there was not enough oil, relative to the population, to permit the PRI to have "limitless" resources it could appropriate to dispense patronage to the Mexican nation. Mexico, quite simply, outgrew the natural limitations of Mexican paternalism as a development model as the twentieth century came to a close.

This is important, for two-thirds of U.S. Hispanics are of Mexican ancestry, and they relate to the cultural and social ideals set forth by the Mexican revolution. "There will no longer be a paternalistic government, but one that shares responsibility," Vicente Fox acknowledged in a televised speech that set out his administration's six-year plan a few months after taking office.[69] The "end" of paternalism, however, does not mean that Mexicans, who have looked to government as a provider (however inadequate it might fulfill that role), reject the *idea* that government should play a central role in the marketplace.

That idea remains central to Hispanic thinking. Indeed, Hispanics believe that there are fundamental "rights" as part of the social contract, and that these include government guarantees for providing a free public education system for children; facilitating mortgages for working-class families; providing basic health care to everyone; offering welfare benefits to the poor and working poor; and defending consumers from predatory or fraudulent business practices. The United States, through public schools, Fannie Mae, federal and state welfare assistance programs, and various consumer protection agencies, taken together, has the trappings of a "social democratic" state, if not in so many words.

What this means for corporate America, however, is that in the same way that African-Americans have long been suspicious of "authority" figures, Hispanics are wary of *non-authority* figures. African-Americans are suspicious of the "public" authorities, for it is the public sector that has rendered legal institutions and policies that have exploited, betrayed, and abandoned them throughout history. Hispanics, on the other hand, are less trustful of the private sector, big business and multinational corporations, since the Hispanic experience has been that, in pursuit of private wants, public needs have been sacrificed.

To a significant degree, this mistrust is a product of decades of official "distrust." Time and again Latin American governments have accused multinationals of not serving their specific nation's best interests; of colluding with "traitors" who have spirited capital out of the country; of taking advantage of consumers by providing goods and services at exorbitant prices. Mexicans, for instance, remain distrustful of foreign oil companies, still cognizant of the predatory practices of American and British oil firms in Mexico in the 1930s. Mexicans have not forgiven Citibank and Texas Commerce Bank, for instance, for the role these financial institutions played in "decapitalizing" the nation in 1982 and in 1994. Mexicans are mindful of the surcharges that American companies placed on goods under the guise of their being "imported" for decades. These are difficult perceptions to overcome, and though they are not articulated in polls and in market research studies, they linger in the subconscious, informing how consumers make decisions day in and day out.

It is clear that demographics across North America are affecting the U.S. and continental consumer market in ways that are only now becoming apparent. Though no market research studies have been conducted on the views of Americans who have moved to Mexico (part- or full-time), or on the views of Americans who, having lived in Latin America, returned to the United States, the emerging anecdotal evidence points to a greater appreciation for Hispanic cultural values. There is no question that Anglophone Americans, both through NAFTA and by simple virtue of being the dominant group during this period of sustained Hispanic ascendancy, are having an effect on Hispanic perceptions, attitudes, and beliefs. The ebbs and flows of these cultural exchanges will ripple through the consumer market in the decades ahead.

Hispanization in Latin America and the United States

The most important effect of changing demographics on Americans, however, has to do with a greater appreciation of what Hispanization entails— and means. Corporate America must appreciate that the same cultural forces that the Spanish used to make Latin America "Spanish" are now being used to make the United States "Hispanic."

When the Spanish extended their authority throughout the New World, they were few in number. Unable to impose their will through force, they had to accomplish their objectives through persuasion and accommodation. The Spanish, in essence, had to acknowledge, and respect, the social and political structures that existed prior to their arrival. Spanish "cabildo organization reflected local traditions far more than they did the Spanish model," historian Robert Haskett writes of colonial Cuernavaca in central Mexico. "Local Marquesado officers prudently refrained from trying to enforce the latter, allowing the ruling group to accommodate Iberian cabildo organization with prehispanic ruling patterns."[70]

What occurred, then, was that the process of spreading "Western" culture—Christianity (Catholicism), language (Spanish), Roman law, and so on—was accomplished through a process of gradual assimilation. What anthropologists now call "acculturation," in fact, was unknown when New Spain existed, simply because the word "acculturation" itself dates back only to 1880. The process, however, was then referred to as "Hispanization." The popes and the kings of Spain, though each had his own objective, negotiated a compromise: establishing missions for the spread of Christianity was the first and foremost. This entailed the spread of the Spanish language, of course. Then, once the indigenous peoples had become both Christian and proficient in Spanish, they could contribute to the process of empire building. The indigenous peoples throughout Spanish America were exposed to European culture and were thus "Westernized," through an extended process of acquiring *normas hispanas.*[71]

The result of Hispanization, not surprising, is uneven. These political arrangements, Haskett explains, "retarded the entry of the Spaniards. [In Cuernavaca, for instance,] no Spanish municipality was ever established in the area during the colonial period. Instead, the region's [native towns] continued to be ruled by indigenous councils."[72] The Spanish had to negotiate the extension of their authority region by region, indigenous people by indigenous people. As a consequence, Haskett explains, the "status of the [Native American] ruling group, who obviously continued to consider themselves a true nobility, was proved by their descent from an earlier hereditary elite whose ascendancy had been recognized by the all-powerful Spaniards."[73]

Cuernavaca was not an anomaly: it was the norm. The fact that acculturation was a gradual process has left a curious legacy. For instance, though the Spanish were successful in converting the indigenous people to Christianity, they were not as successful at getting them to adopt Spanish. Consider one example that will illuminate this situation. In Yucatec Maya, "ek" means "star," which in Spanish is "estrella." As Spanish authority was extended throughout the peninsula, almost all the Maya converted to Christianity. But there was vigorous debate among the Maya about the use, proper or otherwise, of the Spanish language. The elite wanted to solidify their alliances with the Spanish, so sought to learn Spanish and embrace a Spanish "identity." Others decided to refrain from adopting Western ways to such a degree. "Ek" was also a common family name among the Maya. It is not surprising to learn, then, that Maya families that sought to associate themselves to the Spanish decided to "Westernize" their names by changing their names from "Ek" to "Estrella."

A perusal through the telephone book reveals that there are many people named "Ek" and "Estrella" in Mérida, a measure of the historic acculturation embraced by their forebears.[74] This, of course, should not surprise Americans, since in the United States there is a long tradition of immigrants' Anglicizing their names. "Immigrants in America were typically asked their name and entered in official records by those who had 'made it' in America and thus were already English-speaking (i.e., teachers, landlords, employers, judges, etc.)," INS historian Marian Smith, writes. "The fact that those with the power to create official records were English-speaking explains much about small changes, over time, in the spelling of certain names."[75] Throughout Spain's colonies, the process of acculturation, or becoming "Hispanic," was not uniform, it varied from town to town, and even from family to family.

The colonial record reflects the true ambivalent nature of the "conquest."[76] "The voices of the conquered," Haskett writes of New Spain, "are really almost as strong as those of the conquerors."[77] European vanities, however, prevented an admission of these realities to other Europeans. The kings of Spain wanted to rule over "empires," not over a loose federation of subservient indigenous nations. "The notion that Spanish culture was 'victorious' over its indigenous counterpart, to the point that the latter was mostly destroyed by the former, has become mixed up with the so-called . . . 'Black Legend' of Spanish conquest," Haskett writes. "Yet if the Legend is completely true, if the indigenous people were unable to withstand the rigors of invasion, why is it that so much 'Indian' culture can still be found co-existing with other elements in places such as central Mexico?"[78]

In time, as nationalism swept the world and Spanish America broke up into two dozen nations, the Hispanic identity was supplanted by other identities. In the same way that the British colonists rebelled against their English identity and wanted to be called "Americans," so did people in what became Venezuela want to be called "Venezuelans," and with the establishment of the "republic" of Argentina, a new man was born: the Argentine. This process was repeated throughout the hemisphere. "Hispanic," in the New World, was thus demoted from a noun to an adjective: whether or not one spoke Spanish, everyone within the territory of the Mexican Republic was "Mexican," but not necessarily Hispanic.[79]

It was in defense of this Hispanic identity, for instance, that the Hispanic Society of America was founded in New York—dedicated to the study and advancement of *Iberian* culture and society.[80] The process of acculturation by which indigenous peoples came to terms with the arrival of Westerners has been more successful in Spanish America than what was British America, if success is defined as accommodation. That indigenous people were excluded from the societies established by the British has more to do with pragmatism than anything else. The British used their colonies to rid themselves of their discontents, sending entire *families* overseas. Recall the first English to arrive in Jamestown and Plymouth Rock. Those who ventured into Spanish America, on the other hand, consisted of the impoverished multitudes, primarily from Catholic Europe, seeking their fortune. Whereas the Puritans aboard the *Mayflower* included men, women, and children, the Spanish galleons arrived primarily with men. These Catholic men from the whole of Europe were intent on making their fortunes—and returning home to settle down. This was not unlike what occurred in the California Gold Rush after 1849 in the United States. A disproportionate number of men arrived in San Francisco, seeking their fortunes. Few found them, but they accomplished something more important: they found lives for themselves. (Think of how few women appear in Westerns, where the American frontier consisted of many lonely men, desperate for the companionship of "women folk."[81]) Centuries before, of the countless adventurers who went forth into New Spain, very few found fortunes; many were unable to pay for passage back and had to stay.

A social pecking order was established: if one was wealthy enough to bring a bride from Spain—the sixteenth-, seventeenth-, and eighteenth-century version of a "trophy wife"—one could claim a better "pedigree." Only the privileged viceroys and officials accredited to the Spanish Crown were in a position to bring women from Europe to the New World. Thus the term "*criollo*" emerged as a term for an individual born in New Spain whose parents were both European.[82] Most of the Europeans of New Spain, having thus failed to bring their women along, formed relationships with indigenous women. While those born in Europe were at the top of the pecking order, the *criollos* were next in social standing. Those of mixed parentage, or mestizos, occupied positions beneath the *criollos*. Then one found the Indians, and finally, alas, were blacks and slaves.

It is, of course, important to realize that while a *criollo* enjoyed privileges in New Spain, back in Europe he or she was disenfranchised. The Spanish Crown was not prepared to extend the same rights to someone born in the wilderness of the New World that it afforded citizens of a civilized Europe. The viceroys and his top officials who governed New Spain were required to have been born in Europe. This discrimination lay the seeds for rebellion against Spanish authority in the nineteenth century. Latin American independence movements were modeled on the audacious—and successful—American revolt against the British Crown.

In an unkind characterization that defies charity, Americans and Europeans disparaged the habit of European Catholics who married indigenous women, ridiculing the children that resulted from such unions. "A nation of mongrels" is how the British described Mexico to Maximilian, shortly before he set sail from Trieste, Italy, to become emperor of Mexico under the protection of Napoleon. Americans long looked upon Latin Americans as "half-breeds," a cautionary account of the "degradation" that miscegenation produces. And even within Latin America, there have been distinctions. Argentines, who are almost exclusively the descendants of Spaniards, Italians, and Germans, have cultivated a sense of racial "superiority" over their fellow South Americans—mostly Peruvians, Ecuadoreans, and Bolivians—who have been "burdened" by large indigenous populations. Brazilians, where the mixture has included African as well, have been held in even greater contempt by their Argentine neighbors.

There are two points to bear in mind. The first is the question of parental love. Though American historians often describe the indigenous women who bore the children of the European settlers and adventurers in New Spain as "concubines," they were, in fact, "wives." And while, historically, these "mixed race" children were often described as "unfortunate" creatures "neglected" by their fathers, this is not the case. In our own generation, for instance, consider the extraordinary lengths to which American men have gone to find—and claim—the children that resulted from their relationships with Vietnamese women. In the same way that it is almost impossible to find a Vietnamese man who fathered a child with an American servicewoman, in New Spain it was almost impossible to find a similar situation.

Skip Connors, a veteran who retired to Mexico and lived a short distance from my offices, would regale us with stories about the Vietnam War. He would recount, in intimate detail, how haunted some of his war buddies were about their children, how they invested many years in researching their fates, and how willing they were to make financial sacrifices to ensure that they were "taken care of" in Vietnam. If one can understand a father's love, then one can see how the process of Hispanization, which is to say acculturation, unfolded. The Spanish wanted their children to be (Catholic) Christians, to speak Spanish, to become "European." They wanted them to know as much of the world and have as many opportunities as they could. Consider the family of the current American president. "In 1988, when [George P. Bush] was 12, he was an unwitting participant in a short-lived hullabaloo about the way his grandfather, then the vice president, introduced him and his two Mexican-American siblings to President Reagan," Frank Bruni recounted. "Vice President Bush affectionately called them 'the little brown ones.'" [83] At the time, critics noted a racial undertone to these remarks, but it is evident that George and Barbara Bush love their grandchildren equally and want the best for them regardless of their racial heritage. Whatever the hue of George P. Bush's skin, his grandfather, George H.W. Bush, wants to make sure that he has all the privileges and opportunities the family can offer him. George P. Bush's father, Jeb Bush, and one of his uncles, George W. Bush, no doubt agree.

The imperative throughout the colonial period was Hispanization, not as an imperialist tool to subjugate multitudes but as fathers wanting to give their children all the love and opportunity within their means. The Europeans in New Spain, however, were few in number; millions of indigenous peoples had very little contact with the Spanish, apart from the missionaries charged with introducing them to Christianity. Thus, adopting *normas hispanas* outside an official context was an inexact process. Though indigenous rulers aligned themselves with the Spanish—learning the language, adopting the dress and manners, engaging in commerce for their profit—the viceroys soon concluded that the indigenous people *thought* differently, meaning that they were inclined to be "emotional," and not "rational." Whereas Europeans were more inclined to rely on reason, the indigenous people were more inclined to have faith in their passion. From a Western perspective, those who embraced Hispanization, were thus deemed to be "sensible," while those who did not were deemed "unreasonable."

In short order, throughout the colonial period, the Spanish distinguished between people who embraced acculturation from those who did not. "Gente de razón," or "people of reason," on the one hand, and "gente sin razón," or "people without reason," on the other is a distinction that betrays an ethnocentric bias—and a deliberate hierarchy. Recall how D.H. Lawrence mocked the "Indian" worldview: "How tedious of the white [man] coming with the trick of salvation, to rub oil on the baby, and put poultices on it, and make you give it medicine in a spoon at morning, noon, and night. Why morning and noon and night? Why not just anytime, any when? It will die to-morrow if I don't do these things to-day! But to-morrow is another day, and it is not dead now, so if it dies at another time, it must be because the other times are out of hand." [84]

The subtext is that the native people, "people without reason," act on their passions, while Westerners, "people of reason," are moved by reason.

The "conquest" of the New World, then, is the story of Reason establishing its dominion over Passion. That is as apt a description of the "rationalization" that follows the implementation of market reforms as one is likely to find. For American and Canadian managers, this is more than an exercise in historical facts. It establishes the means by which labor relations are understood—and not only for Mexico. With the emergence of Hispanics as a demographic force larger than blacks, the United States is now subject to the same forces of Hispanization that New Spain first experienced in the sixteenth century.

In fact, Americans have been exposed to the differences between "people of reason" and "people without reason" since they first began to settle in the lands that had belonged to New Spain. This is how Douglas Monroy describes Americans' first encounter with this process of acculturation:

> The Anglo presence, then, had a variety of reverberations. Skilled in the manipulation of capital and goods and bent on accumulating wealth to gain status and power, these men further integrated California into the world market. They were, moreover, genuine white people. Their color appealed to the *gente de razon* [Californios and white Mexicans] because it was distinct from that of the Indians. Nonetheless we can imagine that genteel Californio society was hesitant to welcome those whose purpose in life was to make money. Thus, the Anglo merchants both compelled the rancheros because of their whiteness and threatened them because of their business acumen. Intermarriage between the two groups emerged from this context.[85]

The "people of reason" were indistinguishable from the "people of commerce," a fact made biologically definite by the intermarriage of Spanish families (Californios) and Anglo-American immigrants from the East Coast.

In the same way that is not uncommon in our time for nouveau-riche families to marry their daughters off to old money (in the United States) or titled nobility (in Europe), "[American] men ignored their own culture's proscriptions about such racial mixing and entered into Californio society through kinship ties," Monroy concludes.[86] Hubert Brancroft wrote of the miscegenation between Anglos and Spanish Californios: "They have married Californians, have joined the Catholic church, and have acquired considerable property, owing to their possessing more industry, frugality, and enterprise than the natives, and these qualities soon bring the whole trade of the town into their hands. . . . They usually keep shops, in which they retail to advantage the goods purchased in large quantities from vessels arriving in the port."[87] In Latin America, it was not uncommon for the wealthy to travel through Europe in search of young men whose families in Spain, France, and Italy had been bankrupted during the world wars, but who were in possession of titles. From Havana to Buenos Aires, Mexico City to Santiago, Latin American fortunes were "legitimized" through marriage.

In the case of New Spain, it would be a mistake to conclude that Reason always triumphs over Passion. "The Hispanization of the indigenous elites' material culture has often been seen as a negative force," Haskett writes. "From the beginning [of contact with the Spanish], the essentially conservative native elites mediated the intrusion of alien goods and strategies. Consciously or otherwise, they protected themselves and their culture from total disruption."[88] This is instructive, simply because the demographics of the United States record the increasing number of Mexicans—not all of whom may be fully "acculturated" into "reasonableness."

How does this affect the Hispanic consumer market in the United States and throughout North America?

It affects marketing by introducing a "non-Western" perspective to consumer behavior. Consider how the tension between "gente de razón" and "gente sin razón" affects the standard understanding of consumer behavior. A consumer's behavior is influenced by many small groups. A *group* is defined as two or more people who interact to accomplish individual or mutual goals. There are specific formations that can constitute a group:

1. *Membership* groups are those that have a direct influence on a consumer's behavior; they are groups to which a person belongs.
2. *Reference* groups are groups that have a direct or indirect influence on a consumer's attitudes or behavior. An *opinion leader* is a person within a reference group who exerts an influence on others. Reference groups to which a consumer does not belong can influence that consumer's behavior in the following ways:
   a. Expose him/her to new behaviors and lifestyles.
   b. Influence attitudes and beliefs.
   c. Influence product and brand choices.
3. An *aspirational* group is a group to which a consumer would like to belong.

Armed with our understanding of the cultural forces that more clearly define distinctions among Hispanics, the social and individual evolution from being a "persona *sin* razón" to becoming a "persona *de* razón" can be quantified. The failure to understand this diminishes the applicability of much market research to the Hispanic market.[89]

This analysis of consumer behavior is the more accurate assessment of the "aspirational" as a force that affects how Hispanic consumers see themselves, judge others, and tailor their goals. Research on the analysis of consumer behavior is less effective when language can be the primary identifying marker because measure in "spokesperson ethnicity" and "numerically distinctive individuals" is distorted. A white Hispanic youngster, for instance, may identify more with Sammy Sosa, who is black, than he would with Mike Piazza, who is white, if Sosa speaks in Spanish. This contradicts standard literature on "distinctiveness theory," on which "aspirational" consumer marketing is based, assuming that consumers uniformly want to be considered part of the "mainstream" as they define it. This is not the case with many Hispanics, who, consistent with historical norms, as a "reference group" have fixed notions of what it means to be "reasonable."

This is the most crucial lesson to take from Hispanic ascendancy: It changes the way corporate America can understand consumer behavior because current analytical tools do not take into account Hispanics' "deracialized" consumer behavior. In the same way that marketing strategies during segregation reflected the "separate but equal" myth of American society but were rendered obsolete once desegregation became the norm, Hispanics redefine "race" consideration in the United States. The conscientious manager can peruse the issues of the *Harvard Business Review*, or carefully study the literature in research publications, but they have lost their relevance in a post–Census 2000 America. Indeed, most of the research conducted throughout the 1990s, such as, "What We See Makes Us Who We Are: Priming Ethnic Self Awareness And Advertising Response" (*Journal of Marketing Research*), "The Effects of Actors' Race in Commercial Advertising: Review and Extension" (*Journal of Advertising*), "Viewers' Reactions to Racial Cues in Advertising Stimuli" (*Journal of Advertising Research*), and "One-of-a-Kind in a Full House: Some Consequences of Ethnic and Gender Distinctiveness" (*Journal of Consumer Psychology*), speaks of an America that is destined to become as distant as the America that existed when black consumers would not be served a bowl of cereal if they were seated at the counter in a diner.

Reading some of these articles again—in a post–Census 2000 America—they seem so quaint, relics from a time when corporate America was race-obsessed. Now consider how the assumptions used in social research into consumer behavior become archaic when the question of "reasonableness" replaces "race." In the R.J. Reynolds market research, when Cubans agree that Mexicans are "humble," what they mean is that they are closer to being "gente *sin* razón" than they are to being "gente *de* razón." When Mexicans are described as being "accepting, passive, and less inclined to assert themselves," this is consistent with people who are embarrassed about their lack of formal education, not their "character." When Texas Hispanics, on the other hand, are described as fearful of "being taken advantage of by the

'Anglo' establishment," this is the Hispanic reaction to witnessing American racism firsthand.

Cubans baffle non-Hispanics by their apparent paradox of being the most "upscaled," "remarkably aspirational and career-oriented" of all Hispanics, but a group that continues to resist becoming "Americanized." This reveals that Hispanics can succeed on the terms of success as success is defined by the United States without buying into America's mythology of itself and the world. The R.J. Reynolds market research, which is representative of that conducted throughout corporate America, also exposes the limits and consistencies of developing marketing strategies in terms of race. When the research indicates that California Hispanics display a "relative lack of hostility toward the white race," this is peculiar since, according to the U.S. Census, almost all California Hispanics identify themselves as "Hispanic, White." Does R.J. Reynolds mean to suggest that if California Hispanics did display hostility to the "white race," it would be evidence of a form of self-loathing? Or does R.J. Reynolds challenge how the Census and the Immigration and Naturalization Service define "race"?[90]

In traditional corporate marketing analysis, relationships between consumer groups are thought to emerge depending on which characteristics are deemed salient and important to one's self-identity and so give the advertising messages meaning. But when a white Hispanic child prefers a product identified with Sammy Sosa over one identified with Mike Piazza, it undermines a century of consumer behavior theory based on race relations. When it comes to matters of race, Hispanics are telling Anglophone America what feminists have been telling men for three decades: You just don't get it.

Hispanic race-neutral ascendancy, however, cannot be stopped. Consider for a moment Didion's observation, one typical of a non-Hispanic American who doesn't "get it." "There were Cubans in the board rooms of the major banks [in Miami], Cubans in the clubs that did not admit Jews or blacks . . . the entire tone of the city, the way people looked and talked and met one another, was Cuban," she reports.[91]

Miami is a city where city commissioners hold hearings in which city affairs are discussed in a staccato of English, Spanish, and Spanglish that, in reading over the official minutes, baffles anyone who is not bilingual. Hispanic ascendancy entails the assimilation of Anglophone America with Spanish sensibilities and aesthetics. Americans will become more Hispanic as Hispanics become more American, with sweeping effects on consumer markets.

Summary

1. Not since the American Civil War have so many Americans "discovered" Mexico, professionally and personally. The hundreds of

thousands of Americans retiring to Mexico is expected to become millions during the course of NAFTA's second decade.

2. Americans and Mexicans have, as peoples, embarked on a "fast track" cross-cultural course, as each learns about the other, with the old perceptions and misperceptions giving way to realities, most of which are pleasant surprises.

3. Despite the economic gains realized under NAFTA, Mexicans remain apprehensive about the historic "ugliness" of Americans, some of whom have exploited or abused Mexicans.

4. Demonstration effects of Americans—and Americanized Mexicans—are affecting the socioeconomic development of Mexico in ways that were unanticipated by NAFTA, and which shape Hispanic consumer behavior through a process of Hispanization that is emerging as a cultural force in the United States.

5

A Vanishing Border

The Emergence of a North American Consumer Market

Abstract

Canada, to a remarkable degree, influences Hispanic perceptions of the United States and informs Hispanic consumer behavior. By virtue of being the "other" Anglophone people of North America, Canadians are a healthy counterpoint to Americans. Canadians offer Hispanics contact with a kinder, gentler English speaker. For our purposes, the single most compelling impact on Hispanic-Canadian relations is the privileged role of intellectuals in Canada and among Hispanics, and how intellectual debate informs public debate among both groups. As a result, there is a backlash against the United States, a sort of anti-Americanism that further fuels the self-segregation of Hispanics living in the United States. In this phenomenon, Mexican thought plays a disproportionate role; Mexican intellectual traditions still define Hispanic thought in the United States. The role of Mexican history (suspicious of the United States) and Mexican intellectual thought (trusting of Canada) have profound repercussions of the "vanished border" between Canada and Mexico that are great for the United States, for Hispanic intellectual thought in this country reflects the sensibilities shaped by these two nations.

It is an ethnocentric conceit of Americans to view the rest of the world only in terms of our relations with others. Not unlike children who cannot entertain the idea that their parents had relationships long before they were born, so Americans have a difficult time believing that other peoples have relations, good or otherwise, that have nothing to do with the United States. For instance, Americans have a difficult time conceding that the Japanese and Koreans have a long history of relations that have nothing to do with the American occupation of Japan or the cold war conflict on the Korean peninsula. Closer to home, Americans think of Canadians in terms of relations between Washington and Ottawa, and Americans think of Mexicans within the context of U.S.-Mexico relations. But there is a long, splendid history between Mexico and Canada, an elaborate decades-long courtship that defies easy description. As will be demonstrated in this book, the first "vanished" border in North America is the one that separates Canada and Mexico.

The Role of Intellectuals in American and Mexican Public Life

A curious manifestation of American democracy is its signature disdain for and skepticism of intellectuals. The very idea of a democratic society is predicated upon the belief that the average individual, using common sense, is capable of making sound decisions about the common good. Tocqueville commented that this kind of civic intelligence, realized through free public education for everyone, proved advantageous to American democracy. "The great privilege enjoyed by the Americans is not only to be more enlightened than other nations but also to have the chance to make mistakes that can be retrieved," he wrote.[1]

One can now go a step further without being unkind. Unlike Europe or Latin America, the United States was never been "burdened" by an underclass of "peasants" who were illiterate and "unreasonable." This is not to discount the inhumanity of slavery, where social immobility was enforced through the legalization of slavery and draconian laws against teaching slaves to read and write. To a lesser extent, it is not to diminish the Protestant disdain for "superstitious" and "unreasonable" Catholics—Catholic immigrants from Ireland, Italy, France, Germany, Poland, and Mexico among others, continue to suffer discrimination in the U.S.[2] But American democracy is firmly based on the idea that civic "passions"—whether they are of European peasants, or Catholic immigrants, or black slaves—would be "subdued" by reason and common sense which is, in a word, democracy.

Unlike the United States, Canada and Mexico have instinctively demonstrated less enthusiasm in the belief that randomly selecting pedestrians off the street for jury selection, for example, could result in a consensus that promotes superior societal outcomes for the community.[3] Issues are too complicated, and the levels of interest among the public too fickle, and thus the expectation that everyone would be well-versed on civic matters is too unreasonable to form the basis of public opinion.

One manifestation of this difference between the Anglo-American and Hispanic worldview is seen in the public roles of intellectuals. Whereas Americans disdain intellectuals—and suffer few in public life—in Canada and Mexico intellectuals are held in high esteem and have great authority in public matters. In the United States, expressing misgivings about intellectuals is an affirmation of democratic values. Richard Hofstadter's book, *Anti-Intellectualism in American Life*, is a classic examination of this phenomenon. But where it is inconceivable that Americans would allow, for instance, Gore Vidal to sit in the Senate and introduce legislation on all the things upon which he loquaciously pontificates, among Hispanics, their intellectuals are celebrities, and they are tapped for public office and as social leaders.

Mistrust of intellectuals is natural for Americans, and with good reason. Ronald Reagan was so smitten with *Dictatorships and Double Standards* by Jeane Kirkpatrick, then a professor at Georgetown University, that he appointed her ambassador to the United Nations, where she was ineffectual in advancing U.S. interests. The theory on foreign relations presented in her book was discredited, of course, when years later the Soviet Union dissolved peacefully. Despite mounting evidence that her ideas were wrong, she refused to modify her "theory," and American foreign policy at the United Nations was discredited around the world. Her foreign policy fiasco—the United States was found guilty by the World Court at the Hague, Nicaraguan ambassador Nora Astorga trumped Kirkpatrick before the Security Council, and the Reagan administration was accused of duplicity—reinforced Americans' historic mistrust of intellectuals. At the other end of the political spectrum, Daniel Patrick Moynihan was a rare example of an intellectual who is also an effective policymaker. His tenure as senator from New York was an exception because he was both reasonable and persuasive, regardless of whether one entirely agreed with his ideas.[4]

Mexican intellectuals aspire to participate actively and successfully in public life. Mexican public debate, in essence, is dominated by the kind of intellectual vigor similar to that brought to the U.S. Senate by Moynihan. One reason for the respect intellectuals command in Mexico arises from the observation that, where public education has lagged and where there are large numbers of Native Americans who are excluded from mainstream society by virtue of not being fluent in Spanish, people defer to those with formal educations. Intellectuals play an important role in the nation's public life and in setting the debate on public policy. Writing thick tomes on history or the social sciences is a requisite for entering the fray of public life. In the United States, Al Gore is the closest to what is common in Mexico: an individual in public life who writes a book on his ideas, such as *Earth in the Balance*, and then makes his argument into a campaign issue.[5]

Things are markedly different in Mexico. One cultural legacy of the PRI is that, by lacking an ideology, it championed pragmatism, which continues as a characteristic of Mexico's political culture. The PRI, for all its faults, was after all ideologically *inclusive.* It is logical, then, that without fanfare, a democratic Mexico continues this legacy. Vicente Fox, whose experience as a former Coca-Cola executive established his pro-business credentials, surprised no·one when he named Santiago Creel, who had been accused of being a "subversive" by the PRI, as interior minister. Creel began his political career in the 1980s, when he was one of a group of intellectuals and activists who volunteered to be election observers in state elections in Durango and Chihuahua.[6] By 1993 he was helping to organize a plebiscite that would allow Mexico City residents to elect their mayor by direct vote.

More instructive, however, is the appointment of Jorge Castañeda, who in his youth was a communist, as Mexico's foreign minister.[7] "Once a fierce opponent of Mexico's partnership with the American free-trade juggernaut, Mr. Castañeda is now going with the global flow," Tim Weiner reported.[8] His political "conversion" that presumably made him acceptable for the Fox administration was described to Americans as a result of the "growing economic interdependence brought on by NAFTA, the rise of Mexican-American political power in this country and the end of one-party rule in Mexico," the *New York Times* editorialized.[9] That is as reasonable as any other explanation that might be offered. Consider, however, Castañeda's academic prose and manner. In describing the autocratic manner in which presidential candidates were selected prior to Fox's victory, Castañeda wrote: "Beyond these conflicts—which can have calamitous consequences for society—the succession mechanism leads us to reflect on an eternal problem in Mexico's history as an independent nation: the transfer of power."[10] This is the academic tone of official press conferences, management meetings, and serious dinner conversations in Mexico, and it was no surprise when Castañeda, a frustrated policy wonk, resigned his post.[11]

In fact, consistent with the ideological "diversity" of Mexico's government, Fox named Ricardo Pascoe, a Trotskyist, one of the leading architects of Mexico's Left, and one who is curiously at odds with Jorge Castañeda, as ambassador to Cuba, offering a glimpse of the internal problems that arise in Mexican government. "I believe we can play a true role to create a kind of dialogue between Washington and Havana. It's a difficult and crucial moment. But there are also great opportunities,"[12] Pascoe said. Other members of the cabinet include Tourism Secretary Leticia Navarro Ochoa, a former executive of Gillette.

It is, by all accounts, an ingenious administration that brings new meaning to "diversity" and "inclusiveness"—so much so, that National Action

Party, or PAN, leaders have criticized Fox for not having enough members from his own party in his administration. Indeed, diversity is a difficult thing to manage; Ricardo Pascoe was removed from his post in September 2002. Fox's administration is also a government that respects criticism by intellectuals. Of course, writers and intellectuals are not always on the same page, nor on the same side of the political spectrum, but that does not preclude their working together to establish public policy.[13] Political commentator and historian Enrique Krauze, for instance, is lauded for his books, such as *Mexico: A Biography of Power*, which goes on for almost 900 pages, and is tapped for his advice by senior administration officials.[14] University professors, poets, novelists, and economists are expected to put their ideas forward, and then act on them—and not just in government. The exalted role of intellectuals in Mexican society can be readily seen in how poet Homero Aridjis called on 100 intellectuals and artists to sign a declaration demanding that the government do something about pollution in 1985. Declaring that pollution was "killing all of us," his organization, the Group of 100, largely based on Canadian grassroots activism, is credited with being the father of Mexico's environmentalism movement.[15]

But in the United States, with the exception of the Cubans, very few Hispanic intellectuals are on the public stage of civic life in the United States. As Hispanic ascendancy consolidates, however, it is expected that American Hispanic intellectuals will emerge as a voice. For now, corporate America must be mindful that in Mexico, writers write because they are optimistic about making a difference. Intellectuals write in order to make their positions known, and their writings become the "business plans" of their ideas. This, of course, is reminiscent of American writers of a bygone era. Upton Sinclair's *The Jungle*, a call to action, or Sinclair Lewis's social criticisms in *Main Street* defined the writer as, more than society's conscience, a protagonist in social change. As Mexico's struggle for democracy was born in 1968, writers like Elena Poniatowska, Enrique Krauze, Homero Aridjis, Denise Dresser, and Luis Pazos have been at the forefront of participating in change. Others, such as Sergio Aguayo and Luis Alvarez, the former a college professor turned elections monitor and the latter a businessman turned leader of the leading opposition party, have become intellectuals who are at the vanguard of citizen leaders. "People have felt so betrayed by promises from candidates that were never intended to be fulfilled and they not only stopped believing in the government, but they stopped believing in themselves," Julio Faesler, a writer and congressman from the PAN told reporters upon Vicente Fox's election. He reminded the world that in Mexico's progress, it is the intellectual who has kept the faith of the nation alive.[16]

Yet it is important to point out that not all intellectuals have played a constructive role in society. Octavio Paz and Carlos Fuentes, the more well-known Mexican intellectuals outside Mexico, served the interests of the PRI to the detriment of the democratic aspirations of the Mexican nation. When Paz was buried, so was his legacy; Fuentes, since 2000, has been socially ostracized. A fundamental understanding of the role these two men played in shaping (or disfiguring) Mexican democracy, is necessary simply because their presence looms large. Their careers, moreover, paralleled the rise and fall of the PRI, simply because the PRI needed to justify its existence before itself and the world.

"Dictators and authoritarian regimes," Reinaldo Arenas, the Cuban writer persecuted by the Castro regime for writing counterrevolutionary novels, wrote in his autobiography, "can destroy writers in two ways: by persecuting them or by showering them with official favors. . . . those [writers in Cuba] who opted for favors also perished and in an even more deplorable and un-dignified manner: . . . once they embraced the new dictatorship, [they] never wrote anything worthwhile again."[17] This passage succinctly sums up the tragic career trajectories of both Paz and Fuentes. Intellectuals who collabo-rated with the *ancien regime* by becoming the intellectual apologists for the PRI (and whose livelihood depended on the largesse of the PRI's patronage) are now ostracized. That yesteryear's heroes are demonized is a difficult matter, but it is important for American and Canadian executives to understand the forces shaping Mexico's intellectual life, since these two men anticipate what one is beginning to find in the United States. Let us first consider Octavio Paz, then Carlos Fuentes. Paz provided the intellectual arguments necessary to create a schism between Mexicans in Mexico and U.S. Hispanics of Mexi-can ancestry. Fuentes, for his part, defended Mexico's authoritarianism, of-fering arguments that undermined Mexican democratic aspirations. Both men have fallen from grace, not unlike Vladimir Lenin is dismissed by the Rus-sians, who still are recovering from the brutal imposition of a Soviet tyranny on them in the twentieth century. Paz and Fuentes, however, are the ghosts lingering in the background as Hispanic intellectual thought begins to blos-som in the United States.

Octavio Paz, Anti-Mexican Mexican

In 1950, Paz published *The Labyrinth of Solitude*, a book that became a land-mark in analyzing the Mexican character. His essays on Mexico, curiously, began by discrediting Mexicans who emigrated. Considering that Mexican paternalism reached its political apogee during the 1950s, it was in the inter-ests of the PRI to legitimize its development model, in part by advancing the idea that the Mexicans who left Mexico did so not because of the limits of

Mexican paternalism, but because of some individual failures, failures that reflected on their moral character, not on the PRI. "When I arrived in the United States [at the end of the 1940s] I lived for a while in Los Angeles, a city inhabited by over a million persons of Mexican origin," Paz wrote. "At first sight, the visitor is surprised . . . by the city's vaguely Mexican atmosphere, which cannot be captured in words or concepts. This Mexicanism . . . floats in the air. I say 'floats' because it never mixes or unites with the other world, the North American world."[18]

Thus Paz proceeds to characterize Mexicans in the United States as outcasts. He then introduces an element of prejudicial speech—demeaning an entire class of people's self-esteem, emotional stability, and even their spirituality—that culminates in a racial slur:

> Something of the same sort characterizes the Mexicans you see in the streets. . . . When you talk with them, you observe that their sensibilities are like a pendulum, but a pendulum that has lost its reason and swings violently and erratically back and forth. This spiritual condition, or lack of a spirit, has given birth to a type known as the *pachuco*.[19]

In the same way that Americans disparage their countrymen by calling them "trailer trash," the Mexican use of *pachuco* and *cholo* aimed at other Mexicans is derogatory. There is an important point to make here: when Paz used the word *pachuco*, it was he who created those words as slurs.

Paz was not done. He escalated his rhetoric into "accusatory speech." With monumental generalizations that devalue the lives of every Mexican in the United States, the poet proceeds:

> The *pachuco* does not want to become a Mexican again; at the same time he does not want to blend into the life of North America. His whole being is sheer negative impulse, a tangle of contradictions, an enigma. . . . The important thing is this stubborn desire to be different, this anguished tension with which the lone Mexican—an orphan lacking both protectors and positive values—displays his differences. The *pachuco* has lost his whole inheritance: language, religion, customs, beliefs. He is left with only a body and a soul with which to confront the elements, defenseless against the stares of everyone.[20]

Consider the sociological impact of what is being described. Paz deliberately denigrates his fellow countrymen who emigrate to the United States, accusing them of no longer being "Mexican."

Milton Kleg, director of the Center for the Study of Ethnic and Racial

Violence, explains the role of accusatory speech in fomenting prejudice and hatred by noting that "accusations consist of charging a group with some evil act or plot. . . . They are designed to create fear. . . . As an economic and social weapon against racial and ethnic minorities, accusations are extremely effective when combined with stereotypes. Making accusations that fit the traditional stereotype of a group increases the credibility of the accusation—it fits what is already framed in one's perceived reality."[21] Paz then employs the worst stereotype in American culture about Hispanics not only to libel Mexicans in the United States, but also to point out the threat that they pose to Americans.

He concludes his assessment by arguing that the Mexican in the United States is a sociopath:

> The *pachuco* is an impassive and sinister clown whose purpose is to cause terror instead of laughter. . . . As a victim, he can occupy a place in the world that previously ignored him; as a delinquent, he can become one of its wicked heroes. I believe that the North American's irritation results from his seeing the *pachuco* as a mythological figure and therefore, in effect, a danger.[22]

With this conclusion, Paz established his credentials among the PRI as the master of obfuscation, and he was instantly catapulted to the ranks of the elite—an acclaimed intellectual and a media celebrity.

The PRI lavished honors, prestige, and funding on him. While Mexicans in the United States were, in a way, economic "refugees" or "exiles," Paz diminishes their plight and their situation. Exiles, Reinaldo Arenas writes, "have no country to represent" them, for the simple reason that they "live as if by special permission, always in danger of being rejected."[23] Paz, basking in the blank checks to curate museum exhibitions, host literary events, and tour India as Mexico's ambassador, was indifferent to the impact of his manifesto. He was so indebted to the PRI that he turned a blind eye when President Gustavo Díaz Ordaz ordered his interior minister, Luis Echeverría, to open fire on unarmed students demanding greater democracy, who had gathered at the Plaza of Tlateloco on October 2, 1968. This massacre committed by the Mexican Army stood as the most horrific attack by any government on its own students until June 5, 1989, when the Chinese government launched an assault on democracy demonstrators in Tiananmen Square.[24]

The events of October 1968 launched a democratic movement against the PRI, which culminated in July 2000 with Fox's victory. Octavio Paz, however, aligned himself with the forces of repression, and the PRI continued to bestow privilege after privilege upon him. That he turned his back on the democratic aspirations of his own people resulted in a sea change: resentment against him grew, and he was isolated among intellectuals. In 1990, when the government underwrote a series of programs on democracy, for instance, Paz suffered a stunning repudiation from which he never recovered. During a forum that included Peruvian novelist Mario Vargas Llosa, broadcast on live national television, Vargas Llosa confronted Paz. Vargas Llosa congratulated the PRI on creating the "perfect dictatorship" because the Mexican people were oblivious to the nature of their oppression.[25]

It was as if the emperor had been told he had no clothes. Paz stuttered, perspired visibly, and lost his composure. The audience was stunned and silent, and the program abruptly cut to commercials. This incident was the defining moment in Paz's demise, for Vargas Llosa, to the delight of millions of Mexicans, had exposed Paz as a fraud. For the remaining eight years of his life, he was the walking dead, a ghost among the living, suffering the indignities of having his life's work questioned, his only legacy the characterization of U.S. Hispanics of Mexican ancestry as "victims." Two years after his death, the *pachucos* he had so demonized for almost half a century were vindicated and could be now hailed as heroes. "We want to salute these heroes, these kids leaving their homes, their communities, leaving with tears in their eyes, saying goodbye to their families, to set out on a difficult, sometimes painful search for a job, an opportunity they can't find at home, their community, or their own country," Fox said while touring the U.S.-Mexico border days after taking office in December 2000, welcoming his countrymen returning home from their jobs in the United States for the holidays.[26]

Carlos Fuentes, Undermining Hispanic Democratic Aspirations

If Octavio Paz legitimized resentment in Mexico toward Mexicans who emigrated to the United States, Carlos Fuentes built a career undermining Hispanic democratic aspirations. Fuentes' writings reflect the competing interests of Mexico's ruling party throughout the twentieth century. In the same way that politicians can advocate contradictory opinions to suit the constituencies being addressed, or the politics of the moment, the body of Fuentes' work reflects these conflicts. The cognitive dissonance in Fuentes' work, in fact, is of such magnitude that it requires college-level courses at American universities in order to make sense of them.

Maarten van Delden, of Rice University, is to be commended for trying to explain the "fundamental paradox" Fuentes presents.[27] Arguing in *Carlos Fuentes, Mexico and Modernity*, van Delden correctly identifies the "conflict" and "tension" that Fuentes presents in his writings. With "national iden-

tity" on the one hand and "modernity" on the other, the fundamental conflict, of course, is that Fuentes' work seeks to reconcile the impossible: Mexican paternalism and a modern market economy. In his support of the
authoritarianism of the PRI and Mexican paternalism, Fuentes consistently
has attacked the United States and efforts to introduce market reforms in the
Mexican economy. As van Delden writes:

> Fuentes attacks the proponents of modernization in Mexico, with their cult
> of the present and of progress, for having suppressed this feature of Mexi-
> can time. To return to the cultural and historical multiplicity of Mexico
> constitutes an act of liberation, a rebellion against the enslaving prejudices
> of modernity. Fuentes believes that such a rebellion in fact took place dur-
> ing the Mexican Revolution: "Only the Revolution—and that is why, in
> spite of everything it deserves a capital R—made all the pasts of Mexico
> present. It did so instantaneously, as if it knew that there would be no time
> to spare for this fiesta of incarnation."[28]

In his opposition to "modernity," a euphemism for democracy and a capitalist market economy, what Fuentes sought to justify was the failures of
Mexican paternalism. The disenfranchised millions living in poverty were
"defenders" of Mexico's "traditions." It is inconceivable that one can ratio-
nalize efforts to provide material comfort to working families, to poverty-
stricken indigenous peoples, as "unacceptable," particularly when the speaker
enjoys all the creature comforts that world has to offer. It defies credulity that
anyone can excuse the failures of an economic system—where millions languish in abject poverty—as the "price" of "defending" tradition.

Fuentes, however, dismisses all human suffering as the price of "exis-
tentialism." "The distance between desire and its object invests them both
in Mexico with an incandescent purity," Fuentes explains. "The arc traced
from the shore of longing to the shore of fulfillment leaps over any kind of
realistic contingency: in Mexico all encounters are supra-real. . . . All of
Mexico is permeated by an existential avant la lettre. The *now* has always
been the country's response to an insecure, provisional life, without a probable future."[29]

What does he mean? And does it matter? It does, because his thinking
informs the Hispanic thinking—and the consumer behavior of Hispanic consumers throughout the United States. "One of the most common business
phenomena is also one of the most perplexing: When successful companies
face big changes in their environment, they often fail to respond effectively,"
Donald Sull writes in "Why Good Companies Go Bad" in the *Harvard Business Review.* He was commenting on the paradox that it is often the most

successful companies that are the slowest to adapt to change.[30] The same "active inertia" can be said to characterize changes in the Hispanic consumer market, which in fundamental ways is not democratic.

If his defenders argued that Fuentes was a democrat, he would soon disappoint them. He was, and remains, a career opportunist who aligned himself with authoritarian repression. Consider his reaction to the events of October 1968. "Returning to Mexico in 1969 after a number of years spent living in Europe, Fuentes soon came out in strong support of Luis Echeverría, president of Mexico from 1970 to 1976, a support for which he was eventually rewarded with his appointment as Mexico's ambassador to France in 1975," van Delden writes.[31] Luis Echeverría, as interior minister, controlled federal security forces in 1968, and he ordered the military assault on civilian students. He was rewarded for his work by being named to succeed Gustavo Díaz Ordaz. It was during this crisis in credibility that Fuentes returned to Mexico to defend the indefensible: violence directed at unarmed civilians.

His position in Mexican letters during the second half of the twentieth century, however, is instructive. He has lived through Mexico's transition from an authoritarian state with a closed economy to a democratic nation with a robust market economy. He was vocal when Mexico was struggling to open its economy, first by joining the General Agreement on Tariffs and Trade (GATT), and then by negotiating NAFTA. "I had the triple experience of Mexico under Cardenas, revolutionary Mexico; the United States under Roosevelt and the New Deal; and then Chile during the time of the Popular Front," he told *Mother Jones* in 1988. "These were all, in their own ways, exciting democracies."[32] Thus his silence now, when Mexico is an authentic democracy, speaks volumes, for it is the silence of an individual who, like Jeane Kirkpatrick in the United States, has lived long enough to be proven wrong—and is too proud to so admit.

"To account for these contradictions we must see that Fuentes is the inheritor of two separate traditions," van Delden offers, by way of excuse. "On the one hand, he has nourished himself on the skeptical, subversive tradition of modern literature. On the other hand, he has absorbed the traditional Latin American intellectual's sense of responsibility toward the community. The collision of these two paradigms is responsible for the curiously fractured quality of much of Fuentes's work."[33]

Democracy and a modern capitalist economy, however, blossomed despite such "modernity" being decried by Fuentes. "By the 1990s, many of the barriers separating Mexico from the outside world had broken down—a new situation producing a new set of challenges," van Delden explains. "These challenges have provoked in Fuentes a turn to a more nationalist position, something that is particularly clear from his commentaries on political and economic developments, but also emerges from some aspects of his literary endeavor."[34] At a time when Mexico made significant strides in its economic and political process during NAFTA's first decade, Fuentes decries the improvement of the nation's life.

What Sull observed of large companies easily applied to Paz and, especially, Fuentes: "As companies mature, however, their values often harden into rigid rules and regulations that have legitimacy simply because they're enshrined in precedent. Like a petrifying tree, the once-living values are slowly replaced by the cold stone of dogma. As this happens, the values no longer inspire, and their unifying power degenerates into a reactionary tendency to circle the wagons in the face of threats. The result, again, is active inertia."[35]

This reappraisal of Paz and Fuentes is necessary because both men, in their capacities of legitimizing the one-party rule of the PRI's authoritarian regime, offered arguments that devalued and diminished the dignity of U.S. Hispanics. During the second half of the twentieth century, Paz and Fuentes offered arguments that, not unlike the segregationists of the American South, sought to implement public policy that harmed the development of healthy consumer markets. Indeed, in the same way that segregation undermined the development of a black middle class—and a vigorous black consumer market—Mexican policy impeded the development of the Hispanic consumer market in Texas, California, and the American Southwest.

Hispanic ascendancy in the United States, fortuitously, is accompanied by a sea change in Mexican intellectual thought—which is informing the U.S. Hispanic consumer market. How? Through bold initiatives of the Fox administration, such as:

- opening the Institute of Mexicans Living Abroad;
- increasing the number of Mexican consulates in the United States;
- working to enfranchise Mexicans in the United States (through absentee ballots);
- working to have a comprehensive immigration agreement that includes temporary workers;
- working with the Homeland Security office to provide Mexican nationals with legal papers to do simple things that facilitate entering the middle class, such as securing a driver's license or opening a bank account.

These policy changes, in many ways the product of the demonstration effects of NAFTA's first decade, are empowering U.S. Hispanics, changing the fundamental character of the Hispanic consumer market.

With this as background, Hispanic thought continues to be influenced by a continental backlash against Anglophone Americans. It is well established that however much Canadians like Americans, Canada does not always agree with the United States. Whether it is the question of foreign policy toward Cuba, or each nation's position on the death penalty, or comparative approaches to health care, Ottawa often finds itself at odds with Washington. That American high school students believe Canada is one of the fifty states is reason enough for Canadians to be resentful of the United States.[36] "The U.S.-Canada frontier may be the longest undefended border in the world," Anthony DePalma notes, "but that refers only to the absence of tanks and barbed wire. The cultural front has been mined at one time or another with protections, subsidies, tax shelters, and nontariff barriers."[37] There is, in fact, considerable commentary on the ambivalent aspects of the U.S.-Canada relationship. This fosters a mild form of "anti-Americanism," by which Canadians do not agree with Americans.

We have already seen how Hispanics dissent from the American mainstream by speaking Spanish in public, in essence creating a "parallel" consumer market. Hispanic thought and sentiment in the United States are also characterized by historical factors that contribute to anti-Americanism. Whether it is the resentment fostered by Cubans over the Bay of Pigs, or Puerto Ricans who are ambivalent about their status within the United States, or U.S. Hispanics of Mexican ancestry who were stripped of their property and are subjected to racial discrimination, the Hispanic consumer market in the United States is suffused with skepticism about Anglophone Americans.

Indeed, the complicated nature of the U.S.-Mexico relationship shapes Hispanic attitudes in the United States. This has puzzled American commentators for decades and complicated marketing strategies for corporate America. American observers, for instance, presume that lingering anti-American sentiment among Mexicans is a result of the Mexican-American War. Other American commentators, at times, invoke the legacy of racism. There is, undoubtedly, an element of historical resentment among some Mexicans that have their origins in the Mexican-American War and the racism that diminishes American society. There are, moreover, three components to the sentiment that can be described as "anti-American" in Mexico today. These have to do with concerns that the United States is an unreliable partner, and betray the lingering sentiment that Mexico must remain vigilant in defending her own interests. Specifically, the unlawful denial of property rights to Mexican citizens after the conclusion of the Mexican-American War, American complicity in undermining the democratic aspirations of the Mexican people after October 1968, and the on-again-off-again commitment to free trade emerge as points of tension.

To each of these concerns, let us now turn.

Denial of Mexicans' and Hispanics' Property Rights

The Treaty of Guadalupe-Hidalgo concluded the Mexican-American War. Article 9 of that peace treaty specifically protected the property rights of Mexicans and Californios (Californians of Spanish descent). The United States agreed to recognize the deeds and titles to ranches, homes, and businesses of those who lived in lands now under American jurisdiction, but then refused to comply with this provision and embarked on a campaign to seize the properties of Mexicans living in the United States. As historian Douglas Monroy states:

> The Land Act of 1851 wreaked havoc on the rancheros' claims. It created a three-person commission to which all titles of the Spanish and Mexican eras had to be submitted for validation. . . . The commission proceeded from the assumption that all titles were invalid until proved otherwise. . . . The Land Act effectively dispossessed Californios of approximately 40 percent of their lands held before 1846. In the contradictory American tradition of liberty, speculators with cash and shrewdness, not small farmers usually, grabbed the lands.
>
> Article 9 of the Treaty of Guadalupe-Hidalgo declared that Mexicans "shall be maintained and protected in the free enjoyment of their liberty and property." . . . The massive alienation of Californio lands, and their transfer to others, obviously fell outside the letter and spirit of the treaty and American respect for private property.[38]

The campaign against Mexicans became so intense that "Californio elites increasingly called themselves Spanish to distinguish themselves from the disparaged lower classes, whom everyone began calling derisively Mexicans regardless of their origin, economic condition, or moral quality," Monroy writes. "People and things deemed Spanish (food, music, horsemen, and so on) were acceptable to Californians, whereas those deemed Mexican carried negative connotations, a pattern that has persisted to this day."[39]

Throughout California and the American Southwest, the state-sponsored racism became so relentless that, as Monroy explains, a "race war seemed always threatening to break out. . . . The legal culture had coordinated the general assault on Californios and Mexicans. . . . The legal culture accomplished this aim all the while proclaiming in universal terms the virtues of equal protection and justice through the rule of law."[40] Using the law as a weapon to strip people of their property rights created a climate of hostility; without compensation the properties of Mexicans and Californios continued to be seized relentlessly. Where the systematic seizure of Mexican and Californio property met with resistance, a climate of fear was fostered through lynchings. "Unlike in the north [where Chinese were lynched in San Francisco], in Los Angeles all of the spectacular lynchings involved Mexicans."[41]

Though Americans would like to forget the systematic and unlawful denial of property rights, Latin Americans are mindful—and distrustful. Consider how Brazilian public opinion was skeptical of the role the United States played in the establishment of the Amazon Surveillance System in 2002. Breathtaking in scope, the Amazon Surveillance System allows "Brazil to determine for the first time exactly who is flying through the airspace, whether commercial aircraft or drug dealers," Larry Rohter reported from Manaus. "It will also enable the authorities to track illegal logging and deforestation more efficiently, detect foreign guerrilla incursions, protect Indian lands and inhibit smuggling of rare and endangered animal and plant species."[42]

This radar system, however, was financed primarily with a loan from the Import-Export Bank, which is financed by the United States. The construction contract was awarded to the Raytheon Company, and American officials made clear that they expected to receive "intelligence" information that might be useful in the "War on Drugs." These three facts, when placed in a historical context of what the United States did to Mexicans and Califonios in violation of the Treaty of Guadalupe-Hidalgo, resulted in a swirl of speculation in Brazil that the United States had "ulterior" motives. Indeed, the Brazilian press speculated, as Larry Rohter reported, that "the radar was really part of an American plot to seize control of the Amazon and its riches."[43]

"Let's be honest," a columnist for *Folha de São Paulo*, Brazil's largest newspaper said, "it would be wonderful to trust the Americans, but they seldom act honorably towards Latin America. That's why it's only prudent for us to be suspicious of their motives; their intentions have not always been good. All one has to do is look at the shabby way they have always treated the Mexicans and how selfishly they have gone back on their word when it served their own financial interests. I mean, they expropriated the property of tens of thousands of Hispanic families. It would be wonderful to be able to believe the Americans. Maybe one day they'll honor their word."[44]

The "ghost of illegal expropriations past" haunts U.S.-Latin American relations to this day, precisely because it was such an enormous seizure of private property, and done in such a self-serving way.[45] Adjusted for inflation, the cumulative commercial value, in 2003 dollars, of the properties seized in violation of Article 9 of the Treaty of Guadalupe-Hidalgo stands at a staggering $3.8 *trillion*.[46] Americans may have historical amnesia about this incident, but this theft reverberates throughout Latin America—and it affects how American intentions are perceived throughout the entire hemisphere, as the suspicions expressed by Brazilians in the 2000s underscore.[47]

American Complicity in the Suppression of Mexican Democratic Aspirations

On October 2, 1968, Mexican soldiers opened fire on unarmed university students at a rally in the working-class neighborhood of Tlatelolco. The students wanted to use the Summer Olympic Games being held in Mexico City as a way of generating international coverage for their demands that Mexico's political system be opened and made more democratic. The massacre that resulted stunned Mexicans: Never before had the PRI used such naked force to squash criticism and impose its will on the Mexican people.[48]

In the same way that Mexicans often use the accusation of "corruption" against politicians as a form of political protest, Americans have used "stability" as a code word for heavy-handed policies that might offer short-term fixes but create longer-term problems. More concerned with "stability" south of the border than with "democracy," Mexicans believe that the United States undermined their democratic aspirations. Immediately after the massacre, Mexicans blamed the PRI—and the United States for looking the other way. A quarter-century later, revelations about how much Americans knew about the violence directed against civilians continues to be made, as more files released both in Mexico and the United States do, indeed, document American complicity in these events.[49]

In an investigation opened by Fox, for instance, former president Luis Echeverría was asked to testify before congressional investigators. At first he promised to cooperate, but then reneged, reverting to the silence he has maintained for three decades. "Mr. Echeverría now refuses to respond to a special prosecutor investigating the deaths," Tim Weiner reported. "His reversal, made last week through his lawyers, sets up a constitutional confrontation without precedent in Mexico: does a former president have the right to remain silent when called to account for crimes of the state?"[50]

Two reasons cited by associates close to the former president are instructive. First, was a series of disclosures by others, including General José Francisco Gallardo, who served eight years for criticizing the military's human rights violations, and stepped forward with first-hand accounts of the fate of some students who "disappeared" while in military custody. Second, Echeverría is said to be under American pressure to remain silent, lest his testimony result in embarrassing revelations about what the United States knew, and did not know, about what was going on.[51]

The matter reached such a crescendo that many Mexicans are calling for the establishment of a "truth" commission, which might or might not accomplish much. "Truth commissions can aid nations in understanding and remaking a damaged political culture," Tina Rosenberg argued in the *New York Times*. "They

can help victims to heal, create a consensus for democratic reforms and uncover evidence that can be used to prosecute the guilty. But some countries
that establish commissions will not see these benefits, because the new democratic governments lack the desire or clout to sustain their work or have designed truth commissions unsuitable to their societies."[52]

The perception of American subversion of democratic aspirations was not
relegated just to Mexico, but was the norm throughout Latin America during the
1970s.[53] Latin Americans have long been critical of what they see as the U.S.
penchant for turning a blind eye to the crimes against humanity committed by
their own governments. U.S. Hispanics, for their part, harbor a subtle resentment
toward the United States. Mexican Hispanics, for instance, believe American
officials enabled the PRI's repression of their democratic aspirations by support-
ing a government that provided "stability," though not "justice."

As these government documents are released, and principal actors speak
out for the first time, Mexicans find their misgivings about Americans' true
intentions rising. "Quietly, in the last two years, U.S. law enforcement agencies—including the FBI—have trained thousands of Mexican police, forces
which have a history of practicing torture and forced disappearance," Kent
Paterson reported. "Even before the [September 11] attacks, the Bush administration wanted to end all pretense of linking human rights with security
assistance to foreign countries. Since September 11, one of the many emerging anti-terrorism proposals suggests scrapping the 1997 Leahy Amendment
to the Foreign Operations Act, which prohibits U.S. aid to security forces
abroad that engage in human rights abuses and don't punish the responsible
individuals."[54]

Mexican officials face a difficult choice. The establishment of a truth commission would bring tremendous pressure to Mexico's fragile democracy and
unleash a backlash from both the PRI and the Mexican military—and from the
United States.[55] If the truth is not pursued, however, a difficult chapter in Mexican history will continue to fester—and anti-American sentiment will be
strengthened. "One gets the impression that they don't have as a priority the
opening of the files to establish the historical truth," Sergio Aguayo, the political analyst and human rights activist, told the *Washington Post.* "The past has
given us a heritage of bitterness. In any healing process you need the truth."[56]
In either case, "unfinished" business of a bygone era will continue to haunt the
nation's conscience and continue to cast suspicions on American motives.

American Undermining of "Free Trade"

As the 1990s unfolded, time and again trade disputes between the United
States and Mexico tended to arise after the United States took some kind of

unilateral action in violation of a prevailing accord or obligation. Whether it is the establishment of a tuna boycott, or delaying implementation of the provisions for allowing Mexican truckers unfettered access to American highways, or not complying with its contractual obligations to purchase Mexican sugar, Mexico often is forced to react to some action initiated by the United States.

American companies, on the other hand, resort to filing complaints at the slightest provocation. "United States producers have filed dozens of complaints under Chapter 19 of the NAFTA treaty, which spells out a procedure for adjudicating disputes over antidumping and countervailing duties. The complaints cover everything from raspberries to pork to steel," Bernard Simon reported in the *New York Times*, concerning complaints against Canadian tomato growers.[57] But when it comes to protecting American industry, the United States has no qualms about turning its back on the market economies. "The world heard the administration's hypocritical message loud and clear: We are deeply committed to free trade until and unless it affects a major industry in a key electoral battleground," the *New York Times* editorialized in the summer of 2002 after the fracas that followed the Bush administration's decision to impose tariffs on steel imports.[58]

The absence of a dispute-resolution mechanism to expedite negotiated remedies contributes to a lingering resentment. The outcry over the imposition of tariffs on steel imports in March 2002, for instance, was a rare instance in which so many nations were affected that the international pressure proved insurmountable. Five months later, the United States had to rescind most of the tariffs. "The action was the latest twist in President Bush's off-again-on-again commitment to free trade," Edmund Andrews reported in the *New York Times*. "Though administration officials justified their action on dry and technical grounds, it showed that the White House has been forced to backpedal on its protection efforts, for both domestic and international reasons. Domestically, companies that use steel were complaining that they could not obtain the specialty products they needed. Internationally, the administration had been fiercely attacked by almost all of its largest trading partners."[59]

"Free trade" to Americans, many reasonable Mexicans believe, is only enforced when it works to the advantage of the United States. This is anything but fair, and it fosters a backlash that contributes to Mexican skepticism about American motives. "The Americans, in common with all serious and thoughtful nations, have a vindictive temperament," Tocqueville observed, which can be confirmed by Canadians and Mexicans alike. "They hardly ever forget an offense, but it is not easy to offend them, and their resentment is as slow to kindle as it is to abate."[60] Mexicans, in other words, are surprised

prised that the American sense of fair play is oftentimes absent in how Americans approach their relations, political and business, with Mexico.

Summary

1. Since the 1940s, Mexican intellectuals, like their Canadian counterparts, have exerted tremendous influence in forming public policy in their respective countries, with one unintended consequence being that Mexican intellectual thought has informed the development of the U.S. Hispanic consumer market.
2. The role of intellectuals in Mexican public affairs overshadows, at times, that of politicians; intellectuals enjoy privileged roles as policymakers.
3. Lingering "anti-Americanism" resides as much in historical grievances among Mexicans and U.S. Hispanics as it does in the complicity of the United States in undermining the democratic aspirations of the Hispanic peoples, and the willingness of Washington to put domestic politics above the principle of free and fair trade.

6

Mexicans in the United States

Ethnographic Influences on Consumer Behavior

Abstract

Apart from the obstacles posed by virtue of their illegal immigration status, there are considerable challenges for Americans of Mexican ancestry, or AMAs, regardless of what they call themselves, to succeed in the United States.[1] With their estimated purchasing power expected to exceed $600 billion by 2005 and to rise to almost $1 trillion by 2010, these 37 million American citizens and U.S. residents confront similar obstacles that African-Americans have confronted, though not in the form of the crime against humanity that is slavery. These challenges, moreover, arise from the natural state of being diaspora. Corporate America, however, remains so baffled by the demographic ascendancy of Hispanics, that many Fortune 100 companies have availed themselves of anthropologists to understand Hispanics as consumers.[2] For Hispanics of Mexican ancestry, however, it is the nature of being diaspora that is key to understanding them, as people and as consumers. The questions of "rootlessness," the emergence of "victimology" as a form of mythmaking, the dispiriting consequences of racism, a family history where education is not valued, and the social consequences of "lookism," are all *urgent matters. Though these issues have been primarily been presented as social in nature by virtue of their detrimental effects on consumer behavior, these are legitimate business concerns that American companies selling to the Hispanic market in the United States, and Mexican companies expanding into the United States need to understand as they try to meet the needs of consumers whose purchasing power is fast approaching a trillion dollars. To reach this market, it is necessary to understand the social history that has shaped a consumer psyche that is 27 million people strong.*

Racism, Discrimination, and Intra-Hispanic Tensions

What follows is the most difficult part of the discussion presented in this book. It addresses unpleasant issues, such as racism and discrimination. It also discusses the peculiarity of "intra-Hispanic" tensions. Recall Paz's disparagement of Mexicans who moved to the United States, referring to them with a slur and classifying them as "threatening" and "victims." Now recall the incident at the restaurant in Mexico City cited by Anthony DePalma in the introduction. The restaurant manager explained to DePalma that for the "benefit of patrons," the restaurant discriminated about whom it would seat, and that the American businessman who brought along his maid showed a certain "lack" of "discretion," so his party was not seated. The restaurant manager denied this was a racist policy; this had nothing to do with the maid being a Native American woman, the manager protested, but it had everything to do with discrimination. Now consider the Pew Hispanic Center's findings that fully a third of Hispanics living in the United States believe discrimination against them by business and government remains a problem.

What is this all about? How can Hispanics argue they are not racist, when they have no qualms about discriminating? More to the point, what are the cultural ideas that inform the Hispanic worldview? How do Hispanics distinguish between discrimination that is racist and discrimination that is "lookist"?

When I was in college, I dressed as most other young adults did, wearing clothes from Land's End, L.L. Bean, Joseph Bank, Brooks Brothers, Gap, and Eddie Bauer.[3] Once, when my literary agent took me to lunch at the Chemist's Club, which was then located on 41st Street between Madison and Park Avenues in midtown Manhattan, the maitre d' looked at me and said, "Coat and tie are required." After a pause, no doubt designed to impart a lesson, he then offered, "We will gladly provide the gentleman with a jacket, and a tie garish enough to ensure it will be promptly returned." Only after I had donned a dark blue coat and a clip-on tie were we seated. Had I been turned away because the club's extra jackets and ties were in use by other patrons, would this have been an inexplicable form of discrimination?

When I read DePalma's book, I went to three of my favorite restaurants in Mexico City and spoke with the managers. What they said was instructive and, far from being an inscrutable phenomenon, has parallels in American society. The American executive DePalma wrote about was considerate to treat his maid, but that does not mean dress codes will be ignored. "Americans sometimes lack discretion," one of the managers of La Opera told me. "They think that the entire world has gone 'casual.' This is an upscale restaurant, and people here enjoy dressing up for an evening out on the town. On occasion we make exceptions, but we have turned Americans away who are wearing shorts or Hawaiian shirts. While we don't like it, we do sit men wearing khakis—provided these are pressed. And for women, the standards are higher, simply because in the real world, women are still judged more by their looks than are men."[4]

The difference in the role discrimination plays in Hispanic society informs Hispanic consumer behavior. The suggestion, of course, is that discrimination is not about race, but about class. Hispanic consumers who are struggling to make the leap from working- to middle-class, whether in a Latin American capital or a major American city, are conscious of brands. Whatever insecurities a consumer may have, brands confer a kind of confidence. In this regard, Hispanic consumers resemble those of aspiring, mainstream consumers in the United States, and the differences within the cultural and ethnic spectrum of Hispanic consumer approximates the patterns of younger demographics.

To be sure, the Hispanic marketplace in the United States—and across North America—is not uniform. Since the 1970s, in fact, with the success of Cubans in south Florida and Puerto Ricans in the New York, corporate America has realized that the Hispanic market, far from being monolithic, is fragmented.[5] Consequently, different strategies are required for the disparate market segments that together comprise the Hispanic market. Marilyn Halter succinctly describes the process by which social anthropologists have entered the fields of marketing and merchandising:[6]

> The more sophisticated target marketers understand the limitation of too wide a scope for their multinational constituencies. . . . For instance, although both Cubans and Mexicans are classified as Hispanic by virtue of their common language, in reality their socio-cultural histories and patterns of settlement in the United States are quite divergent and demand differentiated marketing approaches.
>
> When marketing specialists at the Bustelo coffee company determined that Mexicans and Central Americans, compared with all other Hispanics, preferred instant coffee to espresso, they developed television commer-

cials depicting their instant varieties to broadcast in Chicago and San Francisco's Bay Area, urban centers with substantial Mexican American communities. Bustelo's market research is so refined that the company has even tracked how tastes in coffee drinking change when people relocate. For example, Mexicans who move to Miami or to New York tend to pick up on the espresso and specialty coffee trends, and subsequently their consumption of instant coffee declines.[7]

Savvy and sensitive marketers, armed with more than a decade in the Mexican market, are familiar with these nuances, of course. As the fields of retail anthropology and ethnography become established in the marketing departments, brand and consumer managers are aware that understanding the cultural preferences within the target group is imperative. Executives at Bustelo, for instance, anticipated what Starbucks subsequently discovered about inculcating a coffee culture among Hispanics.[8] As a result, Bustelo has not lost significant market share to Starbucks the way other coffee brands, such as Maxwell House and Folger's, have lost ground.[9]

In addition, a new challenge for corporate America during NAFTA's second decade, of course, is the "second-stage" phenomenon: Mexican companies expanding their operations into the United States, underscoring the heightened competitive environment. "The steady march of [Mexican] companies northward in the last few years is an outgrowth of the North American Free Trade Agreement," Lee Romney reported in the *Los Angeles Times*. "Some firms benefited directly—from reduced tariffs on imported goods, for example. An even bigger factor: The trade agreement forced a higher level of competitiveness and sophistication on companies long protected by the insular Mexican economy."[10]

Some Mexican companies have become industry leaders in the United States. Niraj Dawar and Tony Frost wrote in the *Harvard Business Review*:

> Although Cemex enjoys low production costs at home, it has had to overcome major disadvantages. To lower its cost of capital, Cemex tapped international markets by listing its shares on the New York Stock Exchange. The acquisition of two Spanish cement producers in 1992 put it in the backyard of a major international competitor, France's Lafarge, and also allowed Cemex to shift its financing from short-term Mexican peso debt to longer-term Spanish peseta debt. What's more, its foreign acquisitions greatly reduced the company's dependence on the Mexican cement market, always a concern given the country's history of economic volatility. In addition, Cemex has aggressively sought to be on the forefront of information technology—a key factor for success in the logistics-intensive cement

industry. Its managers have worked closely on systems development with IBM, and the company has invested extensively in employee development programs designed to support its emphasis on logistics, quality, and service. Through its efforts, Cemex has become one of the world's lowest-cost producers of cement, and it has applied the lessons it has learned to boost efficiency in its acquired companies. Instead of being the target of multinationals, Cemex has since bought additional companies of its own. In the eat-or-be-eaten world of global competition, Cemex is positioning itself at the top of the food chain.[11]

In the 2000s, Mexican consumer and entertainment companies have begun to expand aggressively, from Gigante supermarkets in southern California to Televisa production of television shows on location in Miami. When Mexico's Coca-Cola Femsa acquired Panamerican Beverages, the resulting company had annual revenues exceeding $4.6 billion, and it ranked second only to Coca-Cola Enterprises in Atlanta.[12] Another Mexican multinational making an impressive entrance on the world stage is América Móvil, a wireless telephone company, whose acquisitions in Brazil have been significant. When Grupo Bimbo expanded into the United States, it did so by purchasing Canada's George Weston, Ltd. for $610 million in 2002. What does this mean? It means that every Thomas's English muffin and every Entenmann's cookie, cake, and doughnut baked and marketed west of the Mississippi is baked and sold by this Mexican multinational!

What is clear, then, is that a dozen Mexican multinationals now have more than $35 billion invested in companies throughout the hemisphere, from Canada to Argentina.[13] Hispanics, however, as a cultural force have "arrived." The new Westin Hotel in New York City's Times Square, for instance, is the first skyscraper designed by Hispanics, and has been both hailed and decried as "a Latin American exclamation point" in the heart of midtown, heralding the "undeniable" and "unstoppable" arrival of Hispanic aesthetics in the United States.

Despite these successes—and despite Mexico's enormous potential—Mexicans, as a people, are timid and easily intimidated by mainstream American society. Even when they have had enormous success, such as an enlightened foreign policy that has been instrumental in bringing about peaceful resolutions to regional conflicts, or have succeeded in keeping Latin America one of the largest nuclear-free zones, Mexicans have been reluctant to take their proper place on the stage of international affairs. Mexicans in the United States, likewise, maintain a low profile: their voice is largely absent from the public stage of civic life.

One consequence of being "inaudible," as Joan Didion describes it, on the stage of the nation's political and economic life is that one remains largely unknown. Hispanics, if not from individual success at their economic or social entrepreneurship, now command a higher profile from simple numbers: 37 million Hispanics command over half a trillion dollars in purchasing power in 2003, and that speaks for itself. It is this economics-driven cultural exchange (i.e., the sale of Hispanic music, film, art, and cuisine) that one finds in the proliferation of market research and industry literature about the Hispanic market, which until the late 1990s was rare.[14] Corporate America's commercial interest in understanding the Hispanic consumer market, however, is not shared by mainstream society. (Where R.J. Reynolds commissions a million-dollar study of Hispanic smokers, *Vanity Fair*'s Dame Edna dismisses the Latinos in the United States: "Who speaks Spanish that you are so desperate to talk to? The help? Your leaf blower?")

As a result, there is an impoverished reservoir of literature about Hispanics in the United States. Indeed, whereas historically it is writers and social critics who offer insights into social phenomenon, the appalling lack of credible writing on Mexico by American commentators results in a competitive disadvantage for corporate America; middle-level managers have scarce resources to make informed decisions about Hispanics in the workplace and in the business world. To be sure, Hispanics as a subject matter began to be examined by Mexican writers in the United States as the 1990s came to an end. Jorge Ramos, the anchorman on Univision, has broached these subjects. Mexican investigative reporter Alma Guillermoprieto has her "dispatches" about political, social, and cultural matters published in the *New Yorker*. The emergence of these Mexican voices in the United States reflects the growing clout of Hispanics in the United States.[15]

The lack of "sensible" commentary on the lives and meaning of what the presence of Mexicans in the United States, moreover, is one manifestation of five "issues" that offer significant insights into the historic and cultural issues that have kept Hispanics of Mexican ancestry in the shadows of American life. By speaking Spanish, Hispanics essentially remove themselves from mainstream life; self-segregation inherently excludes. Among Hispanics, those who advocate speaking English and participating fully in American life argue that speaking Spanish in public fosters lingering biases against Hispanics, and that self-segregation is a wound Hispanics inflict upon themselves. Other Hispanics argue that the impulse to self-segregate reflects misgivings and cultural self-doubt natural to those who are minorities excluded from the mainstream of society. Regardless of where one stands on this question, sheer demographics have now shifted the spotlight onto Hispanics as their increased numbers reverberate through the nation's life. These issues, unpleasant as they may be, inform the consumer behavior of tens of millions of Hispanics in the United States, and these cultural, historical, and anthropological issues must be incorporated into successful marketing campaigns.[16]

U.S. Hispanics of Mexican and Central American ancestry—what anthropologists call the "Mesoamerican Culture Area"—represent three out of four Hispanics in the United States. What is going on in their minds? What are the issues they confront? How do these "people of color," who encounter far more obstacles than other Hispanic groups, see themselves and their place in the world? The way they look at the world, the questions that trouble their souls, and how they see themselves in the United States together constitute a consumer profile that needs to be understood more closely, since these issues are the key drivers of the continental Hispanic consumer market.

Specifically:

The "Rootlessness" of the Mexican Diaspora

"I used to stare at the Indian in the mirror. The wide nostrils, the thick lips," Richard Rodriguez wrote in *Harper's* in 1991, to the alarm of Mexicans. "Such a long face—such a long nose—sculpted by indifferent, blunt thumbs, and of such common clay. No one in my family had a face as dark or as Indian as mine. My face could not portray the ambition I brought to it."[17]

What could this mean? What does "ambition" look like? Is ambition something visible in the faces of those who are white—but "invisible" in the faces of those with "Indian" features? Was not Benito Juárez, a full-blooded Zapotec who served as Mexico's president in the nineteenth century, a man of great ambition? Isn't Hugo Chávez of Venezuela as ambitious and "Indian"-looking as one can get? Was Rodriguez a mere dupe of Madison Avenue who, by virtue of not approximating the Greco-Roman or Scandinavian ideal of beauty, was repulsed by his own reflection in the mirror? Or was his statement evidence of the "danger" that "rootlessness" posed for Americans of Mexican ancestry?

This is peculiar, given the history of the Mexican presence in the United States. "Most troubling are the descendants of the Mexican pioneers, for once you admit Mexicans' long history on U.S. soil, you must necessarily accept Hispanic culture and the Spanish language as integral components of our own national saga," wrote Juan González, author of *Harvest of Empire*. "Mexicans, in fact, have lived 'here' since before there was a Mexico or a United States. And they have been immigrating to this country almost from its inception. Since 1820, when the federal government started keeping immigration records, only one other country, Germany, has sent more immigrants to our shores."[18]

For decades, Mexican officials have viewed with alarm the catastrophic loss of culture that Mexicans experience in the United States. To a large degree, they were dismissed as people who had *poca cultura*, or "little culture," which is explained later in this chapter. Appalled by their ignorance, Mexican president de la Madrid launched the "Paisano," or "Countryman," program, aimed at providing information about Mexico to Mexicans returning home from the United States. Since then, Mexican efforts have expanded and now include, for instance, the distribution of Spanish-language textbooks free of charge to students in the San Diego public school system, an attempt to reach out to the children of Mexicans in California.

But there was also the looming fear among Mexican officials that Americans of Mexican ancestry would suffer the fate of America's African diaspora. "Tapping into the blood's memory," as playwright August Wilson says, is a way of reclaiming one's lost identity. Warning of the danger that falls when a group of people is rendered rootless and disconnected from their heritage, Mexicans officials have long worried about the fate of their compatriots in the United States.

These Mexicans arrive in a country where they face racism, where they do not speak the language, and where they witness how indigenous cultures are disparaged. These immigrants, indeed Mexico's most disenfranchised, become "rootless" by living as "outlaws" in an alien country. If it weren't tragic enough that the shortcomings of Mexican paternalism resulted in millions of Mexicans having to search for livelihoods in the United States, their plight becomes worse if they lose their cultural heritage.

As a consequence, one sees the acts of desperation in attempting to *fabricate* an identity by any means possible. Indeed, by creating artificial constructions—in social Darwinist terms—the displaced Mexicans in America seek to substitute a political label for a sense of self. "I think Chicano writers . . . have had to fight to find a place between two cultures," Elena Poniatowska, one of Mexico's leading writers and social critics, observes, dismayed at how quickly Americans of Mexican ancestry have become alienated from their origins. "Americans reject them because they see them as Mexicans and Mexicans reject them precisely because they are not Mexicans. . . . I have had young Chicana writers introduce themselves, and within two minutes declare to me that they are lesbians. I wouldn't come up to anyone and say, 'I am a heterosexual and a grandmother.' This happens only to people surrounded by a culture trying to destroy them and who have created themselves out of this destruction."[19]

Elena Poniatowska is an intelligent, articulate, and thoughtful woman. Listening to her speak and express her views is like tuning in to National Public Radio and hearing a report by Nina Totenberg. What Poniatowska says carries considerable weight. For her to express such astonishment at the way Americans of Mexican ancestry label themselves in such despairing terms is evidence of the racism to which they are subjected in the United States. A kinder explanation, of course, is that labels have become one of the more peculiar ways Americans have created a political construct since social Darwinism, a misguided attempt to apply "scientific" rigor to human society, usually through race-based euthenics. In the American South, proponents of segregation appropriated Darwinian ideas. "Racial hygienists" sought to buttress their arguments for racial exclusion by invoking the "scientific rigor" of social Darwinists and Eugenicists.[20] "As a queer Catholic Indian Spaniard at home in a temperate Chinese city in a fading blond state in a post-Protestant nation, I live up to my sixteenth-century birth," Richard Rodriguez proclaims, as if to mock the American penchant to put a racial label on everyone. He describes himself with the scientific exactitude that one might find in the journal *Nature*, reporting on the plight of a rare endangered subspecies of beetle from a bulldozed section of the Amazon rain forest, though he left out his astrological sign.[21] His is a label that is so absurd as to be rendered meaningless.[22]

That Rodriguez can describe himself in this manner is the logical conclusion of social Darwinist thought in American society. This, of course, was anticipated by Richard Hofstadter in his landmark book, *Social Darwinism in American Thought*. Make no mistake, it is social Darwinism that has denigrated blacks in the United States. Incomprehensible questions of how and why race is "politicized" in America continue to confound Mexicans—and Canadians, who have long protested American racism.[23] When Bush nominated Colin Powell and Condoleezza Rice, for instance, they were denounced by other blacks for not being "really" black. "Today ideology *is* identity. Thus it is not altogether absurd for President Clinton to consider himself black. Nor is it absurd for many blacks to agree with him even as they question Mr. Powell's blackness," Shelby Steele opined. "I know personally that being a conservative minority is a test of character. Identity, after all, is an integral and cherished part of the self. To have someone say in the *New York Times* that you are not really black or Hispanic is to be annihilated on some level."[24]

One can understand the longing experienced by the African diaspora, and how monumental the search for their history continues to be. One can also understand how a cultural disconnection can produce a dispiriting downward spiral for the displaced Native Americans. Mexican officials, who celebrate their indigenous peoples, are at a loss to understand why American Native Americans are demoralized, denigrated, and excluded from the mainstream life of the United States. Although, as Joan Didion suggests in her description of Miami, some Hispanic communities are comprised of the hyper-sophisticated, most Hispanics in the United States occupy the ranks of the working and lower-middle class. These are the people who have been readily dismissed by mainstream America as the busboys, parking lot attendants, and gardeners of Los Angeles.

As Hispanic political and economic ascendancy makes itself felt, there are unexpected reverberations throughout the nation. In California, for in-stance, the "fight" over official history is now unfolding, as Native American groups sue to have the state's historical markers tell their story. The struggle to recognize officially indigenous historical sites is one measure of the ongo-ing fight by Native Americans for a place in the life of America's main-stream. When state officials installed a plaque in Round Valley, near Covelo, that recognized the fate of the original inhabitants, there was an uproar. "The way I feel is the way the East Berliners felt when the wall started getting knocked down. It's a sense of new freedom and the key word is truth," Ernie Merrifield, a Round Valley tribal council member, told the Associated Press.[25] It is only appropriate, then, that it is in California that social Darwinism is being challenged: On April 3, 2001, San Diego City Council voted to ban the word "minority" from city documents and discussions, arguing that the word was "disparaging."[26]

Tensions between Hispanics in Latin America and Hispanics in the United States arise simply because the former see the latter as terribly ignorant. Consider another example, more appalling than that of Rodriguez. "I was born and raised *pocho*—Americanized—and I didn't know much more about Mexico than most: It was where the people who were cooks, custodians, and construction workers were from, *la gente* who ironed and sewed and served food, who weren't afraid of the daylight sun or the nighttime dark," Dagoberto Gilb wrote in *Harper's* one decade after Rodriguez lamented what he saw when he looked in the mirror.[27] Gilb, identifying himself as a *pocho*, is as insulting as if Maya Angelou had described herself as "born and raised a nigger."

"The cliché about Randians is that they are moody youngsters going through a rebellious phase," Christopher Hitchens observed.[28] Mexican offi-cials say the same thing about the Chicanos and Latinos. Gilb's insult, after all, is more than outrageous. It speaks to the concern among Mexican intel-lectuals that the American-born children of Mexicans are "children ignora-mus," in the words of a former official in the Zedillo administration, now in private business. Before one can appreciate the depth of rage Mexican offi-cials have over the legendary ignorance of the Americans of Mexican ances-try, a brief digression is in order.

On more than one occasion, I have had the opportunity to speak to high school students in several cities in the United States. In order to gain an understanding of what our youth are thinking at any given time, I have found it instructive to engage students of all ages in conversation long after my talk. While I am always surprised at their thinking, there are times when it is rather alarming to see the confidence with which some espouse their ignorance. A high school student once "explained" to me that the Declaration of Independence was signed on July 4, 1776, during the Boston Tea Party. When asked why they celebrated such a momentous event by drinking, of all things, tea, she paused, then replied "because of Prohibition. The British didn't allow Americans to buy alcohol."

Let us say you are on company business in, say, Paris. Imagine that this young woman was, inexplicably, invited to a reception sponsored by your firm. Now, imagine what your reaction would be if, with complete certainty, she repeated her nonsense to the French present. If you grew embarrassed as you became enraged in silence, it would be understandable: Here was a foolish student glibly spreading her ignorance while making you into an unwilling accomplice: remain silent and your silence validates; correct one of America's ignorant children and the moment becomes awkward.

Now let us return to our misguided Gilb. After explaining that "Mexico was a story to me, one that I knew not like a Mexican novella but like an American comic book," he sets out in search of "the mother of *mestizo* Mexico." He offers this reason: "Don't I have to see, with my own eyes, where Cortés's first met Malinche's?"[29] Not unlike the high school youngster who proceeded to tell a fabulist tale that explained the signing of the Declaration of Independence, the Boston Tea Party, and the Eighteenth Amendment in one sentence, Gilb proceeds to "explain" the birth of the first *mestizo* with a similarly mistaken invention.

Misattributing Cortés and La Malinche with being the parents of the "first" *mestizo*, he overlooks Gónzalo Guerrero, a Spaniard who, shipwrecked in 1535, eschewed Western civilization and decided to live with the Maya, with whom he fathered the first *mestizo*. Denounced by the Spanish as "evil," and, in the words of Spanish historian Gónzalo Fernández de Oviedo, as having been "brought up among low and vile people," he is today memorialized with monuments that recognize him as father of the Mexican *mestizos*.[30] Guerrero is a *hero* of the Mexican nation, with monuments, schools, and parks named in his honor. By contrast, there is no statue raised to Cortés. Mexican intellectuals are puzzled by some AMA's pursuit of nympholepsy as a form of intellectual thought, and warn Mexican policymakers of the dangers of "rootlessness," not unlike some Americans warn other Americans that their nation's public high schools are giving diplomas to youngsters not because they have mastered the curricula, but for sufficient attendance.[31]

Mexican officials who do look to the United States are stunned to realize that the more intelligent commentators in America on Mexicans are Mexican-born *Mexicans* who work in the United States. "So this was Carlos Salinas de Gortari's contribution to the modernization of his country's politics: to make the party financially independent of the government, and then to extract money from the men who multiplied their wealth through cozy deals with that same government, so that the PRI's candidates could campaign with more funds than ever," Alma Guillermoprieto, who covers Latin America for the *New Yorker*, wrote, in a typically intelligent, well-written sentence.[32]

"Our identity is tied to the land where we were born, or where our families were born, and to the language, Spanish, that has woven one generation to another. Spanish is more alive than ever in the United States. Nine out of every ten Hispanics speak Spanish at home, and this has allowed Spanish language radio, television, newspapers, and magazines to flourish," *Noticiero Univision* news anchor Jorge Ramos wrote. "The Italians and the Poles, for example, never had national television networks in their own language in the United States. Hispanics, however, do, and they are very successful."[33]

It is not without irony that Mexican officials who wish to engage Hispanic opinion makers do so, not by contacting them in the United States, but by calling them up across town—for most live in Mexico City.

Mythmaking and the Cult of Victimology

For forty years, Mexican paternalism employed Octavio Paz as a state-sponsored mythmaker, and part of his task was to demonize the Mexicans who, falling through the economic cracks or not being encompassed by the embrace of Mexican paternalism, left for the United States. Mexican immigration to the United States thus generated great ambivalence. In social terms, the United States acted as Mexico's "safety valve." But politically, it challenged the PRI's paternalistic development model. And the ruling elite wanted nothing more than to prove to itself and the world: whatever failings there were, it wanted to demonstrate, were the failures of *individuals*, but not the *system* itself.

Mexican intellectuals gingerly debated among themselves the merits and shortcomings of Mexican paternalism. But these discussions were academic in tone and skirted around the infuriating possibility that Mexicans were voting with their feet, forced to escape life under the PRI by leaving for the United States. *What was wrong with these people?* the PRI wanted to know, ignoring the remote possibility that there was anything at all wrong with authoritarianism. "Mexico reserved special loathing for the migrant workers—the peasant who traveled back and forth between the United States and Mexico," Richard Rodriguez notes. "The peasant was bilingual, fluent in dollars and pesos, multicultural."[34] Mexicans in the United States—and their children, in turn—lashed back at Mexico. Characterizing themselves as Mexico's "children"—betraying a parent-child relationship that is inappropriate between the individual and her government—they have decried their abandonment by Mexico's failure as a parent.[35] "In Mexico, it's the father who needs to ask forgiveness from his child," Rodriguez demands, which begs the obvious question: If Mexico apologized, how would Rodriguez, who is not fluent in Spanish, recognize Mexico's "biblical confession"?[36]

Mexicans and Mexican-Americans thus face each other across the border, pointing an accusing finger at each other, telling lies about themselves and each other to themselves and each other.[37]

In the United States, recriminations against Mexico have taken one of two forms. First, for more three decades, (leftist) Chicanos have written impoverished arguments in which they have "invented" a new mythology. Chicano writing has long described an "ancestral" land where the Aztecs originated—which is coincidentally located in present-day California. This place, "Aztlán," and the mythology surrounding its description, is designed to advance the idea that Chicanos, far from being unwelcome interlopers in California, are in fact the one "true" and "legitimate" people who have the only legitimate claim to being in California. "Illusions . . . prove that our brain is capable of imposing structure on the world," Josuah Tenenbaum, assistant professor in the brain and cognitive sciences department at MIT, explains. "One of the things our brain is designed to do is infer causal structure of the world from limited information."[38] The fantasies told about Aztlán, however, are important in the psyches of Chicanos.

Second, and more insidious, is the escalation of prejudiced, accusatory, and hate speech directed against Mexico. In the same way that the process of Hispanization, which the Spanish achieved by encouraging indigenous elites to adopt *normas hispanas*, is now understood as acculturation, the cumulative impact of the writings of Octavio Paz in the 1950s is now understood as a form of hate speech. Accusatory speech after accusatory speech, over the decades, not unlike the misogynist themes he explored, stand as an unprecedented attack on Mexicans in the United States, the reverberations of which linger as NAFTA enters its second decade.

Americans of Mexican ancestry have retaliated with venomous speech of their own, which is understandable for a people who are "rootless." "Understanding personal myth is important, psychologists say, because they do more than reveal how a person sees his past: they also act as a sort of script that determines how that person is likely to act in the future," Daniel Goleman reports. "And for those who are living out destructive myths, some therapists are using insights into the myths at the heart of their patients' problems as a key to treatment."[39] Chicano writing, to many Mexican intellectuals who have very little patience for it, is dismissed as a mosaic portrait of the world as seen through the educational limitations of *The Beverly Hillbillies*.

Literature on "Aztlán" is part of the Chicano disconnect from American society, which is so amusing to other Hispanics as to be satirized in the emerging Hispanic literature in the United States. "[E]ver since she discovered the 'Mexica Movement' Amber has lost any sense of humor she used to have," Lauren tells the reader in *The Dirty Girls Social Club*. "The Mexica Movement, for those who don't know, consists of Mexicans and Mexican-Americans who insist on being called Native Americans, and specifically Aztecs, instead of Hispanics or Latinos."[40] There is more, of course, and it is the compelling ignorance of the Aztlán enthusiasts that author Alisa Valdes-Rodriguez exposes. When Amber holds a concert, she boasts that the images projected on the stage behind her were photographs of the "beautiful faces" of the Mexica people she took on a trip to Chiapas. Unbeknownst to Amber, Chiapas is part of the Maya Northern Highlands—where there are no Mexica. The Maya, in fact, were in constant conflict with Mexica. Thus, Amber's breathtaking ignorance of history is as appalling as if she claimed she had traveled to Beijing and returned with photographs of the beautiful faces of the Japanese people (the Chinese and Japanese are historical adversaries), or to London and returned with photographs of the beautiful faces of the Irish people (the English and Irish have centuries of animosity).[41]

Valdes-Rodriguez is merciless in her satire. Later in the novel when Amber's song becomes successful, she is ostracized for that very success by her humorless cohorts in the Mexica Movement. "They're saying you betrayed Aztlán. Like Shakira. I can't live with that," Gato, her Mexican-American boyfriend, tells her before he leaves her.[42] The Mexica Movement accuses Amber and Shakira of betraying "La Raza" by "selling out," which means that they record songs in *English*. This is hilarious because the pop star Shakira, the daughter of an American father (of Lebanese descent) and a Colombian mother (of Catalan ancestry), has no "indigenous" blood in her veins to betray![43] Awash in their monumental ignorance, the joke is on the misguided members of the Mexica Movement. That Hispanics can roll their eyes at the pretensions within the family of Hispanics speaks volumes of the diversity and tolerance that prevails within the community. Lauren, after all, thinks Amber is ridiculous for letting herself be swayed by a group of lunatics on the fringe of *hispanidad*, but they are friends nonetheless and she would never turn her back on Amber.

This diversity has profound political implications. Far from being a monolithic voting bloc to be courted by one political party or another, Hispanics constitute a political mosaic. "Poll after poll shows Hispanics dividing roughly into thirds when asked if they are liberal, conservative or middle of the road," Tamar Jacoby of the Manhattan Institute argues. "Most look first to government to solve the problems of their community—a fundamentally liberal inclination. They are more conservative than most Americans when it comes to social issues like abortion . . . but they invariably place more importance on bread-and-butter issues like education and the economy. And the Pew poll, like others before it, shows that partisan affiliation rarely runs deep."[44]

This is, of course, a way of saying that the term "Hispanic" does more than describe an Iberian linguistic and cultural heritage: it encompasses a constituency that spans the entire spectrum of human opinion. Though Democrats have been first to reach out to Hispanics as a "bloc," their success is in spite of ideological differences: most Hispanics who vote for Democrats have received little in return. "Democrats will try to hold Hispanic support by offering more services that appeal to working-class immigrants, like state-provided health insurance, college tuition subsidies and higher minimum-wage laws," Tamar Jacoby pointed out. "And Republicans are sure to try—and could succeed with—platforms that stress new economic opportunity for students, first-time home-buyers and small business. Either way, Latino power will be a moderating influence as this bloc of voters judges candidates less on ideology than on what they actually deliver for the community."[45]

Indeed, there is a backlash against the perverse "cult of victimology" that Chicano and Latino leaders cultivate. Hispanic cartoonist Lalo Alcaraz's comic strip, "La Cucaracha," which is syndicated nationally, is an attempt to spoof the mythmaking of the "Chicano" persona nurtured by professional "victiomlogists" that populate the Latino/Chicano/Mexican-American community. " 'La Cucaracha' arrives with some big expectations," Natalie Hopkinson reported. " 'He'll rub them the wrong way sometimes,' says Charles A. Ericksen, editor of the Washington-based news service Hispanic Link, which first published Alcaraz's editorial cartoons when he was in college. "But at the same time, they are going to have to recognize him as someone who truly stays in touch with the community and has developed a vehicle to educate the larger audience about what a Chicano is all about.' "[46]

Shades of Racism Against Hispanics

It is not necessary to elaborate on the history of racism that has plagued the United States. Whether in the form of slavery, or the lynching of Mexicans whose properties were seized in California, or the destruction of many indigenous people, there are more than sufficient grievances to illustrate this sad point. While all are deplorable, what is, in fact, admirable is the determination since the 1960s to remedy historical injustices through the emergence of an active civil rights movement that included Hispanics.[47]

Eliminating racism, however, is an ongoing process. As NAFTA moves forward, the subtle nuances of a sustained bias against Mexico pose challenges. To understand how subtle are the biases, consider the curious incident that occurred in April 2001. On April 13, the *New York Times* published an article titled "Florida, Low on Drinking Water, Asks E.P.A. to Waive Safety Rule," by Douglas Jehl. "In a bid to head off drinking-water shortages, Florida is nearing approval of a plan that would allow billions of gallons of untreated, partly contaminated water to be injected deep into the ground in what would serve as subterranean water banks," Jehl reported. The next day, the newspaper published "Mexico Grows Parched, with Pollution and Politics," by Tim Weiner, which reported that "Mexico lies along the same latitudes as the Sahara, and nearly half its land is bone dry. It has less drinking water per capita than Egypt, and 60 percent less than it did 50 years ago." Two days later, the newspaper published Jim Yardley's report titled, "For Texas Now, Water and Not Oil Is Liquid Gold." "For decades the gold beneath the ground in Texas was oil. But if oil built modern Texas, water is now needed to sustain it," Yardley wrote. "Water has become so valuable that a complicated scramble is under way for the rights to underground aquifers . . . there are even 'water ranches' popping up around the state."

The publication of these three reports—within ninety-six hours of each other—suggested that something was happening around the Gulf of Mexico. Why are Mexico, Texas, and Florida confronting water crises? Was it part of global warming, unchecked population growth, or mismanagement of natural resources? Was it a combination of all three, or was something else to blame? A strong case can be made that the United States and Mexico should develop an overall management plan for the Gulf of Mexico as a way of protecting the integrity of that ecosystem. Ignoring the interrelated nature of these events, no editorial content regarding the "crisis" in either Florida or Texas was published.

But of the single commentary published in the *Times*, it was a letter written by Sy Weiss condemning Mexico's population growth as the cause of the water crisis in Mexico.[48] Does this underscore the persistent stereotypes concerning Mexico? By focusing on the nonexistent population "explosion" in Mexico, the *Times* editors neglected to address where the *real* water crisis is prompted by undisciplined population growth: Florida and along the U.S.-Mexico border. Florida, for instance, is expected to experience a population increase of 30 percent over the next two decades; Mexico, by contrast is expected to experience a growth of 15 percent over the same time.[49] That the population along the U.S.-Mexico border has increased a hundredfold since the mid-1940s was never raised by the *Times*. A measure of the population "explosion" in Texas is seen in the price tag on providing water: "Lawmakers say it could cost at least $80 billion to upgrade the state's aging municipal water systems."[50]

Yet the *Times*'s reporting reinforces negative stereotypes consistent with a systematic bias, a tendency to believe the worst of Mexico, a legacy of the "Black Legend" propagated by Britain against Spain during the colonial era. In our current understanding of sociology, the subtle bias evident in this harsh assessment of the water crises affecting the land mass that defines the Gulf of Mexico is what sociologists classify as "prejudiced speech," which constitutes the mildest form of hate speech.[51]

Now consider this example. Where I live in New York, it is not uncommon to see individuals walking about the neighborhood with five or six dogs on as many leashes. If one didn't know any better, the reaction would be to conclude that these people simply have too many pets, and wonder what is wrong with them. Perhaps they should be reported to the Humane Society. They are not reported, of course. People who live in the neighborhood understand that these are professional dog walkers, people who, for a fee, will make sure that their clients' pets are taken for strolls around the neighborhood to exercise, socialize with other dogs, and take care of their needs. None of these people, as it would on the face of it appear, actually own the half a dozen or so dogs they have in tow.

Mexicans in America, isolated from mainstream society primarily by language and culture, tend to live in close-knit communities in the United States. Finding comfort in extended families, it is not uncommon to see siblings, adult children and parents, and cousins and in-laws living together. Amid the presumptions of American life, where the "nuclear" family model remains the norm, cultural misunderstandings emerge, misunderstandings that lead to resentment—and *prejudices*. "Too many babies!" Agustin Gurza, a columnist for the *Los Angeles Times*, reported a caller telling him, admonishing him for an article he wrote about local development issues in Santa Ana, California, where many Mexicans live. "They've always got one in the arm, five or six walking along, two or three in the stroller. . . . And they keep breeding!"[52]

On the occasions when, out of curiosity, I have struck up conversations with these Mexican women with half a dozen children out for a stroll, whether they are out in San Francisco's Mission District or in Queens in New York, I found that most of these women were out with their own—*and someone else's*—children. In an effort to duplicate the familiar extended family, these women were taking care of their own children, along with their nieces and nephews, or neighbor's children. What appears as "too many" children is, in fact, combining child care for friends and "being there" for families, as several households share responsibilities. Census figures confirm these anecdotes: Hispanic couples have an average of 4.1 children, compared with 3.24 for the population at large.[53] Whereas the dog walker is an example of Adam Smith's invisible hand (maximizing her income as best she can), the babysitters demonstrate the importance of Robert Putnam's social capital (contributing to their community as best as they are able). It's the distinction between "fee" and "free." Thus appearances can be misleading; outdated stereotypes, and the failure to grasp simple economic ideas, often contribute to misguided interpretations of reality.

What makes this the more frustrating is the subtle shades of bias, nuances to which one may be blind. Consider how, in an excellent news story in the *New York Times* documenting Mexico's failure to do more for its own migrant workers, Ginger Thompson undermines her own objectivity. "Mr. Fox, the son of ranchers, has not devoted any significant political capital to the abuses against migrants who labor on Mexican soil," she wrote, reporting on the "one million Mexicans who abandon their homes for part of the year to move north with the harvests."[54] But when one compares the living and working conditions of migrant workers in Mexico and the United States, there really is no comparison. In the United States, migrant workers are among the most disenfranchised, having to file lawsuits to obtain access to such basic services as restrooms. In Mexico, on the other hand, housing, medical services, and childcare centers, however imperfect, are made available to migrant workers. Migrant workers in the United States have access to none of these services. Thompson, in fact, reports in the same article how the Fox administration increased by 25 percent federal spending "aimed at building housing, schools, and day-care centers for migrant workers."

This is striking, considering that César Chávez, a Mexican-American labor activist in California, was denounced as a "communist" for demanding that portable toilets be set up near the fields for migrant workers. No reasonable person would disagree with the grim conclusion that the lives of poor people are difficult everywhere. But migrant workers in Mexico suffer demonstrably less than their compatriots who are forced to labor in the United States. "I have been to these facilities in western Mexico, and they are increasing in number and quality every season," Lee Frankel, president of the Fresh Produce Association of the Americas, wrote in response to Thompson's subtle bias against the Fox administration. "You decry the lack of political effort in Mexico to improve the lives of farm workers, yet then describe free housing, free day care, free on-site elementary schools, free medical care, free pension programs and at-home and at-work access to social workers available."[55]

As a consequence, migrant workers who *remain* in Mexico are in *better health* than those in the United States. "Diabetes, high blood pressure and anemia occur at higher rates among California's 700,000 immigrant farm workers, mainly from Mexico, than among Americans, and the workers' health worsens the longer they stay in the United States," Steven Greenhouse reported. "Preliminary findings by the California Policy Research Center in Berkeley indicate that illegal immigrant farm workers, newly arrived from Mexico, have far lower cholesterol, lower blood pressure and less obesity than do farm workers who have lived here legally for a while."[56] This is one reason many Mexicans illegally in the United States want to work long enough to save a little capital and return home. That workers would enjoy better health in Mexico than in the United States is counterintuitive to what one would expect.

Racism against Mexicans has cultural aspects, to be sure. In the ethnic mosaic of the United States, it is not surprising that various ethnic groups are in conflict with each other. "A lot of [Korean] greengrocer owners worked for Jewish and Italian owners," Jonghum Kim, a reporter for *The Korea Central Daily News*, told the *New York Times* about complaints lodged by Latinos against Korean-owned greengrocers in New York City. "And they worked 12 hours a day, their whole families worked together. They gathered up the money and bought the stores. They had no benefits. They didn't even think about that."[57] A tradition of injustice, however, is at conflict with contemporary standards. Korean greengrocers feel they are being unfairly singled out by labor activists, and they do not understand why treating Hispanics the way they were themselves treated when first arriving in this country is no longer acceptable. The dispute over wages and benefits in New York has "pitted Korean immigrants—no strangers to explosive tensions with other ethnic groups—against Mexican immigrants. Sixty percent to 70 percent of the city's roughly 2,000 greengrocers are owned by Koreans, and most of their workers, an estimated 10,000, are Mexican immigrants," Sarah Kershaw reported.[58]

A measure of the depth of challenges Mexican migrants face is seen in the way Hong K. Chun, executive director of the Korean Produce Association, describes how his organization is attempting to reduce tensions. "We are telling [our members], 'Don't look down at them, don't use the bad language.'"[59] One has to be told not to curse at one's employees? The potential for tensions is understandable under such work environments. Tensions are also exacerbated by the low margins on greengrocers as an industry; everyone involved labors long hours for modest profits, which can be wiped out in short order.[60]

Hispanic workers in the United States face threats other than simple work-place discrimination threats that become potentially fatal dangers. In a country where "racial profiling" is a lingering concern, consider the plight of dark-skinned Latinos who work in law enforcement. Noting that "looking like a suspect has its risk" for law enforcement officers of color, Michael Winerap describes the life-and-death danger that minority law enforcement officers of color face in the course of doing their jobs:

> But dark-skinned plainclothes officers have a second, more chilling fear: that someday, a white officer will accidentally shoot them. And that, they said, made them view the [Amadou] Diallo case differently.
> Several years ago, before going undercover, [Officer] Derrick recalls being in street clothes, on his way to work at the 63rd Precinct in Brooklyn, when he saw an elderly woman being robbed by two teenagers. He managed to get the woman into his car, subdue the attackers (though he had no handcuffs) and persuade a passer-by to call 911—an effort that would win him a hero's medal. But as he waited for backup, he was scared. Most officers at the 63rd were away at a funeral that day. He feared that the officers who showed up would not know him, and that he would be in danger—a black man in street clothes with a gun. Seeing a patrol car approach, he waved his police ID over his head and kept screaming: "I'm a cop! I'm a cop!"[61]

It is demoralizing for Mexicans to realize that being "dark-skinned" and being the "good guy" is a counterintuitive connection to make in the United States.

The racism that arises from making "instant" judgments applies not just to dishwashers, farm hands, or stock boys at the neighborhood corner store. "Even the Bush family has not escaped racism and discrimination," Jorge Ramos explains. "During the 2000 Republican National Convention in Philadelphia, George P. Bush, son of Florida governor Jeb Bush and his Mexican wife, Columba, told me he had been a victim of discrimination. 'I have encountered a lot of discrimination in my life,' the young man, then twenty-four years old, told me. The statement caught me by surprise. 'A member of the Bush family was a victim of discrimination in the United States?' I replied. 'Of course,' he said, 'because in our society, unfortunately, people judge you by the color of your skin. I have encountered discrimination my whole life, all around the country. . . .' he responded, without losing his composure, as if this were the more normal thing in the world."[62]

That the American president's nephew is subjected to racism is an outrage, of course. But this is not to say there is no comic relief in this tragic aspect of American life. "Blacks have always known that white folks are crazy," Debra Dickerson contended in Salon.com. "Whenever news breaks of yet another bizarre massacre or hideous chain-saw-and-cannibalism-type crime, we call each other from our cubicles and whisper conspiratorially something like, 'You know that was somebody white. A brother will shoot you for stepping on his new Nikes or to steal a nice jacket. But white folks—they kill people they don't even know, and for no apparent reason, on purpose!'" Then she elaborates on how race determines the type of violence in America. "Blacks routinely characterize certain types of crime as white (and insane) just as whites characterize certain types as black (animalistic)." The reason for this, she argues, is that blacks "lose their minds on a much smaller, much more self-destructive scale. We burn down our own neighborhoods, disable our own elevators and smash the only grocery store for miles. We graffiti the walls we have to look at every day and we make our mothers wade through broken malt liquor bottles to get to the bus stop." White violence, on the hand, is simply insane: "There was never much doubt among blacks that the Littleton killers were white and male."[63] Whether or not one agrees or disagrees with Dickerson, the observation can be made that, in the same way whites hold stereotypes about blacks, blacks also have their own set of preconceived ideas about whites.

Not all blacks, however, are as confident about making racial assumptions based on the color of a person's skin. "Loath as I am to admit it, I must say that I was relieved when I heard that the two teenagers who killed 12 classmates, a teacher and themselves at Columbine High School in Littleton weren't black," Jill Nelson wrote, also in Salon.com the same day. "Why? Because the thought of spending days listening to smug pundits pontificating on black pathology, black predators, black violence, the broken black family and plain old bad black people at maximum volume was too much to bear. It's bad enough that the assumption that black people, and particularly young black people, are either used to or inured to violence is an ongoing subtext in American thought, conscious or subconscious. But frankly, the thought of having Katie Couric and Stone Phillips breaking that old Negro pathology down for us 24/7 was too awful."[64]

Then again, the United States is a country where the Supreme Court rules that the Ku Klux Klan must be allowed to participate in Missouri's "Adopt-a-Highway" program—presumably because keeping highway roadsides clean is an acceptable form of societal cleansing.[65] This also is a country where there is intra-white racism: the Irish encountered tremendous bigotry and prejudice in the United States as they arrived en masse in the wake of the Irish famine of 1845–52; and white Southerners are still held in disdain by white Northerners.[66]

Hispanics suffer from racism, and not just in the workplace at the hands of corporate America. The greatest threat to the development of a vigorous Hispanic consumer market, in fact, arises from racial animus by government. In the same way that, for most of the twentieth century, African-American aspirations were undermined by segregation, in the twenty-first century, Hispanics are subjected to action by government that disenfranchise and devalue their worth as human beings. Consider the actions taken by San Francisco city government. In an effort to protect his supporters who were under investigation for racism against Hispanics, Mayor Willie Brown ordered the San Francisco Human Rights Commission to suspend all ongoing investigations into complaints against partners at two law firms accused of providing legal services to an organization accused of being anti-Hispanic. Here one sees how government's decision to deny Hispanics due process under the law—had Mayor Brown not politicized the matter, the Human Rights Commission would have investigated the issues to determine the merits of the complaints—what emerges is a series of decisions that demean the lives of Hispanics by denying them equal justice under the law. Whether it is a misguided policy to deny Hispanics the right to renew their driver's license in West Virginia, or the right of Hispanics to have their complaints investigated by human rights commissions in California, it is racial animus by government that remains as the most compelling threat to Hispanics—and to the growth of a healthy Hispanic consumer market.

The Phenomenon of *Poca Cultura*

One reason that Mexicans in the United States encounter discrimination is the cultural differences between them and mainstream American society. While the obvious reason (racial differences between whites, blacks, and indigenous people) will be addressed in the next section, it is important to understand the other differences that are as important.

Not everyone in this world is as privileged as this writer, or this reader. There are hundreds of millions of people who lead difficult lives, characterized by dire material need. The illegal immigrants from Mexico are among the most disenfranchised members of Mexican society. Little has been written about the cultural differences of the millions of Mexicans who have attempted to enter the United States illegally. Illegal aliens tend to have an average of four years of schooling, are predominantly from impoverished rural or inner-city communities, and have an indigenous ethnic background. Significant numbers of them are not fluent in Spanish, preferring to speak in one of the indigenous languages, many of which are related to the Nahuatl (Aztec) and Maya family of languages, not widely known outside the immediate geographic area where they originate.[67]

"I live in Marin County, where a part of the community is fighting against the Latin American immigrants," Isabel Allende told *Mother Jones*, surprised at California's continued resistance to the migration of indigenous people across the continent that is as much theirs as it is anyone else's. "People are terrified because they see these dark men standing in groups waiting for someone to offer a job. That's very threatening. Because they don't know them and don't understand their ways or their language, they feel that these men are criminals, that they don't pay their share in this society and yet they benefit. That is not true. . . . They come here to do the kind of work that no American will ever do. You will not be able to stop them. They will integrate. Sooner or later, their children will be with the white children in the schools. It's unavoidable: In 20 years they will be part of this society, just as the Jews are, the Irish, everybody."[68]

Acculturation is a process, and Mexico is a polyglot nation that encompasses more than fifty distinct indigenous peoples and dozens of immigrant cultures, mostly from Europe but also from the Middle East, Africa, and Asia, and the process of acculturation is not a uniform one. The complaint leveled against Mexico as a nation by the Zapatistas, for instance, centers on the fact that many indigenous communities are "excluded" from modernity, which means they are not able to prosper materially in a market economy.[69] When Americans (of Mexican ancestry or not) visit a "village" somewhere in Mexico where not everyone there is conversant in Spanish, this poses a problem. On the one hand, it is a testament to the inclusive nature of the Mexican state, where language is not "imposed" on a people. At the same time, such bold affirmations of identity disenfranchise that community by virtue of their members not being able to participate actively in the nation's socioeconomic life.

That one can be excluded by language is not unique to Mexico, of course. In the United States, debates rage on how both immigrants who do not have a command of English and inner-city black youth who speak Ebonics each encounters obstacles succeeding in life. The importance of being fluent in standard written English is clear to all, especially managers who are frustrated by the lack of reading, writing, and math skills among high school graduates in the United States. Canadians and Mexicans alike are incredulous that the wealthiest nation in the world graduates functional illiterates, young adults who believe Canada is part of the United States and New Mexico is a foreign country.

In Mexico, likewise, there have been opposing initiatives on how best to strike a balance between respecting indigenous cultures and providing the kind of education that is required to participate fully in the nation's life. While the educators at Mexico's National Indigenous Institute (INI), plead for increased funding to publish and teach in indigenous languages, officials at the Education Secretary argue that everyone must be taught to speak Spanish fluently first and foremost. Indigenous elites have, as Haskett explained, understood the importance of being "bilingual," that is, fluent in their own language and that of the dominant society. At one time that meant having a command of Nahuatl, the Aztec language, which after the conquest was replaced by Spanish as the dominant language, the new *lingua franca*.

This process of adopting *normas hispanas* is, in fact, acculturation. It is an uneven process, but a process that has a human face. Consider one young Maya woman who came to work in my grandmother's household. During the 1930s and 1940s, electricity was delivered to many rural communities in the Yucatán peninsula for the first time. Telephone service would follow years later. Sometime around 1937 or 1938, when electricity first arrived in a small Maya hamlet, it caused a great commotion. Among the villagers, it was a cause for celebration which included showing motion pictures projected on the side of the church.

The images of the city captivated the imagination of a young woman named Rosario May. She resolved to visit the large city closest to her village, the city of Mérida. To earn enough for passage on the second-class bus, she set up a table by the speed bumps on the road leading through the center of their town. She sold papayas, oranges, tangerines, jicama, avocados, and tamarinds to motorists who slowed down as they entered the pedestrian zone. When she felt she had enough, without asking permission from her parents, she took off.

Upon arriving in Mérida, she decided to explore the city on foot and was taken aback by all the lights, trolleys, big buildings, cars, and enormous stores around her. In due course, her meager resources were depleted, and she did not even have enough money for a return ticket to her village. She did not want to leave, not only because the city was so exciting, but also because she feared her parents' anger. In the central market she talked to other Maya women and explained her situation. One vendor suggested she go to a neighborhood called García Ginerés and ask, house by house, if there was any housework to be done. She was told not to be intimidated; many of the houses were big, with wrought-iron gates and had dogs, but if she rang gently and smiled, people would be kind. Thus in the course of walking from one gated estate to another, she came to my grandmother's house.

"She must have been fourteen or fifteen," my grandmother said. "There she was, a poor peasant girl, in a dirty *huipil* dress and worn sandals, asking in broken Spanish phrases if there was any laundry she could wash for ten *centavos*." How Rosario May came to enter my grandmother's household and eventually became a member of the staff is not an unusual tale.[70] It has been repeated millions of times by people who wanted to have more options and greater opportunities in their lives.

Imagine if the characters on *The Beverly Hillbillies* had arrived in Beverly Hills—but without a fortune. Indoor plumbing is unheard-of to them, and they call swimming pools "cement ponds." What we consider "culture shock" is what continues to occur throughout Mexico. In Mexico, a kind phrase used to describe the various state of acculturation is referring to situations in which someone demonstrates *poca cultura*, literally, "little culture." More than what Americans refer to as a *faux pas*, in Mexico, *poca cultura* implies that employers have to "educate" workers and servants.

The comic situations in which the characters on the *The Beverly Hillbillies* found themselves is representative of a learning curve that is not uncommon in Mexico. Stories about startling incidents that employers have encountered with their workers and their staffs are legendary. Since the 1980s, however, the phrase *poca cultura* has changed. It no longer refers only to a new employee who has to be told time and again that shoes must be worn at all times, or a new maid who has to be told that one does not use the hot tub for washing clothes.[71] Not all accounts of the shenanigans of people of *poca cultura* are innocuous, however. Writing of the drama that followed the introduction of daylight savings time, a story over the Associated Press wire poked fun at the turmoil. "Imported in 1996 from the United States, the time change has yet to win the hearts and minds of Mexicans, many of whom—most according to some informal polls—feel it disrupts their biological clocks. One leftist congressman even blamed it for stealing sleep and disrupting Mexicans' sex lives."[72]

The phenomenon of "gente humilde," or "humble people" who exhibit "little culture" is not unique to Latin America. "I had decided that St. Louis was a foreign country," Maya Angelou writes of her childhood impressions in her autobiography, *I Know Why the Caged Bird Sings*. "I would never get used to the scurrying sounds of flushing toilets, or the packaged foods, or doorbells or the noise of cars and trains and buses that crashed through the walls or slipped under the doors."[73]

This was the way of the world for most of the twentieth century. In a more general sense today, *poca cultura* is more often used to denote someone who is either not up to the minute with the latest, or displays a garish custom. Someone who throws litter from his car, or lights up a cigarette without asking permission, or commits a social gaffe is described as having "little culture."[74] With greater frequency, one hears this remark made of Americans, especially as NAFTA unfolds, and usually in the context of manners. Sliding business cards across conference tables, failing to shake hands firmly while making eye contact, or displaying other lapses in judgment raises eyebrows.[75]

In my youth, my generation dismissed with the acronym "NQOC" (not quite our class) those we disparaged or ridiculed. The inappropriate putdowns of young, immature adults, however, are not relegated to pretentious snobs. This is true wherever there are people anywhere in the world.[76] When Fidel Castro made a state visit to France in 1995, for example, immediately after a toast in his honor at one event, a Spanish diplomat turned to me and commented on his surprise at Castro's *poca cultura*. I looked up, and sure enough, the Cuban leader was holding his glass of wine improperly.

The plight of people of *poca cultura*, however, suffuses life in Mexico and Latin America. If *The Beverly Hillbillies* stands out as one of the few programs in the United States to address the process of acculturation as society modernizes, consider how in Mexico this process gave rise to an entire *genre* of entertainment. Mario Moreno, the comic and film star, became famous portraying "Cantinflas," a naïve but endearing country bumpkin, or peasant, whose adventures and misadventures in the big city were the stuff of dozens of comedies.[77] The appeal of Cantinflas was that he was a foil to the pretensions of city slickers who looked down on country folk who lacked all manner of sophistication. Like American portrayals of "hayseeds" and "country bumpkins," the conflict between urban "sophisticates" and "simple" country people comes out of the growth of cities and the emptying of the countryside.

In fact, these themes, how country innocence gets the better of city slickers and the misadventures of country people in the big city, affirm that something is lost as one adopts modernity. The city's disdain for the country among Mexican urbanites, however, stood until the late 1940s when Frida Kahlo embraced and popularized native dress as a bold affirmation of indigenous identity. That is not to say that romanticizing "country" values is not without drawbacks; modernity does offer certain advantages, not the least of which is education.

Imagine: Mexico's disenfranchised in the 2000s are not unlike the disenfranchised during the Great Depression. The great failure of Mexico in the twentieth century is that it was not able to give its people an education that allowed them to think analytically and critically. The illiteracy of the most disenfranchised Mexicans stands in sharp contrast to the aspirations of Hispanics as a people; it remains one of the great challenges for officials on both sides of the border. As my grandmother remarked about the multitudes arriving in the cities from the countryside, "This isn't about 'barbarians' being or not being at the gates, but it is about giving the less privileged amongst us an opportunity—and keeping Ellie Mae from hand-washing Jethro's overalls in the cement pond."[78]

The Nature of "Lookism"

It is not enough to repeat the platitude that appearances can be deceiving, or that books can't be judged by their covers. Making rapid-fire judgments based solely on appearances is one skill that allowed early human beings to survive the dangers they encountered in prehistoric times. It is ironic, then, that a trait hard-wired into our brains now threatens our survival as a species. "We perform individual, rational acts of discrimination all the time," Andrew Sullivan notes, criticizing the ban on the use of genetic information to discriminate in either insurance or employment. "In fact, it would be hard to function without them. Deciding not to put an art historian in charge of a nuclear power plant is not bias but common sense. Similarly, discriminating against a blind person when hiring a baseball umpire is certainly not a function of hostility to blind people in general. . . . Sure it's discrimination—but it's rational discrimination."[79] But other forms of discrimination, those based solely on looks, occur every day. "People think if you have black hair you must be Mexican," Ada Aguilar, who lives in Birmingham, Alabama, told *Newsweek.* "But my grandfather was of Spanish descent. [We] Peruvians are a combination of the Incas and the Spanish, and the Spanish come from Germany, France, Italy, Arabia—it's a never-ending story."[80]

So, too, with the distinction between "racism" and "lookism." The former refers to a set of characteristics and assumptions based a person's race. The latter refers to discrimination based on appearances: a person's weight, height, age, and whether or not a person approximates society's ideals of beauty. Women, who are subjected to men's gaze every day, are sensitive to this kind of objectification.[81] The fat, the short, the old, and the homely face discrimination every day of their lives in their professional, social, and private lives.[82]

There are times when biases overlap and it is only from a distance that one gains an instructive perspective. Janet McDonald, an African-American woman who grew up in the projects in Brooklyn, attended Vassar, went on to law school, and went to work in Paris:

> In France, I was liberated. . . . No one judged me on specifics, and I had nothing to prove. The French saw me as just another American, though I didn't see myself that way at all. I viewed Americans as white patriots in "Love it or Leave it" T-shirts, with a flag on their lawns, who didn't want me in school with their children. I was black, period. The French drew no such distinctions, which meant I no longer had to worry about making *African-Americans* look good. Or bad. Whatever I did was attributed to Americanness, not blackness. What a switch—a black person with the power to make white people look bad.[83]

The full implications of these experiences coalesced after Cornell West spoke in Paris. Janet McDonald spoke to him about how the French didn't see her as "black" but as "American"—and how they subsequently treated her as a "full" human being, instead of a macabre stereotype of "blackness."

West suggested that it was because she was educated and well-mannered and carried herself in a respectful and respecting manner. "But I wonder how welcome you would be made to feel if you showed up with some of the girls from your 'hood," she quotes him as asking her. "But if my girls from the 'hood in the Brooklyn projects were treated differently than I'm treated," she wondered out loud when interviewed on *This American Life* on National Public Radio, "then it's not about race, but about class."[84]

"Lookism" succinctly explains Anthony DePalma's anecdote about the American businessman who was turned away at a restaurant when he and his family showed up with their Indian maid. Lookism, of course, works both ways. In the late 1980s I was given a tour of Fiesta America Condessa resort in Cancún as it was being remodeled. As the construction manager pointed out the marble floors in the lobby, one marketing executive, a New Yorker, commented to another, a San Franciscan, that it was "waste" to use marble on the lobby when "obese Midwesterners" were the bulk of the expected hotel guests. "Those people look like baked lobsters" after their first day at the beach, one said to the other. Their fellow citizens, they feared, would "ruin the scenery" by vacationing here, the other replied to the first.

Is the suggestion, then, that only thin people merit marble floors? Or that only Americans from the East or West Coast are entitled to luxuriate when on holiday?[85] The bias against the fat and short (one is reminded of Paul Simon's confession: "Any short man who tells you that it doesn't bother him to be short is lying to you") also applies to those who are "homely."[86] Consider Camille Paglia's criticism of Prince Charles's relationship with Camilla Parker-Bowles. "I think it unsettles people that Camilla Parker-Bowles seems so unbeautiful," Paglia writes. "There's something kind of witchy and harridan-like about her. If she had been a very alluring model or someone of conventional female attractiveness, I think people might have felt, well, now Diana is a mother, it often happens that the husband begins to stray. But to see Charles fall under the sway of this woman without any conventionally appealing female attributes implied to us that there was some strange psychodrama going on in Prince Charles' unconscious. That in some way, what was she—a shadowy image of his own mother? It felt like this unsavory, decadent stuff was going on in the House of Windsor."[87]

Rather than challenging this bias, the editors of Salon.com see nothing wrong with this discussion. In fact, our cultural indulgence in the vanity of appearance is so ingrained that it manifests itself in outrageous complicity in how we value a person's looks.[88] Thus a few sentences later, Andrew Ross makes this statement: "Diana did us all a favor by dying when she did, at 36, with her beautiful image frozen in our minds, before she got older and went even further downhill." Camilla Paglia then reflects, "That's very persuasive." Then she continues, "We look back at James Dean and he's crystallized as how he looked at that moment. *Giant* had just premiered a day or so earlier, and it was one of his greatest performances. On the other hand, Bob Dylan, if he had died in that motorcycle accident in the mid-60s, we would remember him then at his artistic height, rather than now, dragging himself around the world, abusing his own songs and lyrics."[89]

Is looking good, then, more important than having a long, happy life?[90] (In a perverse way this makes impeccable sense: since the old face discrimination, one remedy is not to live long enough to be subjected to the discrimination of "ageism.") Princess Diana is thus deprived entirely of her humanity and reduced to being our muse. The media's emphasis on Western standards of beauty is related in magazines, television, and film, often to the detriment of the self-image of those who do not conform to these standards. Since the 1950s, for instance, young American women have suffered from eating disorders, a byproduct of the poor body image they have when they compare themselves to impossible ideals. By the 1990s, medical problems arising from a negative body image began to affect young American men in record numbers.[91]

For Hispanics, the problem is more acute. Apart from the images the media disseminates, Hispanics have to cope with "lookism," where the short, the dark-skinned, and the overweight are held in disdain. How one looks, and how the media portray beauty, at times intersect at the crossroads of public policy and the language of beauty. In the mid-1990s, for instance, because of lingering issues surrounding apartheid in South Africa, it was difficult for South Africans to secure work visas in the United States, and some were denied tourist visas as well. Through an acquaintance, I learned that several high-powered modeling agencies in Los Angeles found a way around these encumbrances. They arranged for some models to fly to Mexico City, then connect to Tijuana, where they were met by some of the agency's staff, given other young women's California licenses, and simply walked into the United States.

Intrigued, I offered to drive from Los Angeles to Tijuana on one such run. After a drink, the young women—blonde, blue-eyed, slim, and almost all six feet tall—were given the licenses of other young blonde California women. Our entire group of seven was waved on through, presumably because all young blonde women look alike, and also because young blonde women have the look the INS does not scrutinize at this port of entry. Illegal aliens who look like they belong in the *Sports Illustrated* swimsuit issue thus enter the United States with impunity, while other Americans are made to wait in line and are looked over suspiciously.[92] In all likelihood, George P. Bush would be stopped and questioned by the same officials who were waving the South African illegal aliens on through with a smile.

Lookism poses problems for Hispanics. "That cultural swirl is what I've always thought of as the living definition of 'Chicano,' although many who claim the moniker prefer a connection to the mystical Indian past, as in Carlos Castañeda's peyote visions, or urge righteous rebellion against the white man," Rubén Martínez writes in *Crossing Over.* "I think about my own connection to Indian Mexico, if I even have one. My grandfather looked like an Indian—wide nose, bronze skin, short stature. But my grandfather also sang opera and drove a Cadillac in Los Angeles in the late 1950s. Was my grandfather still an Indian? And me—I've got a thin Castilian nose and the hair of a Moor."[93]

Everyone the world over struggles with his or her identity, what it means to belong to a specific group, whether it is racial, ethnic or religious. When darker-skinned Mexicans agonize over being "mixed," what they are speaking about, in reality, is lookism. In Latin America, for instance, the running joke about Argentina is instructive: "An Argentine is an Italian who speaks Spanish, wishes he were English, acts like he is French, and suffers under a German army." (Note, however, that all these "mixtures" are of Caucasians, so there is nothing that would visually differentiate an Argentine of Italian descent from an Argentine of German ancestry.) The oppressive nature of lookism, however, is an obsession for Americans of Mexican Ancestry (AMAs) who do not "look" American.

"I am in the middle of America, in Norwalk, Wis. (population 607), a village nestled in the green hills of Amish and Mennonite country," Rubén Martínez, again, reports. "Norwalk is not exactly the kind of place where you would expect to find America's new paradigm of race. But here it is, before my eyes. Kerry Vian, an affable white woman, is sitting on the front lawn bouncing her 2-year-old son, Chance, in her arms. Javier, Chance's father, a dark brown man a few inches shorter than Kerry, sits nearby with a crew of friends from his hometown in the provincial Mexican state of Guanajuato."[94]

The "look" of mixed-race couples, where one partner "looks" foreign, poses a problem for Hispanic families. In New York City, for instance, federal officials admit that immigration raids "may have violated the federal agency's guidelines for avoiding ethnic or racial profiling," since "agents appeared to rely almost exclusively on Latino appearances or foreign accents . . . to reach a conclusion that workers could be illegal immigrants."

Lookism undeniably plays a significant role in targeting Hispanics and constitutes a form of intimidation. "The I.N.S. seems to equate Latino physical and cultural characteristics with illegality—that is, with being an undocumented immigrant," Michael Wishnie, the director of the Immigration Law Clinic at New York University Law School, told reporter Susan Sachs.[95]

A life-affirming example that illustrates how lookism has nothing to do with race, or ethnicity, but does influence immigrants' success, is in order. While AMAs such as Martínez and Rodriguez write with anguish about their respective dissatisfaction with their looks, not all Hispanics are beholden to the negative impact of lookism. Cubans, who are primarily of direct European descent, Dominicans, who are of mixed white and black ancestry, and Puerto Ricans, who come in every possible hue, seldom harbor negative views about their looks. Miami Cubans and New York Dominicans shine with pride in their physical appearance, something that distinguishes Caribbean Hispanics from Mexican Hispanics in the United States.

It can be argued that a positive self-image translates into success on the public stage of civil life, both economic and political. "The [immigrant refugees] from today's Cuba are the children of a revolution that provided social guarantees but limited opportunities," Mireya Navarro reported. "The people from an earlier Cuba, and their children, have grown into a Miami Who's Who. The mayors of the city and county of Miami, the county police chief and the county state attorney are all Cuban-born or of Cuban descent. So is the president of the largest bank, the owner of the largest real estate developer, the managing partner of the largest law firm, nearly half of the county's 27-member delegation in the Legislature and two of its six members of Congress. About the only accomplishment Cuban-Americans cannot claim is regaining their country."[96]

Now consider Martínez once more. "The sheer power that race still holds on our imagination is the reason America's latest generation of 'foreigners'—Mexicans, Russians, Chinese, Sikhs—has, to greater and lesser degrees, been racialized, even when the shade of difference is not, literally speaking, racial at all. Often when we say 'race' we mean 'nationality' or 'ethnicity' or even 'religion' or 'culture.' We say race when we mean class. We say race when we mean fear."[97]

We say *race*, oddly enough, when we mean . . . *ugly*.[98]

"Certainly, the whitest dinner party I ever attended was a Mexico City dinner party where a Mexican squire of exquisite manner, mustache, and flan-like jowl, expressed himself surprised, so surprised, to learn that I am a writer," Richard Rodriguez, who used to stare at the "Indian" in the mirror, reports. "*Un escritor . . . un escritor . . .*? Turning the word on a lathe . . . until: 'You know, in Mexico, I think we do not have writers who look like you,' he said."[99] Then Rodriguez, a slave to lookism, makes a presumption consistent with the pessimistic spirit that haunts him: "He meant dark skin, thick lips, Indian nose, bugger your mother."[100]

Rather than thinking, as I always do whenever I see Rodriguez walk into a room, that he looks not *oppressed* (Indian), but *depressed* (American), he translates an innocuous statement into a racial one. Being depressed, as part of a professional literary career, is strictly an American phenomenon, whether it is a writer like Elie Wiesel or Andrew Solomon. But depression itself is not a literary genre, despite what Wiesel or Rodriguez would have us believe. In the United States, life-affirming literature about the American experience of Mexico is best exemplified by Sandra Cisneros, whose two novels, *The House on Mango Street* and *Caramelo*, tell stories of dignity, and courage, and record the *meaning* of the human experience of people whose lives are shaped, but are not defined, by the consequences of the Mexican-American War.[101]

Summary

1. The Mexican diaspora has struggled with issues of "rootlessness," one manifestation of which has been the mythmaking literature of the Chicano movement concerning Aztlán, an ancient homeland of the imagination.
2. Mexican officials, seeking to reach out to Americans of Mexican ancestry, continue to grow alarmed at the "cult of victimology" that characterizes many Latino and Mexican-American organizations, a development that makes AMAs vulnerable to being used by unscrupulous political leaders.
3. The prevalence of lookism in the three NAFTA nations increases racism and discrimination that AMAs encounter, simply because the Mexicans in the United States are of Native American ancestry.

Conclusion

The Hispanization of the United States offers a series of unprecedented challenges for corporate America, for never before has such an enormous segment of Americans embarked on becoming a part of the nation's life while linguistically and culturally choosing to remain apart.[1] As we have seen, Hispanics are racially and economically diverse consumers. Baseball great Sammy Sosa, who is black, is as much a Hispanic as is actress Cameron Díaz, who is white; New Mexico Governor Bill Richardson is as Hispanic as socialite Carolina Herrera. This "racial diversity" also holds true for economic status. Cuban-American, white-collar professionals who are well-heeled members of the middle class in Miami are as Hispanic as are Mexican-American blue-collar workers who are struggling members of the working class in Los Angeles.

This is a portrait of a highly fragmented consumer market, one that requires differentiated marketing and merchandising strategies. It also underscores the breathtaking speed with which Hispanic ascendancy is making itself felt throughout the United States. Harvard's Henry Louis Gates Jr. chaired a "black studies" conference in which African-American leaders began to discuss how Hispanics "threatened" blacks' "privileged position" in the United States; Hispanics have never held a similar conference to discuss how to "organize" their ascendancy. It is something that has happened, through the natural evolution of historical forces first unleashed in 1492.

One of my objectives in this book has been to present Hispanics in a way that offers insights and an understanding that has eluded corporate managers. For decades managers throughout corporate America have been undermined by lack of insightful market research—recall the primitive and misguided "findings" in the R.J. Reynolds "analysis"—and by their failure to accept that Hispanics have broken the linguistic model of immigrant behavior that had previously been the norm. Hispanics defy America's black-white racial paradigm that has been the subtext of American life since the arrival of the first slaves, requiring corporate America to, for the first time, think "outside the racial box" that has defined the United States. Hispanics, furthermore, defy acculturation by creating a viable "parallel" economy that is based on the cultural-linguistic heritage that does not accept fully an Anglophone worldview. Not unlike other nations, such as Canada (English-French) or Belgium (French-Belgian), the United States is becoming a bilingual nation, where the battle over how Nielsen Media Research measures television audiences now defines the battle for the Hispanic consumer market.

What does this mean in the Age of Hispanic Ascendancy?

For centuries, throughout the Spanish-speaking world, the phrase "gente sin razón" has been used to differentiate between people who are deemed "reasonable" from those who are "unreasonable."[2] In the same way that American society has obsessed, to the point of pathology—on the nature of race—who is "white" and who is "black"—Hispanics have a long tradition of classifying people into "gente *sin* razón" and "gente *de* razón." Here, however, is where the fluid nature of Hispanic culture offers an epiphany. Whereas a person *without* reason (sin razón) can become a person *of* reason (de razón), in American society it is impossible for one person to go from one race to another. This is fundamental to understanding the breathtaking diversity among Hispanics, where someone like New Mexico governor Bill Richardson and Cuban-American singer Celia Cruz are equally Hispanic. The designation of being "reasonable" refers to a person's way of looking at the world that is consistent with the principles reinforced during the Age of Enlightenment. In much the same way that viewers saw the characters on *The Beverly Hillbillies* become more sophisticated during the course of that television series, similar themes in Hispanic culture center on this kind of progression, of both individuals and a society.

For corporate America, it is imperative to understand the aspirations that characterize American Hispanics, for "reasonableness" plays the same role among Hispanics as "race" does in American society. Indeed, whereas in English America people were defined by the color of their skin, in Spanish America individuals have historically been "classified"—or treated—according to the perceived level of their "reasonableness." The former, like Protestantism, excludes, while the latter, like Catholicism, is inclusive by nature.

To understand the Hispanic emphasis on ascertaining an individual's "reasonableness," consider the frustrations you encounter, both business and personal, that are thrust upon you by unreasonable people!

Hispanics therefore aspire to "belong" by improving their "reasonableness," which is achieved through individual progress. Hispanics are aware that their success is undermined by their lack of a formal education, but they are ambivalent about the obligations to their families that undermine the pursuit of higher education. They are cognizant of the professional limitations imposed by their lack of language skills, and they are frustrated by their inability to master English while losing fluency in Spanish, availing themselves of the slang "Spanglish." They are concerned about immigration laws that discriminate, as they are enraged by the sustained racism of American society (and how discrimination and racism continue to impact their labor rights). They are concerned with reconciling the conflicts that arise between paternalism (the social welfare state) and individual initiative (private-sector enterprise and entrepreneurship).

Taken together, these are the cultural "bleeps" on the radar screen of Hispanic life in the United States that blink brightly. How goods and services that address these concerns are marketed, however, must reflect a fundamental understanding of the essence of these concerns and aspirations. As we examine each of these issues, several surprising—if not unpleasant—facts will be revealed that are as counterintuitive as they are offensive to mainstream sensibilities. For instance, the majority of Mexicans who enter the United States illegally have no desire to remain in this country forever. This challenges the American myth that the world's "huddled masses" who are "yearning to breathe free" wish to make a make a clean break with their past and start new lives in the United States.

Recall in the "How Race Is Lived in America" series published by the *New York Times* how Charlie LeDuff described the emerging racial tensions in North Carolina. Of the surprising arrival of Mexican immigrants to rural North Carolina, lured by radio ads in Mexico promising "good" work at a meatpacking plant in Robeson County, a "young black man had heard enough." The Mexicans, blacks complained, "stood in groups on the street corners." The black residents "never knew what they were saying." The Mexicans "took the jobs and did them for less." While blacks lived in trailers and substandard housing, some of these Mexicans "had houses in Mexico."[3]

These Mexican immigrants, in other words, were working in the United States to maintain—and expand—their homes in Mexico, to which they would return after having accrued enough savings to start their own businesses. The Mexicans in North Carolina arrived there as one arrives in Purgatory: in a state of ambivalence, in the condition of being neither here (in the United States) nor there (in Mexico). When one speaks to these Mexicans, who work long shifts, live in overcrowded conditions, but send their money back home every month to allow those left behind to buy satellite dishes and add new bathrooms, certain things become evident.

These Mexicans are grateful for an opportunity to work and earn dollars in the United States. They regret that their circumstances forced them to leave Mexico in order to get ahead in life. They acknowledge that, had they been afforded an opportunity to get a job or an education in Mexico, they would not have left for the United States. They realize they are "foreigners" in the United States, a country that is not theirs, and a country to which most do not aspire to belong, and the overwhelming majority of Mexicans who enter the United States illegally subsequently return to Mexico. They know they will return to Mexico after having saved a predetermined amount of money ($12,000–$15,000, usually), or after a certain amount of time (five to seven years, usually). They are not "yearning to breathe free," but merely "yearning to be gainfully employed." That they don't see themselves as having moved permanently to the United States is important, for it affects everything about their lives in this country. Indeed, these aspirations change only when there is a life event: that they have a child born in the United States.

Mexico's president Vicente Fox has taken the initiative in undoing the evil advanced by writer Octavio Paz. For two generations, Mexicans have been taught to consider U.S. Hispanics of Mexican ancestry as "turncoats." This view has been encouraged by undeniable, and unpleasant, facts. Mexican immigrants to the United States have been poor, uneducated, largely Native American. In other words, these are *gente humilde* who are of *poca cultura* and whom most Mexicans believe were forced to leave Mexico because they were unable to succeed in Mexico by virtue of being "*gente sin razón.*" Called "victims" by Paz, he claimed they were to be pitied and ignored.

This is all instructive, for it allows marketers to fine-tune strategies for meeting the needs of the majority of this segment of the Hispanic market. The question of education, the surprising issue of language, and how immigration and labor rights have become intertwined, the role of lookism in the United States, and the important ways in which Hispanic "aspirational" behavior defies traditional understanding are all interwoven in the fabric of American life in the Age of Hispanic Ascendancy.

Epilogue

Hispanic ascendancy could not have been possible without the African-American civil rights movement. Hispanics are thus indebted to African-Americans, for they paved the way that Hispanics can now follow as they take their rightful place in the life of this nation. When I return to my home in New York, I am emboldened by defiance: One looks up and the towers aren't there, but that does not mean the World Trade Center is truly gone. There are obstacles that we, as individuals and societies, face, but we can rise above them, to persevere and prevail. A certain patient, nonjudgmental generosity toward each other is in order as Americans—English- and Spanish-speakers alike—embark on this grand experiment that is integration.

"Companies are doing good when they do what they do responsibly, whether it's Ford making cars or Exxon producing oil," John R. Boatright, author of *Ethics and the Conduct of Business,* has argued.[1] It would be unreasonable to ignore the socioeconomic "megatrend" of Hispanic ascendancy in the United States. The only reasonable response is to acknowledge there has never been a better time to live and work in the United States, for there have never been as many promising business opportunities as there are now.

Hispanic ascendancy, finally, demands reflection: How does America's unfinished business in addressing the legacy of slavery affect its future?

A man arrives as far as he can, not as far as he wishes, Vasco Nuñez de Bilboa wrote in the sixteenth century, after giving up his search for El Dorado in his lamentation to the king of Spain. There is something to be said for accepting the way of the world, mindful that by doing right we are doing our part to make this world a better place. In March 2002, in connection with "Missing," an exhibition of the missing persons fliers distributed by the loved ones of those who died in the attack on the World Trade Center then making its way around the United States, I had occasion to have dinner with Kenneth

Kirkley in the nation's capital. We have been good friends since 1991, when I lived for a year in Washington, D.C. We went to a favorite Japanese restaurant in Georgetown and caught up on each other's lives. Kirkley, an attorney educated at Harvard, works for the World Bank. Over dinner, the topics of conversation covered many subjects, from the World Bank's reaction to Argentina's default on its foreign debt, to my being called an "American hero" by White House officials for work organizing "Missing." Kirkley and I have had many long discussions over many things over the years, and as a result, we have arrived at the kind of understanding only possible when you agree and clash with someone you trust. And so there are times when we can communicate with only a short phrase or a slight gesture.

After dinner, as we walked out, it turned out that he had left his car near Union Station, and I had another engagement not far from the Watergate. "Different taxis," he said, then gave a slight shrug and a mischievous grin. Instantly I knew the drill: I stepped between parked cars, raised my hand, and within less than a minute, a taxi stopped. I opened the door. "Always an American hero," Kirkley said, mocking. I then leaned in the front passenger window to tell the driver the destination. Kirkley, shaking his head slightly, waved good-bye, and off he went.

At this point it is almost unnecessary to point out that Kenneth Kirkley is black, and in the nation's capital in the first decade of the twenty-first century, taxis are still reluctant to stop for black men after sundown.

Over the years, in New York, San Francisco, Miami, Chicago, and, of course, Washington, D.C., I have had to hail cabs for black friends and colleagues many times, so much so that the fact no longer needs to be articulated. This tragic situation, however unfortunate, is the way of the world, and it is a fact of life in the United States at the beginning of the twenty-first century. It should not be, and it is a moral obligation of U.S. Hispanics to work to right these continuing wrongs.

This book is dedicated to the legacy of Martin Luther King Jr.

Notes

Introduction

1. Lynette Clemetson, "Hispanics Now Largest Minority, Census Shows," *New York Times*, January 22, 2003.

2. Felicia R. Lee, "New Topic in Black Studies Debate: Latinos," *New York Times*, February 1, 2003.

3. Anthony DePalma, *Here: A Biography of the New American Continent* (New York: Public Affairs, 2001), 235.

4. Randall Robinson, *The Debt: What America Owes to Blacks* (New York: E.P. Dutton, 2000), 90.

5. The westernmost peninsula on the European continent was named "Iberia," a probable reference to the rivers that run through it; "iber" is Celt for "river." "Spain" itself is derived from "Spania," meaning the land of the rabbits.

6. Katharina Wilson, *Hrotsvit of Gandershein: A Florilegium of Her Works* (Rochester, NY: D.S. Brewer, 1998).

7. Christopher Columbus was Italian, of course. The reason it was necessary to have someone fluent in Arabic aboard was simple: In the fifteenth century, Arabic was the language of diplomacy, and it was presumed that, upon arriving in India, communication would be conducted in that language.

8. This excerpt comes from a draft marketing report prepared for R.J. Reynolds Tobacco Company and released as part of the confidential papers made public in the civil trial of *Mangini vs. R.J. Reynolds*. The document is undated but was likely prepared in the late 1980s.

9. Private communication between Putnam and McDonagh, quoted in *Bowling Alone: The Collapse and Revival of American Community* (New York: Simon & Schuster, 2000), 362.

10. DePalma, *Here*, 151.

11. Tim Weiner, "Bank Calls Purchase Way to Woo Hispanics," *New York Times*, December 12, 2002.

12. Robert Rubin's remarks were made at a news conference in Mexico City, May 17, 2001.

13. Weiner, "Bank Calls Purchase Way to Woo Hispanics."

14. Clemetson, "Hispanics Now Largest Minority, Census Shows."

15. Personal communication with Douglas Massey of the University of Pennsylvania's Mexican Migration Project, May 2001.

16. Marvin Matises, "Send Ethnographers into New-SKU Jungle," *Brandweek*, September 25, 2000, 32–34.

17. In theory, however, everyone, by virtue of being born on the planet, has the same right to go wherever he or she pleases; no one has a greater claim to being an "earthling" than anyone else. Whether exercising this right to go anywhere is practical or desirable is another matter altogether.

18. Fernando Margain and Walter Russell Mead, "A Fast Track for Mexico," *New York Times*, June 24, 2001. Fernando Margain, from the National Action Party, is chairman of the Foreign Relations Committee of the Mexican Senate. Walter Russell Mead is senior fellow at the Council on Foreign Relations. Mexican officials continue to express their concern over the persistent violation of the human rights of Mexican citizens entering the United States, despite U.S. legislation aimed at curbing abuses— and deaths—along the border. "Mexico has long insisted that it is one thing to have a person cross the border in search of work," Mexican Deputy Foreign Minister Enrique Berruga told Eric Schmitt of the *New York Times*, "and it is another to have that person be subjected to attacks by authorities. We are most interested in preventing people from being hurt simply because they have crossed the border, and this is a very important advance." Eric Schmitt, "Measures Aim at Violence Along Border," *New York Times*, June 24, 2001.

19. The indictment against officials at Tyson Foods for conspiring to engage in the black-market smuggling of Mexican labor is evidence of the desperate strategies some in corporate America have been forced to adopt. The last time American businessmen were forced to become criminals was during Prohibition. (Other kinds of business-men—drug traffickers—likewise exploit the disparities that arise when private wants are in conflict with public policy.) Smuggling humans is a growing business world-wide. "The human cargo recently seized at sea indicates to some American and Mexican officials that the flow of illegal immigrants may be beginning a new surge and that the heightened land security [after September 11, 2001] may be no more effective than hazard cones on a highway," Ginger Thompson reported. "Rather than stopping the flow of immigrants, the measures may be forcing smugglers onto uncharted, un-marked routes." "Migrants From Afar See Mexico as Steppingstone to U.S.," *New York Times*, March 1, 2002.

20. In the United States it is exceptional to find academics in politics, and for good reason. Henry Kissinger, for his part, remains, in the opinion of greater numbers of people, an unindicted "war criminal." A persuasive argument is presented by Christopher Hitchens in *The Trial of Henry Kissinger* (New York: Verso, 2001). "If killing hundreds of thousands of innocent peasants by dropping millions of tons of bombs on undefended civilian targets is not a war crime, then there are no war crimes," Fred Branfman wrote in his review of Hitchens's book. "Wanted," Salon.com, May 18, 2001.

21. Orlando Patterson, "Race by the Numbers," *New York Times*, May 8, 2001.

Chapter 1

1. There was a certain Cuban resentment in this position, often intended to re-mind Americans that "exile" was a legacy of American intervention in the internal affairs of Cuba.

2. Private communication from Canosa to the author, February 1995.

3. Joan Didion, *Miami* (New York: Vintage International, 1987), 63.

4. Ibid., 63–65.

5. Gary Berman, "The Hispanic Market: Getting Down to Cases," *Sales & Marketing Management* (October 1991).

6. Donatella Lorch, "Is America Any Place for a Nice Hispanic Girl?" *New York Times*, April 11, 1996.

7. Susheela Uhl, "Designing for the Hispanic Market," *Perspectives* (March 1996).

8. Ibid.   ·

9. Robert McCrum, William Cran, and Robert MacNeil, *The Story of English* (Boston: Faber and Faber, BBC Publications, 1986).

10. I doubt Europeans bemoan the introduction of "tomato," an Aztec delicacy: Imagine Italians cooking without tomatoes? I spoke with Phyllis Schlafly in July 2002 by telephone, and she insisted that if "chocolate" is an "Aztec" word, it would have to be replaced. Her organization's Web site is Eagleforum.org.

11. Kenneth J. Cooper, "Reinterpreting Bilingual Classes," *Washington Post*, February 12, 1991.

12. Jacques Steinberg, "Increase in Test Scores Counters Dire Forecasts for Bilingual Ban," *New York Times*, August 20, 2000. Ron K. Unz, the Silicon Valley entrepreneur who spearheaded the campaign to abolish bilingual education, was vindicated. "The test scores these last two years have risen, and risen dramatically," he is quoted as saying. "Something has gone tremendously right for immigrants being educated in California."

13. Pete Hamill, "Henry B. González," in *Profiles in Courage for Our Time*, ed. Caroline Kennedy (New York: Hyperion, 2002), 92–96.

14. Joel Millman, *The Other Americans: How Immigrants Renew Our Country, Our Economy, and Our Values* (New York: Viking), 128.

15. Steinberg, "Increase in Test Scores Counters Dire Forecasts for Bilingual Ban." Tragically, California Democratic leaders have convened several "fact-finding" seminars to study the "problem"—as if schoolchildren learning and scoring higher on standardized tests were a "problem."

16. Marilyn Halter, *Shopping for Identity: The Marketing of Ethnicity* (New York: Schocken, 2000), 56.

17. "The Hispanic market is still somewhat of its own market, but it is making a bridge into the general marketplace," Joe Mandese, editor of *Media Buyer's Daily*, told Elliott. "But the Hispanic networks [Telemundo and Univision] have done a great job marketing themselves by saying, 'These are the demographics who buy your clients' products, and in some instances they're more important than the general market.'" Stuart Elliott, "Hispanic Networks Hone an Edge in a Race for TV Ad Dollars," *New York Times*, May 30, 2002.

18. Mirta Ojito, "To Talk Like New York, Sign Up for Spanish," *New York Times*, October 18, 1999.

19. The complaint also raises the matter of reverse discrimination. There may be no "amigos" on *Friends*, but how many Anglo "friends" are on any of the *telenovelas*, talk shows, and game shows that fill hundreds of broadcast hours on Univision or Telemundo on any given week? Why are Spanish-language networks "ignoring" the non-Hispanic population, which comprises 80 percent of the United States?

20. Mireya Navarro, "Latinos Gain Visibility in Cultural Life of U.S.," *New York Times*, September 19, 1999.

21. Amusement can be found in reading "Conquering Europe, Word for Word," by Peter Schneider, *New York Times*, May 1, 2001, translated into English by Philip Boehm.

22. Jennifer Bingham Hull, "Habla Spanglish?" *American Way*, August 1, 1999. "If you're in South America and you suddenly say something in English, it's a snobby thing to do. It's bad for business. You are going to upset the other person. It sounds like you are trying to show that the person doesn't speak English," Rosa Sugranes, chairman of Miami-based Iberia Tiles Corporation, is quoted as saying in the article, underscoring the challenges of being fluently bilingual.

23. Sue Anne Pressley, "Multicultural D.C. Area Becoming Multilingual," *Washington Post*, February 11, 1992.

24. Robert Putnam, *Bowling Alone: The Collapse and Revival of American Community* (New York: Simon & Schuster, 2000), 371.

25. Hull, "Habla Spanglish?"

26. The nuances of language are such that linguists are now studying how Spanish is changing in the United States. "Now a team of linguists is studying the consequences of the collision of Spanish dialects in New York, looking not only at how that contact is affecting Spanish spoken, but also at what the outcome might suggest about the evolution of Latino identity in the city and beyond," Janny Scott reported in the *New York Times*. One "outcome," of course, is that it is imperative to be proficient in both standard English and Spanish, simply because the inability to converse properly in either is seen as a lack of education. Throughout Latin America few things are as annoying as speaking with a Hispanic who, living in the United States, is unfamiliar with Spanish, for example, using "network" instead of "red" [*red* is Spanish for network! Some will use English "network" when speaking Spanish, which confuses people who speak Spanish but not English]. And in the United States, few things impede one's career advancement as the inability to speak and write in standard English; memoranda with "ain't" does not impress readers in the boardroom. Janny Scott, "In Simple Pronouns, Clues to Shifting Latino Identity," *New York Times*, December 5, 2002.

27. Draft marketing report prepared for R.J. Reynolds Tobacco Company, and released as part of the confidential papers released in the civil trial of *Mangini vs. R.J. Reynolds*. The document is undated, but was likely prepared in the late 1980s.

28. Ibid.

29. This is in contrast to Hispanics in Texas, according to R.J. Reynolds. There, Hispanics have been "here long enough to lose their idealism about this 'land of opportunity.'" As a consequence they see "themselves as a much discriminated-against minority." But they do not riot, which, the tobacco giant argues is "further evidence of the Mexican's passive nature" but, unlike California Hispanics, Texas Hispanics fear "being taken advantage of by the 'Anglo' establishment."

30. Private communication from Lambert to the author, April 1983.

31. Private communication from Cruz to the author, June 2001.

32. Ibid.

33. Roberto Suro, *Strangers Among Us: How Latino Immigration Is Transforming America* (New York: Knopf, 1998), 11–12.

34. Other groups, such as Jews, have for generations also "hidden" their identities to protect their careers. It is not immediately obvious, for instance, that Kirk Douglas [born Issur Danielovitch Demsky] and Winona Ryder [born Winona Horowitz] are Jewish.

35. Personal interview with the author, March 2001.

36. Alisa Valdes-Rodriguez, *The Dirty Girls Social Club* (New York: St. Martin's Press, 2003), 33.

37. Mirta Ojito, "Best of Friends, Worlds Apart," in *How Race Is Lived in America*, introduction by Joseph Lelyveld (New York: Times Books/Henry Holt, 2001), 23.

38. Juan González, *Harvest of Empire: A History of Latinos in America* (New York: Viking, 2000), 92.

39. Ibid.

40. Rodolfo F. Acuña, *Anything but Mexican: Chicanos in Contemporary Los Angeles* (New York: Verso, 1996), 156.

41. Pam Belluck, "Mexican Laborers in U.S. During World War II Sue for Back Pay," *New York Times*, April 29, 2001.

42. Barbara Whitaker, "Judge Dismisses Mexican Laborers' Suit for Savings Taken From Pay in 40's," *New York Times*, August 30, 2002. The braceros were guest workers who entered the United States between 1942 and 1964. "The aim was to keep farms and railroads functioning while Americans went to war," Ginger Thompson and Steven Greenhouse reported in "Mexican 'Guest Workers': A Project Worth a Try?" *New York Times*, April 3, 2001.

43. Alejandro Portes, and Rubén Rumbaut, *Immigrant America: A Portrait* (Berkeley: University of California Press, 1996), 117–18.

44. By the same token, managers charged with the African-American consumer market best be familiar with what terms such as "high yellow," "blue black," and "brown paper bag test" mean within that community.

45. Randall Robinson, *The Debt: What America Owes to Blacks* (New York: E.P. Dutton, 2000), 90.

46. NBC, seeing the future, made a $2.7 billion acquisition of Telemundo in April 2002. "The potential [market] can be measured in dollars," Mireya Navarro reported. "In announcing the sale [of Telemundo], NBC officials noted that the nation's Hispanic population has grown more than 60 percent in the last decade, to more than 35 million. They said that industry research showed that by the end of this decade, Hispanic buying power is projected to approach $1 trillion, twice what it is now." Mireya Navarro, "Promoting Hispanic TV, Language and Culture," *New York Times*, December 30, 2002.

47. Rául Vasquez, "Vanity Fair Apologizes to Latinos," Eastern Groups Publications, February 25, 2003.

48. *Vanity Fair*, February 2003.

49. Procter & Gamble press release, February 21, 2003.

50. Interview broadcast on Univision, February 23, 2003.

51. See www.hispanicprwire.com/release_Crest_Ad_ENG.htm.

52. Marie Arana, *American Chica: Two Worlds, One Childhood* (New York: Dial Press, 2000) 171–73.

Chapter 2

1. Andrew Pollack, "The Fight for Hispanic Viewers: Univision's Success Story Attracts New Competition," *New York Times*, January 19, 1998.

2. The "triumph" of English is consistently being declared. "The rise of English must be counted among the most hopeful developments of the age," Bret Stephens wrote in the *Wall Street Journal*, oblivious to the fact that Spanish is spreading faster *within* the United States than English is spreading elsewhere. "It takes place voluntar-

ily. It allows members of smaller cultures, such as Hungarians or Finns, to jump into the global mainstream without having to make what would once have been a fateful choice among French, German, or Russian. It has done nothing to prevent the simultaneous recovery of Gaelic, Welsh, Basque, and other languages that had withered under the yoke of the nation-state." Bret Stephens, "Ach! That English, It Seduces Tout le Monde," *Wall Street Journal*, April 20, 2001.

3. Joseph Straubhaar, Consuelo Campbell, and Kristina Cahoon, "From National to Regional Cultures: The Five Cultures and Television Markets of Nafta," www.orbicom.uqam.ca/in_focus/publications/archives/straubhaar.html, 1995. They reference M. Ferguson's acclaimed analysis, "The Mythology About Globalization," *European Journal of Communication* 7 (1992): 69–93.

4. Straubhaar et al., "From National to Regional Cultures."

5. Rebecca Gardyn, "Habla English," *American Demographics* (April 2001).

6. Quoted in Suzanne Kapner, "U.S. TV Shows Losing Potency Around World," *New York Times*, January 2, 2003.

7. Ibid.

8. Araceli Ortiz de Urbina and Asbel López, "Soaps with a Latin Scent," *UNESCO Courier*, www.oas.org/culture/series6_f.html. "Brazil's TV Globo is perhaps the most typical of these firms and has sold telenovelas to 123 countries, according to its international sales director, Orlando Marques. . . . Telenovelas were responsible for almost $1.6 billion in billings for 1996, 60 per cent of Brazilian TV's ad billings. 'Without telenovelas, TV Globo might not exist,' says Jorge Adib, the company's former international sales director," the reporters write.

9. "Changing Channels," *World Link*, January/February 1998.

10. Ibid.

11. It needs to be noted that Hollywood blockbusters typically cost more than $100 million to produce and take years before profits materialize. In contrast, Mexican soap operas have low production costs, and the licensing and broadcast fees constitute almost entirely profits. A final point is that people have to pay for movies, while television programs are broadcast free of charge. More people around the world watch Mexican *telenovelas* than Hollywood blockbusters.

12. Even with the trend among European companies to adopt English as the official language, there are other considerations. In fact, the "triumphal march of English through European business is symbolic, born of a wish to shed a parochial image and assume that of a global player," John Tagliabue reported in the *New York Times*. "To this extent, the adoption of one language in business is probably not an indication that Europeans are abandoning their cultural identities as they have surrendered their economic nationalism and adopted a single currency." John Tagliabue, "In Europe, Going Global Means, Alas, English," *New York Times*, May 19, 2002.

13. *Critical Issues* reports:

> Although still far behind Hollywood in absolute sales figures, the rate of export growth for Latin American producers is impressive. They are projected to double every year in the immediate future. Even more significant points out *Forbes* (1997), "For the past 18 months Televisa has been producing telenovelas in English in Mexico City and has sold five English-language programs in Britain, Canada, Australia and parts of Africa. Televisa has negotiated with Fox Television in the U.S. and hopes to air an upcoming English-language soap here before the end of the year." Even though globalization through secondary

circuits is advantageous for emerging producers, it does little for the new target markets. Latin American television soap operas distributed to Eastern Europe are only marginally a form of cultural renaissance in that part of the world. In fact, they are a form of diversification of cultural imports. The peaking and subsequent decline of American TV programming in Western Europe after 1987 proves this point. Because the interest of local audiences in local production is very strong . . . European commercial broadcasters prefer now to invest at least part of the profits in local productions rather than to import everything from the United States, even though it costs more to produce locally. . . . It all boils down, then, not just to economics, but to a mix of cultural tradition, sense of local identity, and entrepreneurial sense.

"Converging or Diverging Culture(s)?: The Impact of Secondary Television Circuits on the Global Community," *Critical Issues*, http://members.tripod.com/sorinmatei/global/world.html.

14. "Changing Channels," *World Link*, January/February 1998.

15. Straubhaar et al., "From National to Regional Cultures."

16. Ibid.

17. The debate within Californio society was considerable. "The Franciscans, on the other hand, virtually all of them peninsulares, were hostile to the revolution, especially after the collapse of Iturbide's empire and the apparent triumph of liberalism, a 'godless' ideology, with the adoption of the Constitution of 1824," Gonzales writes. Manuel Gonzales, *Mexicanos: A History of Mexicans in the United States* (Bloomington: Indiana University Press, 1999), 62.

18. Nancy Gibbs, "A Whole New World," *Time*, June 11, 2001.

19. Mirta Ojito, "Publisher Tries Literary Lightning Rod to Attract Latino Writers and Readers," *New York Times*, September 10, 2002.

20. The Spanish ministries of Education, Culture, and Foreign Relations, for instance, work with Spanish book publishers to promote Spanish-language literature in the United States.

21. Larry Rohter, "Rock en Español Is Approaching Its Final Border," *New York Times*, August 6, 2000.

22. Mireya Navarro, "Promoting Hispanic TV, Language and Culture," *New York Times*, December 30, 2002.

23. Joan Didion, *Miami* (New York: Vintage International, 1987), 52–53.

24. Ibid., 112.

25. At a time when American women were walking around in sweats from the Gap—a bold, though somewhat misguided affirmation of democratic egalitarianism—Cuban women were dressed in clothes "of considerable expense," obviously out of sync with the rest of the United States by virtue of being overdressed.

26. Consider the history of two friends whose families arrived at Ellis Island in the nineteenth century. One, whose grandfather was French, Anglicized his name: D'Avignon became Devino. Another, whose family arrived from Poland, attempted to make the name more "American" by adding a letter "e": Poleski became Poleskie.

27. "Little Havana" was always a way station for Cubans to orient themselves in Miami, and only the very poor remained there. By the 1990s, most of the residents of Little Havana are from impoverished Central American countries, most notably Nicaragua and El Salvador.

28. Didion, *Miami*, 63.

29. Ibid.

30. Michel de Montaigne, *The Complete Essays*, trans. and ed. M.A. Screech, vol. 1 (New York: Penguin, 1991), 231.

31. "You can make your living being a mariachi in New York," Ramon Ponce, Jr. told the *New York Times*'s Seth Kugel. Noting that Ponce's group "has performed not only at Mexican weddings and holiday parties, but also at bar mitzvahs and Chinese weddings," Kugel examines the "shortage" of mariachis in New York. "We've played for Rudolph Giuliani, and on the East Side, where there are a lot of rich people," he said. "But then they call us to go to Brooklyn to play for poor people who have scraped together the money between two or three family members." Seth Kugel, "Mexican Musicians Are Uniting to Meet Mariachi Shortage," *New York Times*, December 16, 2001.

32. Marilyn Halter, *Shopping for Identity: The Marketing of Ethnicity* (New York: Schocken, 2000), 48.

33. For more information, see Robin Finn, "Interview with the Interviewer (Hands to Yourself)," *New York Times*, June 26, 2003.

34. Kevin Starr quoted in Todd Purdum, "California Census Confirms Whites Are a Minority," *New York Times*, March 30, 2001.

35. "A survey released last week of birth certificates statewide showed that for the first time since the late 1850s, just a decade after California was seized from Mexico in the Mexican-American War, a majority of newborns are Hispanic. More than two-thirds of the Hispanic babies are being born here in Los Angeles County and surrounding Southern California," Dean Murphy reported in the *New York Times* in early 2003. "The milestone, though long anticipated, carries great significance in symbolic and real terms, as Hispanics increasingly define what it means to be Californian, and American-born Hispanics assert numerical and cultural dominance over their immigrant counterparts." Dean Murphy, "New California Identity Predicted by Researchers," *New York Times*, February 17, 2003.

36. Susan Sachs, "What's in a Name? Redefining Minority," *New York Times*, March 11, 2001.

37. Lynette Clemetson, "Hispanics Now Largest Minority, Census Shows," *New York Times*, January 22, 2003.

38. Maya Angelou, *I Know Why the Caged Bird Sings* (New York: Random House, 1969), 177.

39. Hispanic cultural ascendancy is seen in other areas. For instance, two of the five films nominated for Oscars in the screenwriting category for 2002 were written in Spanish, a development that startled some Academy members. A Mexican who directed the third installment of the "Harry Potter" movies was nominated. A Venezuelan is editor of *Flaunt*, the "hippest" magazine in Los Angeles. These represent a sea change in the profile Hispanic culture now has throughout the United States.

40. Thomas Schelling, *Micromotives and Macrobehavior* (New York: Norton, 1978), 24.

41. Ibid., 213.

42. Robert Frank, *Choosing the Right Pond* (New York: Oxford University Press, 1985), 225.

43. Milton Friedman, "The Role of Government in a Free Society," in *Private Wants and Public Needs*, ed. Edmund Phelps (New York: W.W. Norton, 1965), 107. First published in Milton Friedman, *Capitalism and Freedom* (Chicago: University of Chicago Press, 1962).

44. Ibid.

45. John Kenneth Galbraith, "The Dependence Effect and Social Balance," in *Private Wants and Public Needs*, ed. Edmund Phelps (New York: W.W. Norton, 1965), 25–28. First published in John Kenneth Galbraith, *The Affluent Society* (New York: Houghton Mifflin, 1958).

46. Hernando de Soto, *The Mystery of Capital* (New York: Basic Books, 2000), 18.

47. Friedman, "The Role of Government in a Free Society," 108.

48. Galbraith, "The Dependence Effect and Social Balance," 29.

49. Barbara Kahn and Leigh McAlister, *Grocery Revolution* (Reading, MA: Addison Wesley, 1997).

50. Andre Schiffrin, *The Business of Books* (New York: Verso, 2000), 121–23.

51. Angelou, *I Know Why the Caged Bird Sings*, 118.

52. de Soto, *The Mystery of Capital*, 17.

53. Galbraith, "The Dependence Effect and Social Balance," 28.

54. Overestimating one's skills was rampant during the Internet boom in San Francisco when, out of dozens of candidates interviewed for several dot-com ventures, Internet entrepreneurs promised the world and then offered little, other than a litany of excuses as to why things would not come to pass as promised.

55. John Kenneth Galbraith, *The Good Society* (Boston: Houghton Mifflin, 1996), 11.

56. The problem with the term "indigenous" is that humans did not "evolve" in ancient Mexico; they migrated there. By virtue of being mobile, humans are not "endemic" to any given geographic location. Whether walking across a continent, or drifting on a raft, or, for that matter, boarding a commercial airliner, humans have always migrated.

57. Silvana Paternostro, "Registering the 9/11 Dead," *New York Times*, June 23, 2002.

58. A measure of how Hispanic culture, one decade into NAFTA and two decades after the end of the Franco dictatorship, is blossoming is found in the simple fact that two Hispanic films—*Talk to Her* and *Y Tu Mamá También*—and an actress—Salma Hayek—were nominated for Oscars, and not in the foreign film category.

59. During the 1982 financial crisis, I recall attending several presentations made by Bank of Mexico officials in Washington and New York. These "presentations" consisted of overhead after overhead of statistics after statistics. Most in the audience quietly walked out before the "talk" was finished.

60. Steven Greenhouse, "Suit Claims Discrimination Against Hispanics on Job," *New York Times*, February 9, 2003.

61. Greenhouse reported, "Workers and federal officials say they are surprised that the factory remains so segregated three years after 91 workers filed charges with the United States Equal Employment Opportunity Commission, accusing the factory's owner, the Quietflex Manufacturing Company, of illegal discrimination. After months of fruitless efforts to negotiate a settlement with Quietflex, the commission intervened last September in a private lawsuit against Quietflex, eager to change what it says is one of the worst cases of work force segregation it has seen in years." Ibid.

62. "The accusations of harassment at the 200-employee bakery, Chef Solutions, reflect a common plight of immigrant workers, who are especially vulnerable to abuse because immigration status, poverty, and language problems often discourage them from speaking up," Steven Greenhouse wrote, reporting on the plight of Mexican sisters in Connecticut who were subjected to sexual harassment. "This is the worst case I've ever seen in terms of the constant sexual harassment, the demeaning conditions the women were subjected to, and the way it was tolerated by the highest officials at the plant," Thomas Meiklejohn, an attorney representing the women, told

reporters. Steven Greenhouse "Immigrants Claim Harassment at Bakery," *New York Times*, February 2, 2003.

63. Jorge Ramos, *The Other Face of America* (New York: HarperRayo, 2002), xxviii.

64. "Our world and perspective are much wider than ABC, CBS, or NBC, and that's what we've been doing the last seventeen years," said Jorge Ramos, who coanchors the *Noticiero Univision* 6:30 P.M. broadcast with Maria Elena Salinas, of his network's coverage of the war in Iraq. *Noticiero Univision* is seen by more viewers in Miami, Los Angeles, and New York than either CBS or ABC. See http://univision.newstrove.com for more information.

65. Mireya Navarro, "Education Gap for Hispanics," *New York Times*, February 10, 2003.

66. Ibid.

67. Ibid.

Chapter 3

1. "For me, I don't care if those workers are from Mars," Eric Schlosser, author of *Fast Food Nation*, said. "It's the way in which using illegals allows them to do all the other practices, like speeding up the production lines, not listening to workers, and having a high turnover rate which reduces the power of the workers." There is, in fact, a consensus on the need for Mexican laborers: "Immigrant labor, whether it's legal or illegal, is critical," Keith Esplin, president of the Potato Growers of Idaho, is quoted as saying. "Most Mexicans here will have papers, but the farmers won't have any idea. There is real good counterfeit stuff out there." David Barboza, "Tyson Foods Indicted in Plan to Smuggle Illegal Workers," *New York Times*, December 20, 2001; and David Barboza, "Meatpackers' Profits Hinge on Pool of Immigrant Labor," *New York Times*, December 21, 2001.

2. Charlie LeDuff, "At the Slaughterhouse, Some Things Never Die: Who Kills, Who Cuts, Who Bosses Can Depend on Race," *New York Times*, June 16, 2000.

3. John Kenneth Galbraith, *The Good Society* (Boston: Houghton Mifflin, 1996), 91.

4. Ibid., 90.

5. Katharine Mieszkowski, "Would You Like Ground Spinal Cord with That?" Salon.com, February 8, 2001.

6. "Last year, two white men hired two brown men on a Farmingville corner with the promise of work. But instead, the Mexicans were taken to an abandoned building and beaten with work tools. News of the attack made it all the way down to San Lorenzo [in Mexico]." Charlie LeDuff, "A Perilous 4,000-Mile Passage to Work," *New York Times*, May 29, 2001.

7. Report quotation provided by Jorge A. Bustamente, professor of sociology at the University of Notre Dame, as published in the *Los Angeles Times*, in response to that newspaper's editorial, "Visas for Mexican Workers," which appeared on August 24, 2000.

8. Ginger Thompson, "U.S. and Mexico to Open Talks on Freer Migration for Workers," *New York Times*, February 16, 2001.

9. "A study by the University of California at Davis found that the number of beds for farmworkers fell from 400 in the 1980s to 250 in the 1990s. The county has 176 beds in four public camps, including the yurt village, managed by the nonprofit California Human Development Corporation; seven camps with about 60 beds are

privately owned." Patricia Leigh Brown, "More Housing for Migrants of Napa Vine-yards," *New York Times*, September 22, 2002.

10. "Mexican Guest-Worker Plan Backed," *Washington Post*, January 11, 2001.

11. Thompson, "U.S. and Mexico to Open Talks on Freer Migration for Workers."

12. "Even in the safest of times, surely there is cause for concern when millions of well-intentioned people are forced by a bad law to view authorities with suspicion and to regard breaking the law as the accepted norm. In times like these, it is arguably suicidal." Tamar Jacoby, "Pressing the Case for Immigration Reform," *New York Times*, September 16, 2002.

13. Mary Jordan and Mary Beth Sheridan, "Mexico Seeks U.S. Shift in Immigra-tion Policy," *Washington Post*, April 2, 2001.

14. "The Sept. 11 hijackers were able to open 35 American bank accounts without having legitimate Social Security numbers and opened some of the accounts with fabricated Social Security numbers that were never checked or questioned by bank officials," James Risen reported, two months before the first anniversary of the terror-ist attacks. That a dishwasher is prevented from opening an account while Al Qaeda operatives are free to transfer tens of thousands of dollars to carry out their terrorist operations speaks volumes about the need for major immigration and banking reform. James Risen, "Sept. 11 Hijackers Said to Fake Data on Bank Accounts," *New York Times*, July 10, 2002.

The hijackers were also able to enter the United States at will. Diane Jean Schemo and Robert Pear reported:

> Two other men the authorities said plowed jetliners into the World Trade Cen-ter, Mohamed Atta and Marwan al-Shehhi, entered the United States on tourist visas. Even without the required student visas, the men studied at a flight school in Florida. . . . Consular officers deluged with visa applications say they gener-ally do not have much time to investigate the applicants. Once foreign visitors enter the United States, immigration officers and law enforcement agencies usually have no idea if they are complying with the terms of their visas.

Diana Jean Schemo and Robert Pear, "Suspects in Hijacking Exploited Loophole in Immigration Policy," *New York Times*, September 27, 2001.

15. Douglas Monroy, *Thrown Among Strangers: The Making of Mexican Culture in Frontier California* (Berkeley: University of California Press, 1990), 173–76.

16. John Steinbeck, *Grapes of Wrath* (New York: Viking Press/Penguin Books, 1992), 315.

17. Barboza, "Meatpackers' Profits Hinge on Pool of Immigrant Labor."

18. "Migrant Deaths and Immigration Laws," Letters to the Editor, *Los Angeles Times*, February 17, 2001. The "eastern" movement of illegal crossing from Califor-nia to the Southwest is well documented. "In the 1988 fiscal year, the 280-mile stretch of Arizona border known as the Tucson Sector, which includes Douglas, overtook San Diego as the busiest sector of illegal entry on the southern border, with 387,406 ap-prehensions," Michael Janofsky reported in the *New York Times*. "The total grew to 470,449 in the 1999 fiscal year—more than twice the number of five years before." Michael Janofsky, "Immigrants Flood Border in Arizona, Angering Ranchers," *New York Times*, June 18, 2000.

Driving illegal immigration away from urban centers to the desert results in cruel deaths, however. Evelyn Nieves reported in the *Times:*

The deaths are full of suffering. People have suffocated in airless trucks, died in vehicle crashes, been struck by lightning, or drowned. . . . Most often, though, they are felled by heatstroke or dehydration. Some carry no identification and, in a tragic irony, end up where they wanted to be, in the United States—but in anonymous paupers' graves. Other migrants, not counted by the Border Patrol, never make it across.

Evelyn Nieves, "Illegal Immigrant Death Rate Rises Sharply in Barren Areas," *New York Times*, August 6, 2002.

19. Tom Zeller, "Migrants Take Their Chance on a Harsh Path of Hope," *New York Times*, March 18, 2001. American ranchers whose properties are crossed nightly confirm these views. "They've decreased the flow of people across my property by maybe 40 to 50 percent," Roger Barnett, a rancher who owns a 22,000-acre spread near Douglas, Arizona, said of the Border Patrol efforts. "But they're just coming on everyone else's place." Eric Schmitt, "A Mexican Border War Turns, but Is Not Yet Won," *New York Times*, February 24, 2001.

Of greater concern is the outlaw violence emerging in the American Southwest. "The police are investigating whether armed vigilantes, self-appointed guardians of the border with Mexico, fatally shot at least two illegal immigrants in the desert last week. . . . Police officers found two bodies riddled with bullets and no sign of the remaining nine migrants," Nick Madigan reported in the *Times*. "It is not known whether they escaped or were loaded into vehicles and taken away, either dead or alive." Nick Madigan, "Police Investigate Killings of Illegal Immigrants in Arizona Dessert," *New York Times*, October 23, 2002. Law enforcement officials were perplexed by the murder of illegal aliens: Was it smugglers who turned on their clients, or drug dealers executing rivals? In either case, the impunity with which these activities occur makes a mockery of "homeland" security, or any pretensions to that effect.

The escalation of violence was followed by increased risk-taking of immigrants crossing the desert. "Local and federal officials painted a devastating picture today of a smuggling operation that killed at least 14 young Mexican immigrants in Arizona, saying a 'coyote' had apparently abandoned more than two dozen men in one of the country's most brutal and desolate stretches of desert on Saturday with little water and no preparation," James Sterngold reported in an all too common account. "A dozen who survived the ordeal, in 115-degree temperatures, were in a hospital in Yuma today. One of them, a 16-year-old, was in critical condition." James Sterngold, "Devastating Picture of Immigrants Dead in Arizona Desert," *New York Times*, May 26, 2001.

20. The representative's basement was remodeled by Creative Drywall Designs and Denver Audio Design, which maintained that the two employees in question were in the United States legally. The *Denver Post* published a story detailing the struggles of one of the employees in pursuing a college education while working a full-time job. Associated Press, "Anti-Immigration Rep. Accused of Hiring Illegal Workers," September 20, 2002.

21. Linda Chávez quoted in Eric Schmitt, "Americans (a) Love (b) Hate Immigrants," *New York Times*, January 14, 2001. Of the Chávez debacle, Grover Joseph Rees wrote, "The good news is that if you should do the right thing by taking a severely abused woman into your home without asking to look at her green card, you will almost certainly not go to jail. The bad news is that you will probably not become secretary of labor, unless you are clever enough, or insipid enough, to have been

nominated for such an office without attracting any strong opponents." Grover Joseph Rees, "Immigration Law Run Amok Claims Another Victim," *Wall Street Journal*, January 11, 2001.

22. Michael A. Riccardi, "New York Judges Call for Action on Fair Pay for Day Laborers," *New York Law Journal* (May 21, 2001).

23. Ibid.

24. Michael Janofsky, "Fired Mexican Quarry Workers in Colorado Say System Betrayed Them," *New York Times*, September 2, 2001.

25. "In a broader action that also raised fears that authorities had begun to enforce immigration laws more harshly, 834 Mexican workers in Portland, Ore., most of them janitors, were dismissed in recent days. But the mass dismissals resulted from an audit of 41 companies by the immigration service, begun in July, which determined that the workers lacked valid work permits, said Karen Kraushaar, a national agency spokeswoman. The agency has not altered its enforcement tactics with regard to Latin American immigrants since Sept. 11, she said." Sam Dillon, "Mexican Immigrants Face New Set of Fears," *New York Times*, October 15, 2001.

26. The violations resulted in lawsuits against Georgia-Pacific, International Paper, and Champion. "They're robbing these workers blind," Mary Bauer, legal director of the Virginia Justice Center, is quoted as saying. "The number of people involved and the number of violations are beyond anything I've ever seen." Steven Greenhouse, "Migrants Plant Pine Trees but Often Pocket Peanuts," *New York Times*, February 14, 2001.

27. Peter K. Nunez, Center for Immigration Studies, "The Deadly Consequences of Illegal Alien Smuggling," testimony before Congress delivered June 24, 2003.

28. John F. Gay quoted in Steven Greenhouse, "Congress Looks to Grant Legal Status to Immigrants," *New York Times*, October 13, 2003. Gay's position is echoed by Nunez: "What is needed is a comprehensive reform of our immigration policy designed to eliminate all of the perverse incentives that continue to draw illegal aliens to this country. If it is true that most immigrants—both legal and illegal—come to this country to work, then it is essential to finally enact an employer sanctions provision that works."

29. "Innocent, hard-working people came here when it was in the interests of both countries [for them] to do so," Matt Piers, an attorney with Gessler Hughes & Socol, a Chicago law firm, told the *Los Angeles Times*. "These folks were totally proper in their entry and their labor. And they got ripped off." Rich Connell and Robert J. López, "Mexico to Look Into Missing Millions Saved for Braceros," *Los Angeles Times*, January 28, 2001.

30. Comments made to reporters in Mexico City on April 18, 2001. Another former critic of Mexico, Texas senator Phil Gramm, flew down to Mexico City to congratulate Vicente Fox, beating out President George W. Bush by a few weeks. At that time, Senator Gramm remarked that "the best way to discourage illegal immigration to the United States is to encourage in Mexico market reforms and economic opportunity. President Fox is committed to this, and I am committed to helping him achieve it."

31. Chris Kraul, "Mexico Visit by Helms Reflects New Realities," *Los Angeles Times*, April 18, 2001. That the outgoing North Carolina conservative—famously critical of Mexico for decades—underscored how Mexico became a priority for American politicians soon after Fox took office was a sea change in how American conservatives saw Mexico. As a measure of the bipartisan stake in a successful Mexico, it was a Democratic White House that arranged for a rescue package in 1995. "Clinton sidestepped an angry Congress to raise the money [for Mexico]. The bailout worked, and

Mexico repaid the loans, plus a billion dollars interest," David Sanger reported. "Rightly or wrongly, Mr. Clinton and his aides contend, the reforms they demanded from Mexico in exchange for the money helped democracy flourish." David E. Sanger, "Economic Engine for Foreign Policy," *New York Times*, December 28, 2000.

32. Diane Coyle, *Paradoxes of Prosperity: Why the New Capitalism Benefits All* (New York: Texere, 2001), 128.

33. "There are days we can't get our crop out," Larry Cox told the *Wall Street Journal*. "What we can't cut in time we leave in the field to rot." Joel Millman, "The Great California Farmhand Debate," *Wall Street Journal*, February 12, 2001.

34. "About 300,000 Poblanos live in the New York metropolitan area," Ginger Thompson reported. "The immigrants, who typically earn more in an hour than workers in Mexico earn in a day, send an estimated $800 million a year back to the state." Ginger Thompson, "Top Democrats Politic Through Rural Mexico," *New York Times*, November 19, 2001.

35. Tamar Jacoby, "Pressing the Case for Immigration Reform," *New York Times*, September 16, 2002. One terrifying consequence of the failure to legalize those who, by virtue of having a job, contribute to the American economy was seen on September 11. "These people will die like they lived—invisibly," Joel Magallan, with the Tepeyac Association in New York, said about the illegal aliens who died in the attack on the World Trade Center. "We have heard disturbing reports that some people whose loved ones are missing have not come forward because of immigration issues," INS Commissioner James Ziglar said in a statement. "We cannot let that happen." Frances Robles, "Families Afraid to Talk About Missing Relatives," *Miami Herald*, September 25, 2001.

36. James F. Smith, "U.S.-Mexico Migration Plan Urged," *Los Angeles Times*, February 15, 2001.

37. Carl Hulse, "Gephardt Is Preparing a Measure to Legalize Illegal Immigrants," *New York Times*, July 23, 2002.

38. Smith, "U.S.-Mexico Migration Plan Urged."

39. Eric Schmitt, quoted in "You Can Come In. You Stay Out," *New York Times*, July 29, 2001.

40. Ibid.

41. Personal interview with Massey by author, March 2001.

42. Paul Donnelly, "Make a Green Card the Real Payoff for Guest Workers," *Los Angeles Times*, February 12, 2001.

43. Douglas Monroy, *Thrown Among Strangers: The Making of Mexican Culture in Frontier California* (Berkeley: University of California Press, 1990), 259.

44. The test of "manhood," as anthropologists would explain, is in being able to return home and provide for their families and communities. See David Gilmore, *Manhood in the Making: Cultural Concepts of Masculinity* (New Haven, CT: Yale University Press, 1990).

Consider a startling case in point, as reported by Ginger Thompson:

> If there is truth in New York City's famous anthem, then Jaime Lucero, a dishwasher turned garment-district millionaire, can make it anywhere. And 25 years after migrating to the city of skyscrapers from the mountains of central Mexico, he seems determined to match his success back home.... Answering his native country's plea for investments to create jobs, Mr. Lucero inaugurated a multimillion-dollar expansion of his clothes manufacturing operations in this tumbledown region of corn and cactus fields. In the next two years, Mr. Lucero

has pledged to spend more than $21 million to build at least six plants, known as maquiladoras, which will assemble women's clothing for export to the United States, in the process creating 7,000 jobs.

Ginger Thompson, "New York Garment Mogul Takes Business Home," *New York Times*, July 30, 2001.

45. Tim Weiner, "Mexico Chief Pushes New Border Policy: Free and Easy Does It," *New York Times*, December 14, 2001.

46. Smith, "U.S.-Mexico Migration Plan Urged."

47. Anthony DePalma, *Here: A Biography of the New American Continent* (New York: Public Affairs, 2001), 167.

48. "A landscaper from Armonk [NY], daunted by the seminar here [on legalizing his workers], said he had one employee, out of dozens, he would apply for. Mr. [Mario] Russell at Catholic Charities said the landscapers and construction workers in the suburbs had the worst chance [of becoming legal] because most employers considered them replaceable 'commodities.' The best chance, he said, would be a small business, like a florist or a deli, where the worker and boss had a 'committed personal relationship.'" Jane Gross, "New Legal Window to Open for Illegal Immigrants," *New York Times*, February 20, 2001.

49. Charlie LeDuff writes about the bias crimes against Mexicans and the climate of hostility in which they live:

> There is the violence. Last year 27 killings were committed in Robeson, mostly in the countryside, giving it a higher murder rate than Detroit or Newark. Three Mexicans were robbed and killed last fall. Latinos have also been the victims of highway stickups. In the yellow-walled break room at the plant, Mexicans talked among themselves about their three slain men, about the midnight visitors with obscured faces and guns, men who knew that the illegal workers used mattresses rather than banks.

LeDuff, "At the Slaughterhouse, Some Things Never Die: Who Kills, Who Cuts, Who Bosses Can Depend on Race."

50. Paloma Dallas, "The Big Apple's Mexican Face," Hispaniconline.com/res&res/pages/8_01/ny_mexican.html.

51. Thompson, "Top Democrats Politic Through Rural Mexico."

52. These demographic changes are startling at times. Consider developments in Connecticut. "Founded by a Dutchman and settled by Puritans, Hartford now has the greatest percentage of Hispanic residents of any major city north of Florida and east of the Mississippi," Paul von Zielbauer reported in the *New York Times*. "Hispanics now account for more than 40 percent of the city's population—the largest concentration among major cities outside California, Texas, Colorado, and Florida." Paul von Zielbauer, "Hartford Bids a Bilingual Goodbye to a White-Collar Past," *New York Times*, May 5, 2003.

53. Pam Belluck, "Chicago Reverses 50 Years of Declining Population," *New York Times*, March 15, 2001. The same was true in other cities, including New York. See, for instance, Susan Sachs, "City's Population Tops 8 Million in Census Count for the First Time," *New York Times*, March 16, 2001; and Dean E. Murphy, "City's Population Changes Are on Vivid Display in Queens," *New York Times*, March 19, 2001.

54. James Sterngold, "Move to Secede Splits Latinos in the Valley," *New York Times*, June 10, 2002.

55. Ibid.

56. Michael Janofsky, "Illegal Immigration Strains Services in Arizona," *New York Times*, April 11, 2001.

57. Juan González wrote, "Color and status so deeply demarcated the English colonies, however, that the free colored class was considered an abnormality only barely tolerated a drop of black in Anglo-Saxon society; while in the Portuguese and Spanish world, *mestizos* and *mulattos*, no matter how dark, were invariably regarded as part of white society, although admittedly second-class members." Juan González, *Harvest of Empire: A History of Latinos in America* (New York: Viking, 2000), 20.

58. Though "Anglo" was used during the first half of the twentieth century, as shorthand for "Anglo-Saxon," as the presence of Spanish speakers has increased, it is now used to denote non-Spanish speakers and culture. Thus, in the same way that Celia Cruz and Antonio Banderas are both "Hispanic," Tom Cruise and Tina Turner are both "Anglo." Throughout this discussion, Anglo denotes an English cultural tradition and Hispanic a Spanish and Portuguese tradition. This is not unique. Among the Amish, for instance, everyone else in the United States is referred to as the "English." Thus, to the Amish, Ricky Ricardo is as "English" as is Fred Mertz; the nomenclature simply identifies the "English" as those who are not "Amish."

59. Stephanie Zacharek, "Crazy/Beautiful," Salon.com, June 29, 2001.

60. Ibid.

61. Robert Samuelson, "America as Mexico's Economic Safety Valve," *Washington Post*, July 20, 2000.

62. Samuel P. Huntington is a professor at Harvard University, where he is also the chairman of the Harvard Academy for International and Area Studies, curiously enough.

63. Ronald Dworkin, "Race and the Uses of Law," *New York Times*, April 13, 2001.

64. Danny Hakim, "Immigration Policy to Bar Canadian and Mexican Part-Time Students," *New York Times*, July 9, 2002. "Not only would the action unfairly penalize law-abiding students who are seeking to further their education, but it would also result in significant economic loss," a letter signed by fifteen college presidents of the Western New York Consortium of Higher Education sent to James Ziglar, commissioner of the Immigration Service, said. The *New York Times* also reported that "on the Mexican border, the University of Texas at El Paso has a special program to train Mexican and United States citizens in mechanical engineering, offering other advanced degrees as well. Eric Tiel, director of the department of international programs, said that if Mexican students were prevented from studying for the degrees, El Paso and neighboring Ciudad Juárez, Mexico, would be faced with a shortage of highly trained workers. 'What affects one side affects the other,' Mr. Tiel said. 'El Paso and Juárez are almost one city.'" The INS reversed its position in August 2002, just in time for hundreds of colleges around the United States to welcome back their Mexican and Canadian students.

65. An arresting development, of course, is that while the Immigration and Naturalization Service (INS) is taking misguided steps that hit American colleges and universities in the pocketbook while depriving Canadian and Mexican students opportunities for higher education, American institutions of higher learning are desperately seeking new sources of revenue.

66. In a compelling example of the absurd, immigration officials in San Diego closed a bicycle lane that, encouraged by officials in both San Diego and Tijuana, had reduced traffic congestion. "As a result [of the closing of the bicycle lane], local [San Diego] lawmakers are boiling, a group of border entrepreneurs are broke [who rented bicycles],

and again it is left to the Mexican workers to suck it up and rise five hours before the workday begins to beat the rush," Charlie LeDuff reported. Charlie LeDuff, "Where Biking Blossomed, Now the Wheels Come Off," *New York Times*, October 8, 2002.

67. Mexico has its own problems securing its southern border, a problem best addressed as part of a continental North American Security Perimeter (NASP) program, despite initiatives by the Fox administration. Ginger Thompson reported:

> In a widely discussed effort called Plan Sur, or Southern Plan, Mr. Fox's government promises to root out corruption among immigration officials, expand the number of agents assigned to defend immigrants from attack, and impose order at the tumbledown, poorly guarded checkpoints throughout the Isthmus of Tehuantepec. . . . At that point, 200 or more miles in from the southern border, the land narrows to just about 100 miles across. And from that area, trains and highways connect to the north. Government officials said the isthmus had been overrun by nearly 100 operations that smuggle immigrants. A deputy in the Mexican attorney general's office said the agency would create a special office for the investigation of immigrant smuggling. Officials at the Federal Preventive Police reported that they had dismantled at least six big trafficking operations from Chihuahua and Coahuila in the north, to Mexico City and to Chiapas in the south.

Ginger Thompson, "Mexico's Open Southern Border Lures Migrants Headed to U.S.," *New York Times*, August 5, 2001.

68. Perhaps most things have to be invented, but not everything.

69. Ginger Thompson, "Big Mexican Breadwinner: The Migrant Worker," *New York Times*, March 25, 2002.

70. Charlie LeDuff, "With War in the Air, Home Is but a Dream," *New York Times*, September 28, 2001.

71. Sam Howe Verhovek, "Immigrant Laborers Feel Stranded in Pacific Northwest as Day Jobs Dry Up," *New York Times*, January 27, 2002.

72. Rubén Martínez, *Crossing Over: A Mexican Family on the Migrant Trail* (New York: Picador USA, 202), 142.

73. Various aspects of the role stress of racism among American black men is found in the following sources: R. Dennis, "Social Stress and Mortality Among Non-white Males," *Phylon* 33 (1977): 408–28; L.E. Gary and B.R. Leashore, "The High-Risk Status of Black Men," *Social Work* 27 (1982): 54–58; M. Geerken and W. Grove, "Race, Sex and Marital Status: The Effect on Mortality," *Social Problems* (1974): 567–80; W. Jones and M.F. Rice, *Health Care Issues in Black America: Policies, Problems, and Prospects* (New York: Greenwood Press, 1987); J. Rimmer et al., "Alcoholism, Sex, Socioeconomic Status, and Race in Two Hospital Samples," *Quarterly Journal of Studies on Alcohol* 32 (1971): 942–52; and J.B. Stewart, "The Political Economy of Black Male Suicides," *Journal of Black Studies* 11, no. 2 (1980): 249–61.

74. Russell Thornton, "What the Census Doesn't Count," *New York Times*, March 23, 2001.

75. The question of credibility arises, for instance, in the racism by Hispanics against whites. In a review of the book, Tim Golden noted that while Martínez "has a fine ear for language, but the poor Mexicans he meets sometimes speak in strangely lyrical sentences. At times, Martínez's great sympathy for the immigrants is undercut by his cartoonish rendering of the people they encounter in the United States—

the cruel white bosses, the racist white neighbors, the shock troops of the Border Patrol." Tim Golden, "'Crossing Over': North of the Border," *New York Times*, March 10, 2002.

76. Rachel L. Swarns, "Immigrants Feel the Pinch of Post-9/11 Laws," *New York Times*, June 24, 2003.

77. Mary Beth Sheridan, "An Entry Card for Immigrants," *Washington Post*, July 26, 2002.

78. In an about face, however, New York has refused to accept the consular IDs. "Citing security concerns, Police Department officials said they had rejected requests from the [Mexican] consulate to accept the new 'matricula consular,' or consular ID card, as proof of identity for Mexican immigrants," Susan Sachs wrote. "The [New York] State Department of Motor Vehicles also has refused to recognize the consular card, issued since March [2002] by Mexico's 43 consulates in the United States, to its list of approved identity documents for obtaining a driver's license." Susan Sachs, "New York, Citing Security, Rejects Mexican ID Cards," *New York Times*, December 28, 2002.

79. Graham Gori, "A Card Allows U.S. Banks to Aid Mexican Immigrants," *New York Times*, July 6, 2002.

80. Ibid.

81. The acquisition of the house, however, was not the end of Reyna Guzmán's problems. Martínez writes, "At first, the chilly reception from Reyna's neighbors depressed her to the point that she begged the realtor to tear up the contract. But then she reminded herself that she had worked all her life to buy the house, and she swore to herself that the ones to move would be the neighbors. Five years later, her wish came true: the neighbor she believed was behind most of the harassment, a white police officer, has placed a For Sale sign on his property." Martínez, *Crossing Over*, 315.

82. Figures provided by the U.S. Census Bureau, Washington, DC, Summer 2002.

83. Eric Schmitt reported:

> Groups that back restrictions on immigration, like the Federation for American Immigration Reform and Project U.S.A., which had lost much of their audience in the past five years, have gotten a second wind. They are seizing on the new fears of immigration and providing money and advisers to local campaigns, including the one here in Mason City, a town of 29,000 people that is 93.4 percent non-Hispanic white, according to 2000 census figures. . . . In the past two years, groups advocating restrictions on immigrants have sprung up in Colorado, Georgia, North Carolina, Oregon, and South Carolina. A national coalition that opposes increased immigration, led by the federation of immigration reform, ran more than $500,000 in radio and print advertisements in 10 states in April and May condemning any new agreement with Mexico to expand immigration. The same group paid for new advertisements broadcast in New York City last week.

Eric Schmitt, "Pockets of Protest Are Rising Against Immigration," *New York Times*, August 9, 2001.

84. "Today, many Mexicans live below the poverty line because they perform jobs that Americans do not want or that pay too little, a fact that is the driving force behind several bipartisan proposals in Congress to give them worker rights," Pamela Falk wrote in a letter to the *Los Angeles Times*. See "Mexicans in the U.S.," *Los Angeles Times*, May 17, 2001.

85. Tim Weiner, "Bush, Fox Hope Nations Will Become Better Friends," *New York Times*, February 4, 2001.

86. Chris Hedges, "Where Affection Is Peddled by the Drink, Lonely Immigrants Provide a Market," *New York Times*, March 19, 2001. This loneliness is exacerbated by the holidays—and their inability to travel back home before returning to work. "Juan wished he could spend Christmas with his family instead of with other lonely men like himself," Yilu Zhao writes. "But he and his four roommates, immigrant day laborers far from their sunny Central American homes, did their best to make the holiday festive. . . . On Christmas Eve, a woman who is their friend cooked tamales for the men, a generous gesture that only reminded them that their wives' or their mothers' were more delicious. Then Juan's roommates departed for a holiday party, and he turned to the telephone, his surest tie to his wife and three children in Guatemala." Yilu Zhao, "Christmas Is a Lonely Day for an Immigrant Laborer," *New York Times*, December 26, 2002.

87. Hedges, "Where Affection Is Peddled by the Drink, Lonely Immigrants Provide a Market."

88. Eric Schmitt, "U.S. and Mexico Agree, in Principle, on Temp Workers," *New York Times*, August 9, 2001.

89. "Death on the Border," *New York Times*, May 19, 2003.

90. The *New York Times* editorial was prompted by the death of nineteen undocumented workers in Texas in May who suffocated when locked in the back of a trailer.

91. Kate Zernike and Ginger Thompson, "Deaths of Immigrants Uncover Makeshift World of Smuggling," *New York Times*, June 29, 2003.

92. Thompson, "U.S. and Mexico to Open Talks on Freer Migration for Workers."

93. Carol Hancock Rux, "Eminem: The New White Negro," in *Everything But the Burden: What White People Are Taking from Black Culture*, ed. Greg Tate (New York: Broadway Books, 2003), 36.

94. Argentina's Saul Menem is of Syrian descent; Mexico's Benito Juárez, a full-blooded Zapotec Indian, was president while Americans were fighting the Civil War.

95. Beth Coleman, "Pimp Notes on Autonomy," in Tate, *Everything But the Burden*, 70–71.

96. Certain things, such as the twentieth century's American practice of lynching, are best left in the past and not dragged into the current century.

97. Randall Robinson, *The Debt: What America Owes to Blacks* (New York: E.P. Dutton, 2000), 8.

98. Felicia R. Lee, "New Topic in Black Studies Debate: Latinos," *New York Times*, February 1, 2003.

99. Raymond Hernández, "Rangel's Star Grows Dim as Democrats Lose Ground," *New York Times*, November 30, 2002.

100. Henry Louis Gates Jr. "New Topic in Black Studies Debate: Latinos," *New York Times*, February 1, 2003.

101. Maya Angelou, *I Know Why the Caged Bird Sings* (New York: Random House, 1969), 178–79.

Chapter 4

1. Mary Jordan, "American Retirees Flock to 'Paradise' in Mexico," *Washington Post*, February 5, 2001. Those Americans who settle in Mexico, interestingly, find a kind of life that is superior to what is possible in the United States. Vera Engle, a

retired nurse from Cumberland, Maryland, is a case in point. "Engle said she would not trade her Mexican life, where she lives in a stunning home with a blue tile pool and papaya trees. She said her loyalty to Mexico is due in part to the medical care her husband, who died in 1999, received while suffering from cancer. Engle recalls that on one particular bad day, the doctor came to their home four times," Jordan reported.

2. Margot Roosevelt, "No Bad Days," *Time*, June 11, 2001.

3. "In January 2000, a government committee found that the average prices for the top five drugs for the elderly were 83 percent higher in the United States than in Mexico," Sarah Lunday reported. "But those savings can be risky, pharmacists at American hospitals near the border said." Representative James C. Greenwood is quoted in Sarah Lunday's article, "When Purchasing Medicine in Mexico, Buyer Beware," *New York Times*, April 17, 2001.

4. Another American pioneer is Barbara MacKinnon Montes, who, along with her husband, the late naval captain Alfredo Montes, worked to establish "biosphere reserves" south of Cancún, ensuring that millions of acres of tropical habitats were protected from development.

5. One couple, Joe and Flavia Keenan, have since moved to Brazil; Joe Keenan was assigned there by his employer, the Nature Conservancy. There are three other interesting couples, an Irish-American married to a Lebanese-Mexican; a Czech woman who is divorced from her Mexican husband; a Frenchman and his Mexican wife, whose parents came from New York and Brussels.

6. Mary Jordan and Kevin Sullivan, "Diary," Slate.com, November 13, 2000.

7. When the Loma Prieta earthquake struck on October 17, 1989, I was unprepared for such disasters, but my neighbors kindly provided flashlights, drinking water, and sake.

8. Tony Cohan, *On Mexican Time* (New York: Broadway Books, 2003), 12.

9. Edward Cody, "Shades of Mexico Past," *Washington Post*, November 4, 1991.

10. This is not to imply there is anything wrong with paganism, of course. It should be noted that it fell on my sister to explain the innocuous inclusion of "pagan" symbolism in Easter celebrations among American Christians. I have to admit, however, it's the commercialization of pagan elements notwithstanding that remains personally discomforting. One final comment is in order. The idea of a Jewish couple trying to make their new European neighbor feel welcome by giving her an Easter basket is a splendid one.

11. Cohan, *On Mexican Time*, 16.

12. Ibid., 145.

13. Ibid., 180–81.

14. Richard Rodriguez, *Days of Obligation* (New York: Viking, 1992), 92–93.

15. Ibid., 9.

16. Paul Krugman criticized the Bush White House for putting domestic politics (electoral votes, to be precise) over honoring trade agreements when tariffs on steel imports were imposed. See "America the Scofflaw," *New York Times*, May 24, 2002. More importantly, the Bush administration continues to alienate Brazil, which is taking a greater role on the world stage—and Brasilia now rivals Washington for leadership position in South America, surprisingly, by championing free trade.

17. The United States and Chile did not reach a free-trade agreement until the end of 2002, almost a decade behind the most optimistic estimate. "The Chilean government reacted more with relief than exhilaration to the announcement of the trade agreement," Elizabeth Becker reported. "The accord caps nearly a decade of negotia-

tions in which frustrated Chilean officials have often questioned the seriousness and sincerity of their American counterparts. . . . The first contacts about an agreement took place in 1990 under the first Bush administration. When the Clinton administration secured passage of the North American Free Trade Agreement, Chile was told it would be next in line for trade liberalization, but little progress was made because Republicans in Congress refused to approve the fast track authority that Mr. Clinton was seeking." Elizabeth Becker, "U.S. and Chile Reach Free Trade Accord," *New York Times*, December 12, 2002.

18. Colombians, understandably, were stunned when George W. Bush declared war on "terrorism." Why? "There is no match for a united America, a determined America, an angry America. . . . If we fight this war as a divided nation, then the war is lost," the *first* president Bush said on September 5, 1989, announcing the "war" on drugs. "Victory, victory over drugs is our cause, a just cause." Latin Americans realized that the "war on terrorism" would be an unending nightmare, the way the "war on drugs" is a conflict without end. In the intervening decade Colombia descended into virtual civil war, with no end in sight. This is one reason why Mexico and Chile, both sitting on the UN Security Council, did not endorse military intervention in Iraq; they feared it would exacerbate problems by trying to offer military solutions to very complex problems. See George H.W. Bush's interview with *Time* magazine, September 5, 1989.

19. "Now the resistance [to Vicente Fox] is rising right and left, as skeptics ask what Mr. Fox has to show for his stances beyond pleasant promises from his friend President Bush. His fiercest critics say he is making Mexico a 21st-century banana republic, at the service of the United States," Tim Weiner wrote. This sad assessment was widespread. "The terrorist attacks of September 11 gave President Fox an excuse for not achieving his promises. Now he's having to accept that his friendship with President Bush has great limitations. That's a major setback," Jorge Montano, a former Mexican ambassador to Washington, said. Tim Weiner, "Fox's Wooing of America Brings Him Woes at Home," *New York Times*, April 26, 2002.

20. "Some critics in Latin America are annoyed at what they say is the administration's strategy of dealing first with small countries that have fewer trade disagreements with the United States rather than including bigger trading rivals like Brazil," Elizabeth Becker observed. "And the initiative intensifies competition between Washington and the European Union for access to the Latin American market, where Europe is the second-largest trading partner after the United States. . . . Critics, particularly in Brazil, say they fear that this regional agreement is an attempt by the United States to divide and rule, forcing the bigger Latin nations to accept Washington's dictates in the wider negotiations." Elizabeth Becker, "U.S. Begins Talks for Trade Pact with Central Americans," *New York Times*, January 9, 2003.

21. Dexter Filkins reported:

Since they arrived, the four nuns have cut their own paths through the borough's gritty precincts. They visit immigrant families late at night, often the only time the families can be together to meet with them. They poke around local grocery stores in search of the most piquant chilies. "When we first got here, everyone just stared at us," said Sister Lucila, describing their daily strolls. "Now, everyone waves and says, 'There go the sisters.'" In a neighborhood where many residents are poor, the nuns stand out—part oddity, part inspiration—for having willingly chosen a life of poverty.

Dexter Filkins, "Mott Haven Journal: Four Nuns Serve in a Place of Need," *New York Times*, April 1, 2001.

22. Another grand-uncle struggled with his oldest daughter, a young woman who accomplished little more on any given day apart from dressing herself—and painting her toy poodle's claws red with nail polish—before midday. Fast on her way to acquiring an eating disorder, this young woman decried the materialism of the "capitalist system" that made her leisure possible, while longing for the opportunity to learn ballet with "doña Alicia"—famed Cuban ballerina Alicia Alonso—in Havana. Also shipped off by her frustrated father, she was sent to study and live among the deprivation of true "Socialist realism in Cuba."

23. Charlie LeDuff, "At the Slaughterhouse, Some Things Never Die: Who Kills, Who Cuts, Who Bosses Can Depend on Race," *New York Times*, June 16, 2000. In a subsequent case against the Smithfield Packing Company, Judge John H. West found "egregious and pervasive" labor law violations. "Among the judge's findings was that company officials had sought to scare the plant's sizable Hispanic work force by warning that the union, if successful in organizing the plant, would report workers to the Immigration and Naturalization Services," Kevin Sack reported. Kevin Sack, "Judge Finds Labor Law Broken at Meat-Packing Plant," *New York Times*, January 4, 2001.

24. This is consistent with the Mexican view that the United States is the "purgatory" one must endure to arrive at Canada.

25. Personal interviews with Sydnor by the author, March and April 1995.

26. It was Aristotle who first observed that humans are political animals. Thus it follows that if misanthropy is the hatred of humanity, it is also a hatred of politics. That is itself admirable in its own way: hating what we are as a yearning for what we could be.

27. Alexis de Tocqueville, *Democracy in America*, ed. J.P. Mayer and Max Lerner, trans. George Lawrence (New York: Harper & Row, 1965), 569.

28. Deborah Tannen, *I Only Say This Because I Love You* (New York: Ballantine Books, 2002), 7–8.

29. On the rare occasion when the American government does apologize, it presumes that this entails writing checks, as was the case when the United States formally apologized for the internment of Japanese-Americans. Even then, however, historical documents to memorialize American injustices are rare. "Whispered Silences: Japanese-American Detention Camps, Fifty Years Later," an exhibition of the photographs of Joan Myers, is a welcome exception.

30. Indeed, consider the absurdity of America's reluctance to apologize for what we have done wrong as a nation: We would rather apologize for and recognize the Irish famine than apologize for and recognize slavery. "The Irish Hunger Memorial opening today on the edge of the Hudson River near Manhattan's southern tip could be New York City's equivalent of the Vietnam War Memorial in Washington, an unconventional work of public art that strikes a deep emotional chord, sums up its artistic moment for a broad audience and expands the understanding of what a public memorial can be," Roberta Smith reported. The Irish Hunger Memorial is a few city blocks from the archaeological site of New York City's first cemetery for black slaves, which has no memorial. Roberta Smith, "A Memorial Remembers the Hungry," *New York Times*, July 16, 2002. An outrageous example is that in November 2000, the U.S. government apologized to Germany for the state of Arizona's executing two German citizens in 1999 in connection with the killing of a bank manager. That the United States routinely fails to inform foreign nationals arrested in this country of their right

to avail themselves of their consular officers is sufficiently egregious. Worse yet, the imposition of the death penalty in the United States is in violation of the Universal Declaration of Human Rights, to which the United States is a signatory nation. When the United States was voted off the UN Human Rights Commission in Spring 2001, it caused outrage among Americans. Yet, a convincing argument can be made that three of the nations elected at that time—Austria, France, and Sweden—all have better records on human rights than does the United States. American outrage over being denied a seat on the UN Human Rights Commission was expressed by William Safire in "Slavery Triumphs," *New York Times*, May 7, 2001.

31. *American Prospect* was started by Robert Reich, former labor secretary under the Clinton administration. Franke-Ruta, Meyerson, and Reich were granted the right to reply.

32. From the first page of Ann Coulter, *Slander: Liberal Lies About the American Right* (New York: Crown, 2002).

33. Personal interviews with Giberstein by the author, March 2000 and June 2001.

34. Ibid.

35. Rebecca Gardyn, "Habla English," *American Demographics*, April 2001.

36. "Latinos are here to stay," Raquel Welch told her audience at a National Press Club luncheon, embracing her heritage. "As citizen Raquel, I'm proud to be Latina." Mireya Navarro reported:

> That Ms. Welch feels comfortable calling herself Latina and has found solid Latina roles to play reflect fundamental changes in Hollywood. Latinos have been part of motion pictures since the industry's inception, but their depiction in movies has fluctuated wildly, from amoral bandits to aristocratic Latin lovers, for instance, depending on the politics and events of the time, film historians say. Some portrayals were so offensive that in the 1920s Mexico and other Latin American countries called for a boycott of American films. But there were also periods when Latinos were popular—the Latin lover craze, the Carmen Miranda comedies—particularly in World War II when much of Europe was closed off as a market and movies turned to Latin America instead.

Mireya Navarro, "Raquel Welch Is Reinvented as a Latina," *New York Times*, June 11, 2001.

37. Quoted in Rebecca Gardyn, "Habla English." See also *Hispanic MONITOR* at http:/secure.yankelovich.com/solutions/monitor/his-monitor.asp.

38. Gardyn, "Habla English," April 2001.

39. Josh Tyrangiel, "Warhol's Border Patrol," *Time*, June 11, 2001.

40. Ibid.

41. Josh Tyrangiel, "The New Tijuana Brass," *Time*, June 11, 2001.

42. Virginia Woolf, *Mrs. Dalloway* (London: L.&V. Woolf at the Hagarth Press, 1925), 10–11.

43. Robert Putnam, *Bowling Alone: The Collapse and Revival of American Community* (New York: Simon & Schuster, 2000), 376.

44. Douglas Monroy, *Thrown Among Strangers: The Making of Mexican Culture in Frontier California* (Berkeley: University of California Press, 1990), 158.

45. Mexico's PRI was humane compared to the Soviets, of course. "You have to remember that this country was torn away from the rest of the world for 70 years, during which there as a virtual genocide of the best and the brightest, the most tal-

ented," artist Mihail Chemiakin told the *New York Times*, explaining the difficulty Russia has encountered since the demise of the Soviet Union. "To expect that suddenly, all at once, democratic norms will restore the culture is impossible. The country was too disfigured." Celestine Bohlen, "In Russia, a New Vulgarity and a New Freedom," *New York Times*, August 19, 2001.

46. Ginger Thompson, "Mexicans Wrestle with Their Own Border Issues," *New York Times*, August 27, 2000.

47. Jamie Allen, "Luis Barajas: Founder, Flaunt Magazine," CNN.com, February 6, 2001.

48. Nancy Gibbs, "A Whole New World," *Time*, June 11, 2001.

49. Larry Rohter, "Rock en Español Is Approaching Its Final Border," *New York Times*, August 6, 2000.

50. Ibid.

51. Ibid.

52. "Music from the Motherland," *New York Times*, May 14, 2001.

53. "In many ways, history is repeating itself," Nancy Foner, an anthropologist at the State University of New York at Purchase and the author of *From Ellis Island to JFK: New York's Two Great Waves of Immigration*, is quoted as saying. "Like today, immigrants a hundred years ago often settled near their relatives and friends from their home communities—in the same neighborhood and sometimes on the very same block. In New York's Little Italy a century ago, you might have found people from one small district clustered on one side of a city block while people from another district lived on the opposite side." Kevin Sack, "Far From Mexico, Making a Place Like Home" *New York Times*, July 30, 2001.

54. Stefan Thomke and Eric von Hippel, "Customers as Innovators: A New Way to Create Value," *Harvard Business Review* (April 2002): 79.

55. The examples are dizzying. In my neighborhood, Roberta Graham married Alfonso Escobedo; Joe Keenan married Flavia. The Escobedo and Keenan children are, respectively, the true NAFTA generation.

56. Monroy, *Thrown Among Strangers*, 158.

57. "It was a slam-dunk for Petrobras," Walter Molano of BCP Securities in Greenwich, Connecticut was quoted as saying of Petroleo Brasileiro's purchase of a 58.6 percent stake in Pérez Companc, Argentina's leading energy concern. Tony Smith, "Latin Companies are Bargain Hunting in Argentina," *New York Times*, July 24, 2002.

58. Alsea's marketing savvy was rewarded when in September 2002 it opened its first Starbucks in Mexico City, a few blocks from the American embassy. "We don't have to go up a learning curve with them," Howard Schultz, chairman and founder of Starbucks, said. Associated Press, "Alsea to Aid Starbucks in Mexico," September 10, 2002.

59. Richard Rodriguez, "Go North, Young Man," *Mother Jones* (July/August 1995).

60. Personal interview, March 2001.

61. It goes without saying that one unexpected benefit of NAFTA is that my grandmother's gardens are being tended by someone who has also worked on Steven Spielberg's gardens, and the masonry work is now being performed by someone who improved his technique after being yelled at by Martha Stewart. ("All these years I have been asking nicely," my grandmother observed. "To think that what I really should have been doing is acting vulgar and yelling at the help!")

62. For an amusing account, see Eric Umansky, "With Fidel's Blessing," *Brill's Content*, January 2001.

63. For example, Mexicans who are legal residents of the United States cannot vote in the United States, thus creating a floating population of people in the United States who pay taxes but have no say in government. Taxation without representation proved intolerable to American colonists in the eighteenth century. Mexican consular officials, in another initiative, lobbied members of the American banking system to have them accept Mexican consular identification to have these individuals open bank accounts, thus sparing them the expenses of having to deal in a cash economy, or pay exorbitant fees at check cashing services. Another noteworthy program involved the Mexican government providing tens of thousands of bilingual textbooks to help the school systems in border cities teach the Hispanic students enrolled in their districts.

64. This is what is presented as insight: "Mexicans drink more Coca-Cola than Americans drink," Richard Rodriguez states. Mexican officials find such declarations amusing. Rodriguez forgot to state, however, that this result was only after a Cuban, Roberto Goizueta, was in charge of Coca-Cola and executives like Vicente Fox, Mexico's current president, worked together to implement a comprehensive marketing campaign. And what, pray tell, is one to make of the corollary fact that Americans spend more on Corona beer than Mexicans do? What is one to make of other meaningless facts? Consider: Though California is west of Nevada, Los Angeles is further east than is Reno. And while Mérida lies south of Mexico City, Mexico City is further from the North Pole than is Mérida. Richard Rodriguez, *Brown: The Last Discovery of America* (New York: Viking, 2002), 161.

65. Personal communication, aide to Sergio Acosta, foreign relations committee secretary of the House of Deputies, April 2002.

66. Shelby Steele, "When the Going Gets Messy, There's Jesse," *Wall Street Journal*, December 1, 2000.

67. Associated Press, "Mexico Names Man to Direct Agency," September 19, 2002. From the start, expectations were raised high. "What I'd like to see from this guy is that he stays here in the United States, that he helps organize Mexicans here, and that he serves as a liaison to not only the Mexican government, but to the American government," Guadalupe Gómez, president of the Council of Presidents of Mexican Federations of Los Angeles, said at the time of Morales's appointment.

68. John Kenneth Galbraith, *The Good Society* (Boston: Houghton Mifflin, 1996), 8.

69. Fox's speech, delivered in a national address on May 29, 2001, set out a twenty-five-year projection consistent with developing a post-paternalistic modern nation, fully integrated into NAFTA. His lack of political experience, however, resulted in a treacherous learning curve, one that was anticipated by European observers. "Alongside slick marketing, what is needed is the skilful choice of priorities, the nurturing of alliances for change, and persistence as well as popularity-seeking," the London *Economist* observed when Fox took office. "Fox's Political Challenge," London *Economist*, December 2, 2000.

70. Robert Haskett, *Indigenous Rulers: An Ethnohistory of Town Government in Colonial Cuernavaca* (Albuquerque: University of New Mexico Press, 1991), 21.

71. There were, of course, vigorous debates and famous clashes of opinions. Church and state conflicted when bishops and viceroys clashed; the former wanted a gradual process, and the latter wanted to be done with it, the better to promote commerce.

72. Robert Haskett, "Indigenous Rulers: Nahua Mediation of Spanish Socio-Political 'Evangelism' in Early Cuernavaca," Unpublished paper, 1994, 6.

73. Ibid.

74. The same holds true for many other names, of course. The Yucatec Maya surname "Cantu" became oftentimes "Canto," and so on.

75. Marian Smith, "American Names/Declaring Independence," www.ins.usdoj.gov/graphics/aboutins/history/articles/NameEssay.html.

76. One manifestation of that ambivalence is seen in the brand of Christianity practiced in Mexico. The devotion to the Virgin of Guadalupe reflects the fusion of both Western and indigenous traditions, where a European saint appears as a person of color. "This seems to be so kinetic, so deep," Timothy Matovina, a theology professor at the University of Notre Dame, told the *New York Times*. "In Mexican society, Guadalupe is everywhere—on tattoos, on T-shirts, on dashboards, in stores, in homes, in churches. She's the daily companion to Mexican people no matter whoever or wherever they are." Mireya Navarro, "In Many Churches, Icons Compete for Space," *New York Times*, May 29, 2002.

77. Haskett, "Indigenous Rulers," 6.

78. Ibid., 24.

79. With national identities supplanting the forces of acculturation, certain terms were rendered archaic. When an American, such as Richard Rodriguez, walks up to a Guatemalan of indigenous descent and asks, "Are you Hispanic?" he gets no reply. (The question is as insulting as if he had asked, "Are you acculturate?" or if he had asked an African-American, "Are you civilized?") The answer to his insensitive question, of course, is "I'm Guatemalan."

80. Though hardly known among "Latinos," the Hispanic Society of America enjoys great renown around the world as a leading center of Hispanic studies. Indeed, it is often compared to the Victoria and Albert in London, but with a focus on Spain and Spanish studies.

81. Think of how the cowboy culture exalts solitude and individualism in a rugged terrain, both physical and emotional.

82. In New Spain, "criollo" carried with it a certain snob appeal, much the same way that in nineteenth-century America, the term "WASP" came to carry an elitist distinction.

83. Frank Bruni, "Another George Bush, P., on Political Stage," *New York Times*, April 18, 2000.

84. D.H. Lawrence, "The Mozo," in *Mornings in Mexico* (London: Martin Secker, 1927).

85. Monroy, *Thrown Among Strangers*, 158.

86. Ibid., 160. It would appear that every California daughter was married to an American arriving from the East. Abel Stearns married Juan Bandini's daughter, Arcadia, in 1841. Cave Couts and James B. Winston married two other daughters. Jon Forster married Pio Pico's sister, Isadora. Antonio Maria Lugo's daughters were married to William Wolfskill and Stephen Foster. John Temple married Rafaela Yorba.

87. Monroy, *Thrown Among Strangers*, 161.

88. Haskett, "Indigenous Rulers," 161.

89. The relevance of much research is diminished because it imposes a white-black racial paradigm that does not apply to Hispanics. Among the more conspicuous literature thus affected includes the following:

Aaker, Jennifer L., Anne M. Brumbaugh, and Sonya Grier. "Non-Target Market Effects and Viewer Distinctiveness: The Impact of Target Marketing on Advertising Attitudes." *Journal of Consumer Psychology* 9, no. 3 (2000): 127–40.

Forehand, Mark R., and Rohit Deshpandé. "What We See Makes Us Who We Are: Priming Ethnic Self Awareness and Advertising Response." *Journal of Marketing Research* 28 (August 2001): 336–48.

Grier, Sonya A., and Rohit Deshpandé. "Social Dimensions of Consumer Distinctiveness: The Influence of Social Status on Group Identity and Advertising Persuasion." *Journal of Marketing Research* 38, no. 2 (2001): 216–24.

Grier, Sonya A., and Anne L. McGill. "How We Explain Depends on Who We Explain: The Impact of Social Category on the Selection of Causal Comparisons and Causal Explanations." *Journal of Experimental Social Psychology* 36 (1997): 545–66.

Whittler, Tommy E. "The Effects of Actors' Race in Commercial Advertising: Review and Extension." *Journal of Advertising* 20, no. 1 (2001): 54–60.

Whittler, Tommy E., and Joan DiMeo. "Viewers' Reactions to Racial Cues in Advertising Stimuli." *Journal of Advertising Research* (December 1991): 37–46.

Williams, Jerome D., and William J. Qualls. "Middle-Class Black Consumers and Intensity of Ethnic Identification." *Psychology and Marketing* 6, no. 4 (1989): 263–86.

Williams, Jerome D., William J. Qualls, and Sonya A. Grier. "Racially Exclusive Real Estate Advertising: Public Policy Implications for Fair Housing Practices." *Journal of Public Policy and Marketing* 14, no. 2 (Fall 1995): 225–44.

Wooten, David B. "One-of-a-Kind in a Full House: Some Consequences of Ethnic and Gender Distinctiveness." *Journal of Consumer Psychology* 4, no. 3 (1995): 205–24.

90. More amusing, if the "characteristics" identified by R.J. Reynolds are applied to other groups, bizarre outcomes are possible. Market research, for instance, describes Italians as being "loud" and the Japanese as being "timid." R.J. Reynolds indicated that Caribbean Hispanics, such as Puerto Ricans, were "loud" and that California Hispanics were "timid." Using the transitive property of mathematics (if A = B and B = C, then A = C), does R.J. Reynolds suggest that Puerto Ricans are Italian, or that the Japanese are California Hispanics?

91. Joan Didion, *Miami* (New York: Vintage International, 1987), 53.

Chapter 5

1. Alexis de Tocqueville, *Democracy in America*, ed. J.P. Mayer and Max Lerner, trans. George Lawrence (New York: Harper & Row, 1965), 225.

2. Conservative commentator Patrick Buchanan is legendary for counting the ways Catholics are "second-class" citizens in American political life, for instance.

3. Canadian writers and intellectuals, such as Al Purdy, Margaret Atwood, and Pierre Trudeau, have played more visible roles in their nation's life. Much to Canadians' chagrin, however, Americans have insisted on dismissing the role of intellectuals, often disparaging Canadians themselves. For instance, Jeff Hale mocks Canadians in "Worrying About Hockey Is Canada's National Sport," *New York Times*, February 10, 2002.

4. Among the more engaging books Daniel Patrick Moynihan wrote are *Miles to Go: A Personal History of Social Policy* (Cambridge, MA: Harvard University Press,

1996); *Maximum Feasible Misunderstanding: Community Action in the War on Poverty* (New York: Free Press, 1969); *Pandemonium: Ethnicity in International Politics* (New York: Oxford University Press, 1993); and *On the Law of Nations* (Cambridge, MA: Harvard University Press, 1990). An exceptional collection of his work is found in *Daniel Patrick Moynihan: The Intellectual in Public Life*, ed. Robert A. Katzmann, (Washington, DC: Woodrow Wilson Center Press, 1998).

5. Consistent with American values, critics then labeled Al Gore a "nerd" and a policy "wonk" as a way of disparaging him and attacking his "conceit" in putting his ideas in a book.

6. It took this long for Mexicans to challenge the mantra of dictators everywhere first spoken by Porfirio Díaz: "He who counts the votes, wins."

7. The remarkable "evolution from hard-line Marxist to pragmatic power broker" of Jorge Castañeda is reported in Peter Fritsch and José de Cordoba, "A Mexican Official Travels from the Left to the Center of Power," *Wall Street Journal*, April 10, 2001.

8. "Blurring right and left ideologies, Mr. Castañeda tilted Mr. Fox toward great promises of social and political justice," Weiner wrote. "Mr. Castañeda is already contemplating running for president himself. It is not easy to imagine a man whose tastes run to fancy suits and fine wines pressing the flesh in a dusty village. But then, a few years back, no one foresaw Mr. Castañeda standing shoulder to shoulder with the American secretary of state, whispering in his ear." Tim Weiner, "When He Talks for Mexico, Washington Pays Attention," *New York Times*, March 19, 2002.

9. "An Unlikely Mexican Foreign Minister," *New York Times*, May 12, 2001.

10. Jorge Castañeda, *Perpetuating Power: How Mexican Presidents Were Chosen* (New York: New Press, 2000), 22.

11. Consider a representative sentence in one of his books. "Despite its marked contrasts with the Anglo-Saxon, conservative free-market paradigm—amply documented by Margaret Thatcher's constant, lost battles over restricting the community's encroachment into social, political, and legal realms—the EC is certainly not a perfect model of social, regulated, planned, environmentally sound, and politically democratic and accountable integration," he wrote in *Utopia Unarmed: The Latin American Left After the Cold War* (New York: Knopf, 1993), 318. This is a sentence only an academic could write—and it reflects Mr. Castañeda's admirable stubbornness. Who else could write almost 500 pages on the future of Latin America's "Left"—which has, in fact, no future, but only a rather sorry past?

12. Mark Fineman, "Mexican Envoy Seeks to Forge U.S.-Cuba Ties," *Los Angeles Times*, March 18, 2001.

13. For instance, despite my respect for the journalistic skills of Andres Oppenheimer, I did not agree with his dim assessment of Mexico during NAFTA's first decade, which he presented in *Bordering on Chaos: Mexico's Roller-Coaster Journey to Prosperity* (Boston: Little, Brown, 1996).

14. American commentators, for some inexplicable reason, often note that Enrique Krauze is Jewish, as if that would somehow preclude his participating fully in Mexico's civic life. Artist Frida Kahlo was half-Jewish and she was adored, and Jacobo Zabludovsky, also Jewish, was, for decades, the Mexican equivalent of Dan Rather, the anchorman reporting the news on national television. These are the rule, not the exception.

15. When Vicente Fox defeated the PRI, the *New York Times* profiled the singular role of intellectuals as agents for democratization, a compelling tribute to the role

writers and thinkers are expected to play in public affairs. Julia Preston, "The Defiant Ones: Four Mexicans Exult in Party's Fall," *New York Times*, July 12, 2000.

16. Ginger Thompson, "Mexico's Voters Spoke. Now the Victor Must Act," *New York Times*, July 9, 2000.

17. Reinaldo Arenas, *Before Night Falls* (New York: Viking, 1993), 90.

18. Octavio Paz, *The Labyrinth of Solitude* (New York: Grove Press, 1962), 12–13.

19. Ibid., 13.

20. Ibid., 14–15.

21. Milton Kleg, *Hate, Prejudice and Racism* (Albany: State of New York University Press, 1993), 179–80.

22. Paz, *The Labyrinth of Solitude*, 16.

23. Reinaldo Arenas is writing not about Mexicans, but about his fellow Cubans— and his observations hold true for all immigrants. Arenas, *Before Night Falls*, 301.

24. "For three decades, one of Mexico's most explosive secrets has been the identity of the snipers who carried out the country's worst massacre since the 1910 Revolution, firing machine guns from rooftops into a crowd of peaceful protestors on the eve of the 1968 Olympics," Sam Dillon reported when General Marcelino García Barragán broke his silence. "These documents are of extraordinary importance, because they fill one of the largest gaps in our knowledge of the 1968 violence," historian Sergio Aguayo told Dillon. "Sam Dillon, A General Illuminates '68 Massacre in Mexico," *New York Times*, June 29, 1999.

25. A decade later, Vargas Llosa was delighted as the PRI was defeated. "Such is the heavy mortgage that weighs upon the shoulders of Francisco Labastida, the PRI candidate. He confronts a tough choice: Lose, so that his country may at last be free, or win a Pyrrhic victory, which everyone will consider a swindle, and whose immediate consequence will be to turn Mexico away from what seemed to be her first firm steps toward real democracy," he wrote from Mexico City on the eve of the election that brought Vicente Fox to power. Mario Vargas Llosa, "Freedom's Stake in Mexico's Election," *New York Times*, June 30, 2000.

26. Tim Weiner, "Mexico Chief Pushes New Border Policy: Free and Easy Does It," *New York Times*, December 14, 2001.

27. Maarten van Delden, *Carlos Fuentes, Mexico and Modernity* (Nashville: Vanderbilt University Press, 1998).

28. Ibid., 31.

29. Carlos Fuentes, "Notas de un novelista: La revolución cubana," in *Novedades*, February 2, 1959, quoted in van Delden, *Carlos Fuentes, Mexico and Modernity*, 90–91.

30. Donald N. Sull, "Why Good Companies Go Bad," *Harvard Business Review* (July–August 1999): 42.

31. van Delden, *Carlos Fuentes, Mexico and Modernity*, 31.

32. Stephen Talbot, "The Dangerous Mind of Carlos Fuentes," *Mother Jones* (November 1988): 24.

33. van Delden, *Carlos Fuentes, Mexico and Modernity*, 168.

34. Ibid., 169.

35. Donald Sull identifies the four "hallmarks of active inertia" this way: (1) strategic frames become blinders, (2) processes harden into routines, (3) relationships become shackles, and (4) values harden into dogmas. Sull, "Why Good Companies Go Bad," 48.

36. Curiously, some American high school students think Canada is a state, but

think New Mexico is a foreign country. Officials at the Convention & Visitors Bureau in Las Cruces, for instance, amused me with incredible tales. "Yes, the U.S. dollar is legal tender in New Mexico. No, you don't need a passport to enter New Mexico" would very well do as the state motto.

37. Anthony DePalma, *Here: A Biography of the New American Continent* (New York: Public Affairs, 2001), 274.

38. Douglas Monroy, *Thrown Among Strangers: The Making of Mexican Culture in Frontier California* (Berkeley: University of California Press, 1990), 203–4.

39. Ibid., 207.

40. Ibid., 218.

41. Ibid., 210. A riveting account of lynching in the United States, Philip Dray's *At the Hands of Persons Unknown: The Lynching of Black America* (New York: Random House, 2002), should be required reading in every high school.

42. The Amazon Surveillance System is impressive: 900 listening posts on the ground, 19 radar stations, 5 airborne early-warning jets, and 3 remote-sensing aircraft. The $1.4 billion system monitors 1.9 million square miles, an area larger than half the continental United States. Larry Rohter, "Brazil Employs Tools of Spying to Guard Itself," *New York Times*, July 27, 2002.

43. Ibid.

44. The reporter, fearful that his access to members of the American business community would be affected, requested that his name not be used. His sentiment, however, is representative of how many Brazilians, if not most, feel.

45. Brazilians are particularly wary of making Mexico's mistake in trusting the United States. Brazilians fear being bamboozled by Americans, and often point to Americans' betrayal of their word in the Treaty of Guadalupe-Hidalgo as a cautionary account. Brazilians, in fact, point to present-day American duplicity. Of the U.S. farm subsidies passed in 2002, Brazilians were enraged. "Farmers here [in Brazil] are still seething about the farm bill that the United States Congress passed this spring [of 2002], which authorized more than $100 billion in subsidies for cash crops, including cotton, soybeans and sugar," Edmund Andrews reported from São Paulo. "Cotton farmers say the cotton subsidies sent world prices plunging and wiped out most of their profits this year. Brazil's soybean farmers, who are second only to the United States in production, say they would have suffered an even worse fate had it not been for bad weather conditions and low output in the United States." Edmund L. Andrews, "As U.S. Seeks Trade Accord, Brazilians Recall Discord," *New York Times*, October 30, 2002. This fundamental dishonesty when it comes to playing fair continues to undermine American credibility around the world and foster resentment from our allies.

46. See International Credit Monitor report, 1989; adjusted for inflation by the author. As one Mexican official quipped, "The White House is free to send us a check, payable to the 'Bank of Mexico' whenever it chooses."

47. It is not without irony that some of the Brazilian farmers hurt by American farm subsidies—are Americans! Simon Romero reported, "More than a century after his ancestors began farming in the Midwestern United States, Dan Carroll's best hope of bringing his son into the family business is to buy land in the savannas of Brazil. 'I have no doubt that Brazil is the future of global agriculture and I want my son to be part of that,' Mr. Carroll, 46, said in an interview. 'It's prohibitively expensive for him to buy land in the States right now.'" For an increasing number of Americans, the pursuit of the American dream leads them outside the United States.

Simon Romero, "U.S. Farmers Put Down Roots in Brazilian Soil," *New York Times*, December 1, 2002.

48. Ginger Thompson reported:

[The] photographs give new life to the testimonies repeated year after year by the students who were there, and raise fresh questions about the credibility of past government denials. In one frame after another, the photos show the faces of frightened young men paraded before a camera by plainclothes gunmen wearing one white glove, the signature of the special force. Published on Sunday in *Proceso*, the 21 photographs were anonymously delivered to the magazine's correspondent in Madrid. A caller, who refused to identify himself, told the correspondent that a government photographer had been assigned at the time to document the operation.

Ginger Thompson, "Flashback to Deadly Clash of '68 Shakes Mexico," *New York Times*, December 13, 2001.

49. "In recent months, [Interior Minister Santiago] Creel has allowed government human rights investigators to review secret files on protesters and guerrillas missing since the 70s," Ginger Thompson reported. "On the anniversary of the student massacre in Tlateloco, Creel announced that the government would open its archives on that tragedy." Ginger Thompson, "Mexicans Move to Pry Open Potentially Explosive Files," *New York Times*, October 12, 2001.

50. Tim Weiner, "Mexican Leader, Reneging, Bangs Door Shut on a Violent Era," *New York Times*, August 21, 2002.

51. In September 2002, three officers, General Francisco Quiros Hermosillo, Brigadier General Mario Arturo Acosta Chaparro, and Major Francisco Barquin, were charged with the murder of leftists in the 1970s and went before a military court. For General Gallardo's story, see Ginger Thompson, "12 Who 'Disappeared' in Mexico: A General's Sinister Story," *New York Times*, July 16, 2002. In Mexico, *Proceso* continues to run investigative stories examining the links between American officials and the PRI's repression. In the United States, the New California Media has run a number of stories by Reding. "The first document [released] is a confidential telegram from the U.S. embassy in Mexico City to the State Department in Washington," Andrew Reding reports. "It says that Mexico's foreign minister visited the U.S. ambassador with a message from President Echeverría to President Richard Nixon. The message was to reassure Nixon, who was worried about the possibility of communism on the U.S. southern flank, that Mexico would never tolerate communism within its borders. . . . The second document is a lot more damning. . . . It said [Mexican security forces] were under orders to take drastic measures against the 'terrorists,' who were 'expendable' as 'garbage.'" Andrew Reding, "Declassified Documents Point to the Top in Mexico," *New California Media*, ncmonline.com, January 25, 2002. For an account of the three officers being charged, see Tim Weiner, "Three Mexican Army Officers are Accused in 70's Killings," *New York Times*, September 28, 2002.

52. Tina Rosenberg, "Truth Commissions Take on a Local Flavor," *New York Times*, February 26, 2001.

53. In recent years, declassified documents are shedding light on the extent to which American officials knew of the systematic violations of human rights. In a typical story, Diana Jean Schemo reported, "A recently declassified State Department document shows that Latin American officers involved in Operation Condor,

the joint effort in the 1970s by right-wing opponents to crush left-wing opposition, used an American communications installation to share intelligence." Diana Jean Schemo, "New Files Tie U.S. to Deaths of Latin Leftists in 1970s," *New York Times*, March 5, 2001.

54. Kent Paterson, "Anti-Terrorism: U.S. Police Training in Mexico May Clash with Human Rights," Pacific News Service, Pacificnews.org, September 26, 2001.

55. "The military had an unwritten agreement with the government: give us complete autonomy, and we will leave you alone," Raúl Benítez, a leading national security scholar at the National Autonomous University of Mexico, told the *New York Times*. "This system is changing, but slowly." Others argue that Mexico should follow Costa Rica's lead and abolish its army. "Why do we have an army?" Alvaro Vallarta Cecena, a retired general who heads the congressional armed services committee, is quoted as saying. "To invade the United States? To invade Guatemala? No, we need it inside Mexico, to solve internal problems." Tim Weiner and Ginger Thompson, "Harsh Spotlight Shines on Mexico's Army," *New York Times*, July 9, 2002.

56. Mary Jordan, and Kevin Sullivan, "Mexico Moves Slowly to Confront Past," *Washington Post*, January 2, 2001.

57. Bernard Simon, "U.S.-Canada Tomato War Heats Up," *New York Times*, December 7, 2001.

58. "Steel Pandering," *New York Times*, August 26, 2002.

59. Edmund Andrews, "Bush Scales Back Steel Tariffs," *New York Times*, August 23, 2002.

60. Tocqueville, *Democracy in America*, 567.

Chapter 6

1. Americans of Mexican ancestry use various labels to describe themselves, each one with distinct political or socioeconomic overtones: "Mexican-American," "Hispanic," "Latino," or "Chicano." Five derogatory terms are also used: "pocho," "cholo," "wetback," "taco," and "spic."

2. Marvin Matises, a cultural anthropologist who studies American consumers, personal communication with author, July 2000.

3. In an effort to make a gentlemen of me, it was my uncle Teddy who introduced me to Paul Smith, Bergdorf Goodman, Paul Stuart, and his tailor, all to spare me further embarrassments.

4. Personal communication, February 2003. The observation that women are judged more harshly than men transcends how one is dressed to go to a restaurant. "Women tend to be forgiven for their ambition if they apologize for it," Linda Wells, editor of *Allure* magazine said, commenting on the misogynistic delight men showed for Martha Stewart's legal troubles. "Martha refuses to apologize and she still hasn't and she is paying a price for that." See David Carr, "For the Press, a Case That Is an Irresistible Draw," *New York Times*, June 5, 2003.

5. Consider, for instance, the demographic changes in New York's Spanish Harlem. As Puerto Ricans entered the ranks of the middle class, many moved out of Spanish Harlem to Queens or northern New Jersey. Puerto Rican success and exodus coincided with an influx of Mexicans—mostly from Puebla and Oaxaca states—into that community. The incoming of Mexicans into what had been a Puerto Rican neighborhood created its own phenomenon: Puerto Ricans, nostalgic about the neighborhood that had been their parents' and grandparents' home, have, in the 2000s, found re-

newed affection for Spanish Harlem. "No matter where you lived, even if people lived in Brooklyn or the Bronx, they always came here," Nicholasa Mohr told a reporter. "They came to La Marqueta or they would come to see relatives, or go to church at St. Cecilia's. This was the capital, the heart of the Puerto Rican community." Felix Matos Rodriguez, director of the Center for Puerto Rican Studies at Hunter College, agreed. "You have a community here that on many fronts is feeling threatened. So the need to protect the base becomes very important because that's how you make a claim on the political structure." In other words, some Puerto Ricans fear that Mexicans moving into their former neighborhood undermines the community's historic identity as a place where Puerto Ricans lived in New York City. Joseph Berger, "A Puerto Rican Rebirth in El Barrio," *New York Times*, December 10, 2002.

6. Armed with video cameras installed in the homes of American consumers, cultural anthropologists are studying how Americans live with the same curiosity usually reserved for contributors to *National Geographic* magazine. Video clips are now routinely presented in marketing meetings throughout corporate America, which is particularly instructive when merchandising to ethnic groups, though it is rather unsettling. Describing how anthropology has invaded marketing in the United States, Lawrence Osborne writes:

> Housecalls, which borrows the techniques of academic ethnography and anthropology to study the intimate (and sometimes secretive) behaviors of those strange, exotic tribal units known as consumers [are now used throughout corporate America]. Wiry and fit-looking despite his gray hair and 71 years, [Bill Abrams] chats amiably about his latest suburban expedition. Abrams knows that the Housecalls approach seems invasive—but aren't anthropologists who camp out with remote tribes pretty pushy, too? "There are things that you just can't learn from questionnaires," he says. "You have to see people with the product at the very moment they're using it." Abrams looks back at Macri's house and smiles. What consumers say and remember and what they actually do are often two totally different things.

Not all anthropologists are pleased by these developments.

> Some academic anthropologists have lamented that their discipline—one predicated on an appreciation of individual cultures—has been appropriated by advertisers intent on creating global markets. That said, many besides Janet Allen have crossed over to the corporate side. In the early 1990s, for example, Nissan hired a team of anthropologists to help redesign its Infiniti line of cars. The researchers helped Nissan understand that Japanese notions of luxury were radically different from those of Americans: the Japanese crave simplicity, Americans visible opulence. Nissan's method was promptly imitated by Volkswagen and others.

Lawrence Osborne, "Consuming Rituals of the Suburban Tribe," *New York Times*, January 13, 2002.

7. Marilyn Halter, *Shopping for Identity: The Marketing of Ethnicity* (New York: Schocken, 2000), 50.

8. Starbucks outlets in Miami, for instance, have tailored their products to reflect Hispanic cultural preferences where coffee is concerned. Among Hispanics, for in-

stance, coffee is a "drink," whereas for Anglo-Americans, coffee is a "beverage." How one consumes a drink differs from how one consumes a beverage; a drink is consumed in one sitting, while a beverage is carried away.

9. For more information on how non-Hispanic coffee brands are faring now that Starbucks has inculcated a coffee culture among American consumers, please see www.associatedcoffee.com.

10. Lee Romney, "Mexican Businesses Push North of the Border," *Los Angeles Times*, February 19, 2001.

11. Niraj Dawar and Tony Frost, "Competing with Giants: Survival Strategies for Local Companies in Emerging Markets," *Harvard Business Review* (March/April 1999): 128–29.

12. "The deal puts Coca-Cola Femsa in a strong position to combat increasing competition from Pepsi-Cola," Elisabeth Malkin reported. "Mexico will continue to be the most important country for the combined company, providing 63 percent of revenue. Coca-Cola Femsa also has a franchise in Buenos Aires, while Panamco's franchises cover all of Venezuela, most of Colombia, parts of Brazil and parts of Costa Rica, Guatemala, Nicaragua and Panama." Elisabeth Malkin, "Latin American Coca-Cola Bottlers in Giant Merger," *New York Times*, December 24, 2002.

13. In November 2002, América Móvil won an auction for three mobile phone licenses in Brazil, one that included the prized São Paulo metropolitan area. "Latin America contrasts sharply with the major developed economies, where growth in wireless phone service has slowed markedly and companies are retrenching after over-investing wildly in new licenses and new digital services in the late 1990s," Elisabeth Malkin reported. "The technology proved slow to meet expectations and even slower to generate interest among consumers, while prices for existing services were beaten down by intensifying competitive pressures. That bubble never reached Latin America, where more than half the population lives in poverty and for many people, cell phones are their first phones." Elisabeth Malkin, "Big Mexican Cellphone Company Moves Into Brazil," *New York Times*, November 23, 2002.

14. Insightful writing on the Hispanic market is primarily produced by marketers, two of whom are Ed Morales and Arlene Davila. Corporate managers are advised to read Morales's *Living in Spanglish: The Search for Latino Identity in America* (Los Angeles: LA Weekly Books, 2002), which offers an urbane, refreshing and thoughtful discussion; and Davila's *Latinos, Inc.: The Marketing and Making of a People* (Berkeley: University of California Press, 2001), which is an exemplary discussion of the Hispanic market in the United States.

15. One Mexican-American voice, Richard Rodriguez's, enjoyed widespread dissemination, both in the PBS *News Hour* and in his anguished writings published in *Harper's*.

16. Corporate America has successfully met these challenges in the past. Compare the racial and ethnic inclusiveness of contemporary advertising campaigns with those of a quarter century ago, where Asians, Hispanics, and African Americans were almost invisible.

17. Richard Rodriguez, "Mixed Blood," *Harper's*, November 1991.

18. Juan González, *Harvest of Empire: A History of Latinos in America* (New York: Viking, 2000), 96.

19. Tim Rutten, "Literary Candor, Straight from Latin America," *Los Angeles Times*, April 9, 2001.

20. For the history of how social Darwinism was used to justify segregation, see

Daniel J. Kevles, *In the Name of Eugenics: Genetics and the Uses of Human Heredity* (Cambridge, MA: Harvard University Press, 1985); Robert C. Bannister, *Social Darwinism: Science and Myth in Anglo-American Social Thought* (Philadelphia: Temple University Press, 1979); Edward J. Larson, *Trial and Error: The American Controversy Over Creation and Evolution* (New York: Oxford University Press, 1985); and John Higham, *Strangers in the Land: Patterns of American Nativism: 1860–1925* (New Brunswick, NJ: Rutgers University Press, 1994).

21. Richard Rodriguez, *Brown: The Last Discovery of America* (New York: Viking, 2002), 35.

22. Those inclined to examine queer Latino letters would be advised to read Jaime Manrique, *Eminent Maricones* (Madison: University of Wisconsin Press, 1999), which is a significant discussion on Manuel Puig, Reinaldo Arena, and Federico García Lorca.

23. Canada has long protested the application of the death penalty in the United States as being both a violation of human rights, and racist in application. Canada has sided with third countries, such as Germany and Mexico, who have challenged the right of the United States to execute their citizens, and Canada has protested the racist treatment of Canadian citizens at the hands of American officials. Most recently, Canada has complained formally of the mistreatment of Canadians of Arab ancestry who have attempted to enter the United States lawfully.

24. Shelby Steele, "Ideology as Identity," *Wall Street Journal*, January 11, 2001.

25. "Californians are unaware, generally, that our forebears committed themselves to the literal extermination of the California Indian people," historian James Rawls of Diablo Valley College said. The conflict over who has the right to claim history affects the entire state. In San Francisco, for instance, statues of Juan Bautista de Anza, who led the first European settlers to the area from Mexico, and King Carlos III languish in a warehouse. Associated Press, "of Californians Fight Over History," July 22, 2002.

26. "San Diego Council Bans the Word 'Minority,'" CNN.com, April 3, 2001.

27. Dagoberto Gilb, "Blue Eyes, Brown Eyes: A *Pocho* Tours Mexico," *Harper's*, June 2001.

28. Christopher Hitchens, "Why So Many Tech Executives Are Smitten with Randian Objectivism," *Fast Company* (August/September 2001): 132.

29. Gilb, "Blue Eyes, Brown Eyes."

30. J. Holbrook Johnson, "Father of the Mexican *Mestizos*," Stevensonpress.com, May 1996.

31. Dagoberto Gilb was granted the right to reply in September 2002 but declined to comment.

32. Alma Guillermoprieto, *Looking for History: Dispatches from Central America* (New York: Pantheon, 2001), 283.

33. Jorge Ramos, *The Other Face of America* (New York: HarperRayo, 2002), xxii.

34. Richard Rodriguez, "Prodigal Father," Salon.com, December 7, 2000. "Her English is about as bad as my Spanish," he says of the young woman whose task is to escort him around Tijuana.

35. In his book, *Days of Obligation: An Argument with My Mexican Father* (New York: Viking, 1992), for instance, Richard Rodriguez has a chapter called "Mexico's Children."

36. Rodriguez, "Prodigal Father."

37. The recriminations and accusations are consistent with those of dysfunctional families. "You were a rotten father who never loved me," Americans of Mexican an-

cestry lash out. "You were an ungrateful kid who dropped out of school, and that's why you're a loser," Mexico shouts back.

38. Quoted in Lisa Belkin, "The Odds of That," *New York Times*, August 11, 2002. "But have we evolved into fundamentally rational or fundamentally irrational creatures?" he ponders. "That is one of the central questions."

39. Daniel Goleman, "Myths Bring Cohesion to the Chaos of Life," *New York Times*, May 24, 1988.

40. Alisa Valdes-Rodriguez, *The Dirty Girls Social Club* (New York: St. Martin's Press, 2003), 25.

41. The fictional Amber is as misguided as real-life Dagoberto Gilb in writing his Mexica nonsense in *Harper's*.

42. Valdes-Rodriguez, *The Dirty Girls Social Club*, 216.

43. Indeed, in the case of Shakira, her linguistic heritage consists of English and Arabic from her father, Catalan and Spanish from her mother. Shakira can thus sing in Arabic, Catalan, English, and Spanish with equal legitimacy.

44. Tamar Jacoby, "A Voting Bloc Without a Party," *New York Times*, October 28, 2002.

45. Ibid.

46. Natalie Hopkinson, "Stinging Insect: Lalo Alcaraz's 'La Cucaracha' Hits the Funnies," *Washington Post*, November 25, 2002.

47. Early leaders of the Chicano movement included César Chávez, and Dolores Huerta. Their pioneering work centered on the Bracero Program and the Community Service Organization (CSO). Early successes included the Delano strike that resulted in the Agricultural Labor Relations Act of 1975.

48. Sy Weiss, "Mexico's Water Problem," Letter to the Editor, *New York Times*, April 17, 2001.

49. "With its population expected to grow to 20 million from 15 million over the next 20 years, forecasts say that without new sources of supply Florida by 2020 would face a water deficit of as much as 30 percent," Douglas Jehl wrote in his report. Mexico's Inegi forecasts, by comparison, that Mexico's population will rise to 115 million by 2020, from its current population of 101 million.

50. Jim Yardley, "For Texas Now, Water and Not Oil is Liquid Gold," *New York Times*, April 16, 2001.

51. Erratic weather patterns extended geographically and were of unusual duration, suggesting such factors as global warming were the cause and not Mexican "overpopulation." "A persistent drought in rural Arizona [for instance] and large parts of most other Western states [up and down the U.S.-Mexico border] is bearing down on Arizona's largest population centers, Phoenix and Tucson," Michael Janofsky reported. "Cities where green golf courses, swimming pools, and shopping mall fountains have long been taken for granted are worrying for the first time that a shortage of water may end the days of unbridled growth. They are facing hard decisions about water use as the state confronts the drought's long-term effects on farms and forests, including dwindling crops, a growing threat of devastating wildfires and a worrisome infestation of tree-killing beetles." Michael Janofsky, "Arizona Starts to Feel Impact of Long Drought," *New York Times*, January 27, 2003.

52. Agustin Gurza, "Facts Disprove Stereotype of Large Mexican Families," *Los Angeles Times*, February 20, 2001.

53. In Mexico, after three decades of an unwavering national campaign, families are smaller. The average Mexican couple has 2.4 children in 2002, compared with 7.2

in the 1960s. More than 70 percent of fertile married women take birth control, despite opposition by the Catholic Church. The National Population Council in Mexico City hails this achievement as a "silent demographic revolution." The gravest population problem in Mexico, in fact, remains that 80 percent of the children are being born to the poorest 20 percent of the population.

54. Ginger Thompson, "At Home, Mexico Mistreats Its Migrant Farmhands," *New York Times*, May 6, 2001.

55. Lee Frankel, "Mexico's Farm Workers," Letter to the Editor, *New York Times*, May 13, 2001.

56. "It's an appalling picture," Robert Ross, president of the California Endowment, a foundation that specializes in health issues, is quoted as saying. "These are people who help keep our food prices low for American families, and I have a hard time figuring out why their health should be so poor." Steven Greenhouse presents cultural biases and America's inadequate health system as factors. "Many growers acknowledge that their workers' health is substandard, but they blame an inferior health system in Mexico and the failure of the workers to take care of themselves. Many growers say they cannot afford to provide insurance," he writes. Steven Greenhouse, "Fear and Poverty Sicken Many Migrant Workers in U.S.," *New York Times*, May 13, 2001.

57. Sarah Kershaw, "Union Drive Collides with Korean Grocers," *New York Times*, February 15, 2001.

58. Ibid.

59. Ibid.

60. It is not small businesses where profit margins are tight that exploit workers. "We think that there probably are a lot of contractors who hire day laborers on public works projects, pay them the $120 a day they're promised, and those workers don't know they're not being paid the wages" as required under the law, M. Patricia Smith, chief of New York State's attorney general's labor bureau told reporters. "We are very concerned that there could be a trend, especially in places like Long Island, where there are a lot of day laborers." These comments were made after a New York contractor agreed to pay $75,000 to eighteen immigrant laborers; day laborers are often paid $120 a day, while the contractor receives anywhere between $130 and $160 for each laborer. Elissa Gootman, "Contractor Is to Pay $75,000 Owed 18 Immigrant Laborers," *New York Times*, October 4, 2002.

61. Michael Winerap, "Why Harlem Drug Cops Don't Discuss Race," *New York Times*, July 9, 2000.

62. Jorge Ramos, *The Other Face of America* (New York: HarperRayo, 2002), xxiv–xxv.

63. Debra Dickerson, "Crazy as They Wanna Be: Black People Take Secret—and Unwarranted—Comfort in the Fact that Mass Killers Tend to Be White," Salon.com, May 4, 1999.

64. Jill Nelson, "White Lies: Asking 'How Could it Happen Here?' Reveals the Racism Behind Our Thinking About Violence," Salon.com, May 4, 1999.

65. The March 2001 ruling came after a seven-year battle between the State of Missouri and the Ku Klux Klan. The suit, filed by Klansman Michael Cuffley in 1994, sought permission to have the KKK clean up a half-mile stretch of Interstate 55 near St. Louis. The Missouri Department of Transportation sought to block approval of the request, but was overruled in November 1999 when a federal judge ruled that the KKK had a right to participate. The KKK sought to have a sign erected that read,

"Adopt-a-Highway. Next mile adopted by Knights of the Ku Klux Klan, Realm of Missouri." The problems continued, of course, when the *Jefferson City News Tribune* reported in August 2000 that the Klansmen had failed to pick up litter, mow grass, or perform any of the required beautification duties, such as planting flowers, presumably white.

66. "For all the derision it provoked, Hillary Rodham Clinton hit on much of the basis of that hatred when she said that the prejudice against her and her husband was because they were Southerners," Charles Taylor wrote in his farewell to the Clinton presidency. "As LBJ had before him, Clinton encountered the still prevalent belief, on the left as well as the right, that white Southerners are trash, degenerate hayseeds who will muddy the carpet if you let them into the house." Charles Taylor, "Farewell, Charming Pragmatist," Salon.com, January 13, 2001.

67. Figures are provided by the Mexican Migration Project codirected by Jorge Durand of the University of Guadalajara and Douglas Massey of the University of Pennsylvania. The project began in 1982.

68. From an interview by Bob Baldock and Dennis Bernstein for "Skirting the Brink: America's Leading Thinkers and Activists Confide Their Views of Our Predicament," a public radio project in progress.

69. Some changes are lamentable as Mexico becomes "modern." On January 1, 2001, for the first time in 127 years, passenger train service to Mexico City was suspended, ending an era, for passenger trains had rolled dramatically both through Mexico's landscape and history.

70. In a matter of days, after she demonstrated her work ethic and skills, my grandmother's driver took her back to her village to let her parents know she was safe. It was agreed that she could remain in Mérida, provided she was allowed to return every two weeks for three days. In the decades that followed, Rosario May took care of her parents and continued to work until she married and returned to her village.

71. In the United States, there is comic relief in films that show the frustration that Americans, particularly in southern California, encounter when teaching their Latina maids how to use washing machines, vacuum cleaners, microwave ovens, or dishwashers.

72. Associated Press, "Mexico Debates Daylight-Savings Time," January 25, 2001.

73. Maya Angelou, *I Know Why the Caged Bird Sings* (New York: Random House, 1969), 58.

74. Mexican parents often use the accusation of having "little culture" to shame their children, such as telling a ten-year-old that people will think she has "little culture" should she fail to send thank-you notes after receiving birthday gifts.

75. As Mexico becomes more successful on the world stage, it is clear that identifying an instance of *poca cultura* is used as a form of snobbery among Mexicans and Mexican Hispanics.

76. "NQOC" stands for "not quite our class," and remains one of the more affected American imports from class-conscious Europe. One manifestation is Maureen Dowd's crass attempts to depict George W. Bush as a "hick" from Texas in her *New York Times* column.

77. Mario Moreno as "Cantinflas" is best known to American audiences in the film *Around the World in Eighty Days*, in which he costarred with David Niven in 1956.

78. In her autobiography, Maya Angelou tells the same lesson imparted by her own grandmother: "She said I must always be intolerant of ignorance but under-

standing of illiteracy. That some people, unable to go to school, were more educated and even more intelligent than college professors. She encouraged me to listen carefully to what country people called mother wit. That in those homely sayings was couched in the collective wisdom of generations." Angelou, *I Know Why the Caged Bird Sings*, 83.

79. Sullivan also differentiates between racism and the use of genetic information: "The point of laws against racial bias is to outlaw irrational discrimination based on irrelevant characteristics. The point of laws against genetic discrimination is to outlaw rational bias based on relevant information." Andrew Sullivan, "Promotion of the Fittest," *New York Times*, July 23, 2000.

80. "The New Face of Race," *Newsweek*, September 16, 2000.

81. Western feminists who denounce the "oppression" of women in Muslim countries being required to wear a chador or other garments fail to consider that many women find it "liberating" to be able to go in public without having to fend off unwanted stares. In some ways, Muslim women are freed from the dehumanization of being a sex object.

82. Ursula Adler Falk and Gerhard Falk, "Ageism," discrimination against the old, for instance, has been analyzed in minute detail in *Ageism, the Aged and Aging in America: On Being Old in an Alienated Society* (Springfield, IL: C.C. Thomas, 1997).

83. Janet McDonald, *Project Girl* (New York: Farrar, Straus and Giroux, 1999), 91.

84. The impact of lookism can be insidious. In *Ghosts of Manila: The Fateful Blood Feud Between Muhammad Ali and Joe Frazier* (New York: HarperCollins, 2001), for instance, Mark Kram describes Joe Frazier's "anger at Muhammad Ali's attacks on him, attacks that often disparaged his looks, particularly hurtful since Ali was so often celebrated in the press for being exceptionally 'good' looking." In *Driving While Black* (New York: Broadway, 2000), Kenneth Meeks writes, "The statistics speak for themselves, eloquently. But this book is not a sermon; it does not preach. What it does—very effectively—is put information into the hands of those whose rights are violated, and provide them with the means to resist, to fight back, to promote themselves. It is a handbook more than a call to arms, a manual of instruction and self-help more than a political tract" (xi).

85. I, for one, have always admired the values of small-town life. In the summer of 2002, when I had occasion to travel to Wichita, Kansas, I found the people and their community charming. In downtown Wichita, at the intersection of Douglas and Topeka Streets, the Rotary Club posted a sign proclaiming that at that intersection, in 1885, the first light bulb was demonstrated to residents. That charming detail is a refreshing and gracious pleasure so often missing from our lives.

86. Lori Leibovich, "Fat People, Get Real!" Salon.com, September 12, 1997.

87. See Andrew Ross's review of Camille Paglia, "They Destroyed Her," Salon.com, September 2, 1997.

88. Literature on how one's appearance enhances one's chances of getting ahead in the world is now emerging, as more scientific analysis of the economic consequences of lookism begin to be conducted. An article on lookism begins:

> If you're attractive, you stand a better chance of making more money than your less attractive colleagues, says Dr. Daniel Hamermesh, a labour economist at the University of Texas at Austin. He found that, for men, those who were below average in looks made about nine per cent less a year than average-looking men. And good-looking men were making about 5.5 per cent more

than average-looking men. The effects were smaller for women (5.5 and 3.9 percent, respectively). "This was adjusting for other variables, such as age, location, education, health and marital status," says Hamermesh.

"Good Looks Pay Off—Literally, Says Labour Economist," http://communications.uvic.ca/Ring/98oct30/looks.html.

89. Ross, "They Destroyed Her."

90. It is frightening to read a conversation between two intelligent, educated, thoughtful and informed individuals who, without a qualm, suggest that we owe it to ourselves to die when we are at our most "attractive." Or to read their argument that aging naturally diminishes the value of our lives because our looks invariably go "downhill."

91. For more information on the "epidemic" in negative body image, contact National Eating Disorders Association at 603 Stewart St., Suite 803, Seattle, WA 98101.

92. In my capacity as an observing journalist, it would be wrong to argue that I was in a "getaway" car involved in an operation to smuggle illegal aliens, who happened to be gorgeous models, into the United States.

93. Rubén Martínez, *Crossing Over: A Mexican Family on the Migrant Trail* (New York: Picador, 2002), 30–31. Martínez claims to have the hair "of a Moor," which is itself a peculiar statement because that derogatory term, now archaic, was used by Europeans to describe North African Arabs.

94. Rubén Martínez, "America's Next Great Revolution in Race Relations Is Already Under Way," *New York Times*, July 16, 2000.

95. Susan Sachs, "Files Suggest Profiling of Latinos Led to Immigration Raids," *New York Times*, May 1, 2001.

96. Mireya Navarro, "Miami's Generation of Exiles Side by Side, Yet Worlds Apart," *New York Times*, February 11, 1999. Recent arrivals, however, are at times taken aback by how "Americanized," which they equate with materialism, their compatriots have become in the United States. "People are so materialistic," Olga Rodríguez is quoted as saying. "It's like they have a dollar sign on their forehead. It hasn't happened to me yet. I offer rides to classmates in language school even if I have to go out of my way."

97. Martínez, "America's Next Great Revolution in Race Relations Is Already Under Way."

98. Discrimination against the unattractive is so widespread, in fact, that ABC News 20/20 devoted an entire segment, "The Ugly Truth," produced by correspondent John Stossel, to this phenomenon.

99. Rodriguez, *Brown*, 131–32.

100. Ibid., 132.

101. "I never saw an upholsterer in American literature," Sandra Cisneros told the *New York Times*. "He was such an example of generous and honest labor. I didn't want people to erase him." Mireya Navarro, "Telling a Tale of Immigrants Whose Stories Go Untold," *New York Times*, November 12, 2002.

Conclusion

1. In the American experience, only small, primarily religious groups, such as the Amish, have eschewed becoming part of the "mainstream."

2. In the English-speaking world, the terms "peasants" and "simple folk" have been used to distinguish between those deemed to be unsophisticated.

3. Charlie LeDuff, "At the Slaughterhouse, Some Things Never Die: Who Kills, Who Cuts, Who Bosses Can Depend on Race," *New York Times*, June 16, 2000. "Among the judge's findings was that company officials had sought to scare the plant's sizable Hispanic work force by warning that the union, if successful in organizing the plant, would report workers to the Immigration and Naturalization Services," Kevin Sack reported in "Judge Finds Labor Law Broken at Meat-Packing Plant," *New York Times*, January 4, 2001.

Epilogue

1. Personal communication from Boatright to the author, May 2002.

Index

About the Author

Louis E.V. Nevaer is an economist, author, and consultant, and formerly a publisher of newsletters for top management in international finance. He has written two books examining the Hispanic and Mexican marketplace: *New Business Opportunities in Latin America* (1996) and *Strategies for Business in Mexico* (1995). One of his more recent books, *The Dot-Com Debacle and the Return to Reason,* was named one of the Recommended Business Books of 2002 by the *Harvard Business Review.* In addition to this book on Hispanic ascendancy and the emergence of a unified Hispanic consumer market throughout North America, an additional book examining NAFTA's first decade is forthcoming. He divides his time between New York, Miami, and Mexico City. He can be reached at HispanicEconomics.com.